Everybody Says Freedom

Everybody Says Freedom

PETE SEEGER   BOB REISER

Including Many Songs Collected by Guy and Candie Carawan

New York   W·W·NORTON & COMPANY   London

Published simultaneously in Canada
by Penguin Books Canada Ltd.,
2801 John Street, Markham, Ontario L3R1B4.
Printed in the United States of America.
The text of this book is composed
in 11/15 ITC Clearface
with display type set in ITC Clearface Bold.
Composition and manufacturing by
The Maple-Vail Book Manufacturing Group.
Book design by Margaret M. Wagner.
*Since this page cannot legibly accommodate all the
copyright notices, page 259 constitutes an extension
of the copyright page.*

First Edition

Library of Congress Cataloging-in-Publication Data
Seeger, Pete, 1919–
Everybody says freedom /
by Pete Seeger, Bob Reiser.
p. cm.
Includes index.
1. African Americans—Civil rights—Songs and
music—History and criticism.
2. African Americans—Civil rights—
Songs and music.
I. Reiser, Bob.   II. Title.
ML3550.S43   1989
784.6'83234'0973—dc19   88–23341

ISBN 0-393-02646-9
ISBN 0-393-30604-6 {PBK}

W. W. Norton & Company, Inc.
500 Fifth Avenue, New York, N.Y. 10110
W. W. Norton & Company Ltd.,
37 Great Russell Street, London WC1B 3NU

1 2 3 4 5 6 7 8 9 0

FRONTIS.
*Freedom Singers, Georgia
1963. © Joe Alper, courtesy
Jackie Gibson Alper*

Contents

PART ONE: THE WALL

PART TWO: BREAKING THE WALL

PART THREE: BEYOND THE WALL

Foreword

*E*very generation needs the instruction and insights of past generations in order to forge its own vision. The places, personalities, and events of the Civil Rights era, with all the real-life drama it embodied, have forever left their imprint on the national psyche of the American people. The commitment, spirit, and creative energy embodied in the day-to-day battles to abolish the racist institution of segregation in our country represented one of the finest chapters in our nation's history.

Pete Seeger, artist, legend in his own time, and his colleague Bob Reiser, have done a remarkable job capturing this time, this particular moment in our lives—a moment we now realize was one of great complexity. Yet, with all its complexity it yielded to the power of the simple truth articulated by the African American community: "We want to be free!" In the following pages of this narrative we revisit all the places along the Freedom Road that were the landmarks from Montgomery to Memphis. Yet quite aside from the nostalgia that someone who was involved like myself may feel, it is a testament of such power it causes us to reflect upon the deeper meaning of that movement. It leads us to a new recognition that there is more to American history than the Bill of Rights, the Constitution, the Declaration of Independence, and the Statue of Liberty. These are monuments to our National Purpose.

Yet despite and in defiance of these monuments, the insult of racial segregation remained an institution for nearly a century. Created by an economy of exploitation and greed, sustained by the politics of divide-and-rule, defended by the pronouncements of law that had no moral foundation, nurtured by the religion of "white supremacy," it was enforced, on a daily basis, by a police state. This is one of the fundamental lessons of the American national experience.

Our nonviolent mass movement of resistance confronted this Closed Society, opened it up to scrutiny by the world community, and moved the nation's conscience in the process. This is an historic contribution to the people of our country that has achieved international recognition. While the story of the details has been told many times, the unique contribution of the present book is the way it lifts up the role of music in our struggle—the music that kept our spirits strong and kept our movement moving. Old songs that had their roots in the black church or the struggles of labor of past generations were altered to fit the needs of the current struggle, and new songs were creatively emerging out of the struggle. Mass action created the body of the movement and the music breathed its soul.

Pete Seeger and Bob Reiser have created a work of both culture and history and they have underscored for us the fact that the movement and its culture are inseparable.

> Oh Pritchett, you never can jail us aa-a-a-a-alllllll,
> Oh Pritchett, segregation's got to faa-a-a-alllll.

That spirit of Albany, Georgia, typified our movement's attitude, as the black citizens of that city filled the jails in a nonviolent witness for freedom. The eye-witness accounts lend an aura of authenticity to the events. As a case in point, Ed King's description of the funeral march that accompanied the martyred Medgar Evers's body to the cemetery in Jackson, Mississippi, reads like a report coming out of apartheid South Africa today. No wonder; they are forged in a common experience with institutional racism.

Today we are building upon that legacy of struggle. The challenge facing this generation is for the achievement of economic justice for the unemployed, the working poor, the farmers who have lost their land, and the millions in our country without medical care. This is at one and the same time a challenge to end the arms race, to free our nation from the addiction to military spending that we have inherited from forty years of the Cold War. Economic justice means stopping the flow of drugs into the country and stopping the flow of jobs out of the country. It requires the empowerment of the millions who are now locked out from a real voice in the affairs of our nation. *Everybody Says Freedom* is a gift toward that peaceful future. It will help in every way to enlighten our minds, lift our spirits, renew our determinations, and inspire us to *Keep Hope Alive!*

—*Jesse Jackson*

Introduction

The civil rights movement was a victory not only for African Americans but for the rest of America as well. As its effects sent ripples out through the world, it was a victory for every human being in every land, whether they know it or not. That is why we two white people have undertaken this book.

Most of the songs in this book came directly from the mouths and hearts of people in the civil rights movement. Some of the songs exploded spontaneously during the heat of demonstrations and marches and church meetings. Some of them were spun during the lonely hours of solitary confinement in Hinds County jail and Parchman penitentiary. (Thank you, Mississippi prison system, for helping to give us this music.) Rarely were they written down. They survive thanks to the good memories of the singers and to the efforts of people like Guy and Candie Carawan, who traveled across the South, recording and transcribing what they heard. Guy and Candie's books, *We Shall Overcome* and *Freedom Is a Constant Struggle,* which provided us with many of the songs included here, have just gone back into print. You can obtain these invaluable books, which together have 106 freedom songs, by writing to the We Shall Overcome Fund, Highlander Center, RFD 3, Box 370, New Market, TN 37820.

Many of the men and women who created the music in this book are gone now. We may never know all of their names. Let's pause to thank them, and also to ask any reader who has information about them to get in touch with us so we can give the proper credit in later editions of this book.

We hope people in far-flung corners of this earth will take courage, and will attempt some action, translating old stories and songs for new situations, new ears, new consciences. Almost any one of these songs could be rewritten for a new situation. We can imagine an ecology group like the Clearwater singing, to the tune of *We Are Soldiers in the Army,* "We-are-sailors-on-the-ocean. The calms, the storms, we'll take it all in stride." (The ocean could be the world of controversy they immerse themselves in.)

The story is not told in strict chronological order. Each chapter focuses on a particular area or situation; sometimes several chapters recount events that are of the same period, but have different characters or settings. As much as possible we have tried to use the words of those who made the movement possible—young people, some only in high school at the time, old people, those whose names are known only among friends and family. We have found them in coffee shops in Jackson, Mississippi, in churches in Brooklyn, New York. We've neglected many of the famous, but their words are already familiar. We've also neglected many of the unnamed and unknown, who gave the most and often gained the least. But to all those thousands—they know who they are—who took beatings or went to jail or lost their homes or their jobs to change the lives of people in this country, to them, to those who gave their lives, and to future generations of activists, we dedicate this book.

—Pete Seeger and Bob Reiser

Acknowledgments

*T*his book is possible because of the painstaking work of people like Guy and Candie Carawan who collected freedom songs and helped save them from being lost forever.

We thank Avon Rollins for his time and help and for allowing us to use papers from his personal files. We thank Matt Jones for pointing us toward many of the people who made the movement. We thank Joanne Grant, Hollis Watkins, Bob and Dottie Zellner, and Jack Chatfield for their help and encouragement. We thank Ed King of Jackson, Mississippi, for taking the time and effort to bring to life in our imagination his city of the 1960s.

Our thanks to Jackie Alper for giving us access to her husband's great store of photos, and to Flip Schulke, Dan Budnik, Danny Lyon, and Bob Fletcher, who allowed us to use many of their extraordinary pictures. We also thank Paul DeLeon, Hubert and Jane Sapp, Myles Horton, and the staff of Highlander for giving their time and help, and allowing us to use their facilities, their library, and their photo collection. We thank the librarians at Tougaloo College and Howard University for giving us access to their extensive collections of civil rights material.

We thank Bill Ferris of the University of Mississippi's Center for Southern Culture, Professor Ron Bailey, Professor Charles Eagles and his wife Brenda, and Arun and Sunanda Gandhi for their help and hospitality in Oxford, Mississippi.

Thanks also to Diane Nash, Bernard LaFayette, and Dr. James Cone for reading over portions of our manuscript and helping to keep our poetic license in check, to Hubert Babinski for proofreading, and to Juli Goldfein for expertly double-checking the music.

We thank Connie Hogarth and Jack O'Dell of the Rainbow Coalition, Bernice Johnson Reagon of the Smithsonian Institution, Judy Bell and Jay Marks of the Richmond Group, and Joy Graeme of the Harold Leventhal office; we thank our wives Toshi and Sandy for putting up with us. Most of all we thank the tens of thousands of people, black and white, who continue to work to make this a nation and a world with liberty and justice for *all*.

A Musical Note

*W*e have included only a few dozen of the hundreds of songs sung in the civil rights movement. We hope that readers will look up some of the recordings still available. A school, a church, any organization, could put on a program of these songs, perhaps using slides on a screen to help carry the story line forward. A chorus or duo, a group of amateurs who like to sing, could do this, with a little time for rehearsals. A family could spend an evening singing their way through this book.

You'll have to read through it "creatively." We've printed in parentheses words which song leaders could use to encourage group response on the first verse, but have usually left it up to the song leaders to find their own words for subsequent verses, if they are needed.

If you can't read music, but would like to learn some of these songs, there are several possibilities. You could get someone who can read music to go slowly through the music with you, while you use a tape recorder to get the tunes down. You could borrow some of the records of the songs (buying them is possible too, but can get expensive). Or you could learn how to read music yourself. This could take at least a couple of months, maybe more, but if you like music, the effort is worth it. You'll gain a lifetime of pleasure.

I realize that we are asking singers to do two almost contradictory things: first, to reflect those turbulent times, when these songs were an important part of the American civil rights movement; and second, to keep the feeling of spontaneity and improvisation which caused these songs to never be sung the same way twice.

My guess is that if people in later decades would like these songs to live again in the truest sense, they may start singing them as they were sung, and then frankly change them, adding extra verses, stretching melodies, voices, and harmonies. This may be a little confusing to some listeners, but as the listeners start participating, joining in the choruses, they'll start to understand.
　　　　　　　　　　　　　　　　　　　　　　　　　　　　　　　　　　—*Pete Seeger*

Guide My Feet While I Run This Race

Ella J. Baker's life work—to improve the lives of ordinary people—came to fruition in the 1960s, when she played a key role in the movement for civil rights. She had worked in the movement for most of her adult life, first as director of branches of the NAACP, then as executive secretary of Martin Luther King's Southern Christian Leadership Conference.

She became known as the godmother of SNCC, the Student Nonviolent Coordinating Committee. Instrumental in establishing the organization in 1960, she fostered its growth over the next few years, helping its members grapple with the problems of a young, brash, and brave organization.

The tenets which she had held throughout her life became a part of SNCC. Her emphasis on developing local leadership, her belief in people's ability to change their own lives, her sense of community, became integral to the young people who fought so hard for dignity, justice, and equality.

In all her work, Ella Baker stressed the worth of the ordinary person and his or her potential for leadership. Perhaps her most heartfelt credo was expressed in her keynote speech to the 1964 state convention of the Mississippi Freedom Democratic party: "Until the killing of black men, black mothers' sons, becomes as important as the killing of white men, white mothers' sons, we who believe in freedom cannot rest."

When necessary, her vibrant voice rang out in speech or in song. But Ella Baker became a calming, questioning, quiet counselor whenever she was called upon to give advice, guidance, sustenance to another human being.

She was a teacher, an organizer, and more: she was a nurturer.

—*Joanne Grant,*
author of *Fundi,* the film tribute to Ella Baker

Ella Baker's favorite song was a spiritual sung in black churches throughout the South and then adapted for the movement, *Guide My Feet While I Run This Race.* This transcription is by Ethel Raim.

Ella J. Baker.
© *Diana Davies / Insight*

Guide my feet . . .

Guide my heart . . .

Guide my tongue . . .

Guide my vote . . .

Guide my mind . . .

Everybody Says Freedom

Myles Horton, Knoxville,
Tennessee. Courtesy Highlan-
der Center

Prologue
Highlander

Profile: MYLES HORTON

*M*yles Horton, founder of the Highlander Folk School (in 1963 renamed the Highlander Folk Center), sits in a little garden in front of a small three-room house at the Center, just outside of Knoxville. Despite his eighty-three years, Myles is not a sitter. He is always moving—picking up weeds, hoeing, answering mail, running inside to get the phone. For over fifty years, Highlander has been a learning and planning center for people in the South who have been working for social change in their own communities. The Center has moved twice since it served as a meeting place for the southern college students who would create SNCC and SCLC, but the passion is as it was fifty years ago.

I got involved in the movement before there was even a movement. Highlander was born out of the 1930s. Back then it looked to us that the world was either going to be Socialist or it was going to be Fascist. We didn't know there would be an FDR who could help make the old system more tolerable, at least for a while.

Highlander was a way to use education to change society—not to reform the old one cosmetically, but to build a new and more humane society. But we have always believed that you don't force your program down people's throats. You go to the people who are suffering, and you work with them, their ideas, their leadership, their program. What you do is just nurture the development of those things.

In the thirties we felt that unions could be schools of democracy, where union members could get used to a much fairer and more democratic society than the one they were used to. We didn't want Communist unions or Catholic unions or white unions or black unions, because we felt that you couldn't make large, effective, democratic unions unless you took in everybody—men, women, black, white—everyone.

So all through the thirties people from the unions would come here for workshops, to work out their plans and strategies—whatever. Our philosophy was always that we might give our two cents and do what we could to help the people work together, but we would never interfere with their plans. After 1950 the political climate changed and many unions were afraid of our radical ideas, afraid to be associated with us. So we started looking for another way in which we could be a force for positive change.

We realized that one area in which we could help was racism. We had already done a lot to bring blacks and whites together in the South. Our workshops and seminars were always interracial, and there were more blacks and whites together in unions here than there were in the North. But it was still the biggest barrier to democracy here in the South. Employers, anyone in power, would always play whites against blacks and vice versa, to keep people divided.

So, back in the early fifties we officially made it our goal to fight racism in any way we could. We didn't know how yet, but we knew we had to do it. Now we had a problem. We had a predominantly white school here—faculty, the board, was about 85 percent white—and we were taking on a problem where the people who were hurting were black. Up till then, any political or religious group that had worked with racism had demanded that whites and blacks work out the problems and strategies together. We said, "Hell, that's no good. The people who are suffering, the black people, should liberate themselves. We'll encourge the black community to develop its own movement, its own leadership. Then we'll join in and follow them."

Consequently, we had a relationship with black groups that was different than anyone else's. They could make use of Highlander, our library, our staff, our faculty, but they didn't have any fear we would take over. They knew other groups would try to share power and wind up controlling them, because white people control amost everything in this society.

We made an educated guess in 1953 that the Supreme Court decision would be to integrate schools, and we started workshops right away. A lot of the people who later became active in the civil rights movement came to Highlander. Rosa Parks came to several seminars because she was interested in education. She said this was the first place she ever met any white people with whom she could relax.

Once the movement began, we just made ourselves available. The people will put you to work, they'll work the hell out of you. The greatest danger is making yourself the expert. People will come to you, expect the answer, and when they don't get it from you, they'll go look for a slicker expert instead of learning to make their own answers.

By the late fifties, they started red baiting us again—calling us Communists. They figured that was a sure way to split us off from the black movement.

One time, Senator Eastland called me up to his investigative committee. They knew I was no Communist. They had investigated me so many times in the forties and the fifties, they must have had a drawerful of FBI files showing I wasn't a party member. But the point is I wouldn't condemn Communists—I felt they had a right to believe same as anyone else. Those days, if you didn't condemn Communists they called you Communist.

So I got in front of the committee and they asked me, "Do you know so-and-so? Did they say such-and-such?" So I said, "I believe I have freedom of speech. I can speak about what I choose, and not speak about what I choose. Now, if I have that right, so do other people. I can't speak for them. If you have a question about what they believe or what they said or what they did, ask them."

Eastland said he'd cite me for contempt. So I said, "Let me help you out. I am in contempt of you and this committee and everything it is trying to do, and I am proud to be in contempt." Well, he just stuttered and sputtered and sputtered some more and finally he yelled, "Throw him out! Throw him out!" They picked me up, marched to the marble front of the courthouse, and threw me down the steps.

They sent some guy to our twenty-fifth anniversary meeting to sneak around and take pictures. I didn't know who he was—he said he was a free-lance photographer. Some other fellow was there, the husband of a woman who was attending a seminar. His name was Abner Berry, and he was Communist. As I say, we don't keep people away because of their political beliefs. So, as the speeches were about to get under way, I asked the photographer to take some pictures for us to use at Highlander. Right there in the front row was Rosa Parks and Martin Luther King, Jr., and some other notable people. It would make a good picture. He kept fiddling with his camera. When Mr. Berry came to the front to set up a recording machine, the photographer started snapping away. A few weeks later, that photo was on Citizens Council billboards all over the South, with the words "Martin Luther King at Communist Training School."

Billboard in Tennessee, 1961. Dale Ernsberger, The Tennessean / *courtesy Highlander Center*

The upshot of this red baiting was that we were more respected by the black community than ever before. See, anytime anyone ever helped black people, the politicians would scream "Communists"—so as far as local black people were concerned, "Communist" was a name for people who would help them.

I'd say just about the most important thing we did in the movement was start the citizenship schools. In 1956 Septima Clark, our director of education, and Esau Jenkins, a bus driver on John's Island, near Charleston, South Carolina, started coming to Highlander and bringing some neighbors with them. It was a poor kind of place, most people earning their living by picking cabbage from morning to night. The people there wanted to vote—but they couldn't read and write. They asked Highlander to help them set up a school. We helped them raise the money, and gave whatever help we could, but everything about the school was up to the people. They found Bernice Robinson, a beautician, to teach. Bernice and her "students" worked out a curriculum. They had to teach it all in only two months, January and February, between the picking and the planting seasons. They started by learning to read and write their names, then the words to hymns they knew. They learned to hold a pencil and read and write stories about the work that they did; finally, they tackled the Constitution, and the actual registering to vote.

That school went on year after year—I remember people like Bob Moses and Fannie Lou Hamer coming down to see it. And then they would go back to Mississippi and other places and start their own schools. Martin [Luther King] asked us to set up schools for them.

Eventually this became the model for the Freedom Schools that SNCC and CORE set up all through Mississippi and the rest of the South.

What hurt me so badly was to see the brutality that would happen to people after they left, when they tried to set up their own schools. I met Mrs. Fannie Lou Hamer when she visited with us. She wasn't yet known. The night before she left John's Island we went to a voter-registration drive to give a little support, and the people in the bus started worrying and getting pessimistic, saying things like "We couldn't do that. Nobody would follow us and blacks wouldn't stick together." Things like that. She just started to sing: "We shall overcome—We shall overcome—" She was a spirit, an incredible spirit.

Then she gets on the bus to go home to Mississippi and they drag her off the bus in Winona and they put her in jail and they beat her terribly. I got a call from some of the people who were with her, and so I went down there.

Their purpose was to terrorize black people, to keep them from trying to register to vote. By the time I got down there just the reverse was happening. People were flocking in. They were beaten up and they were jailed, but they just kept coming. Just unnamed, unknown people from these plantations. The FBI watched them getting beaten and just took notes and pictures. No pictures of the police doing the beating, just of the people getting beaten—because those were the "troublemakers."

What a contrast—one side the courage of people like Fannie Lou Hamer and hundreds of others whose names we'll never know against all the power of the state and all the power of the police and all the power of the FBI and the jails. And all those powers were just helpless because the people had decided to move. The beating didn't frighten the people; it released something in them, it made them stronger.

In 1965, there was another change.

Our philosophy was just to train leaders who would run their programs themselves. It was clear by 1965 that the black people were more than ready to take over the full running of the movement. If we helped in any more than a supportive way, we would just be interfering.

The movement was moving in a new direction, an economic direction—a fight for economic quality involving not only the black people, but native American people and Chicanos and people from Puerto Rico and white people from Appalachia, which had the largest number of poor whites in the country. It was a coalition called the Poor People's Campaign. So we concentrated our efforts in Appalachia, which is our base. If you can't work with your own people, you can't be respected by anyone else. People say, "Who are you?" So we worked with the problems of toxic dumping and strip mining and cooperatives for farmers and cultural projects. Now that we have a growing sense of an Appalachian community, we can work with the other groups. I have a simple theory about this: if you can't work where you are, you can't work where you ain't. In other words, if you can't work on your troubles at home, you can't really work anywhere else. People who come in without any kind of a base—in other words, the outside experts we are always hearing about—are useful, but nobody really listens to them.

With new trainers and teachers, Highlander thrives today.

There are peaks and there are valleys. Right now we are in a valley. Not many radicals today—a lot of reformers, but not many radicals. I've had two wonderful experiences, two social movements—the union movement in the early days and the civil rights movement. I keep hoping I can get in on another one. But it better hurry. . . . I'm ready and waiting.

We Shall Overcome

The history of *We Shall Overcome* is a beautiful example of the interchange between black and white musicians in creating American music.

I'll Overcome, more often called *I'll Be All Right,* was a gospel hymn sung in black churches through much of the South. It was usually sung rather fast, with hand clapping on the second and fourth beats of the $\frac{4}{4}$ measure.

In 1945 several hundred tobacco workers, mostly women, mostly black, were on strike in Charleston, South Carolina. To keep their spirits up they sang on the picket line. One of the workers, Lucille Simmons, loved to sing this hymn in the extremely slow "long meter" style, and the first words became *"We will."* A white woman, Zilphia Horton, music director at the Highlander Folk School in Tennessee, learned it from them. It became her favorite song. In '46 she taught it to me in New York, and in 1950 I taught it to Guy Carawan and Frank Hamilton in California. Zilphia had a lovely alto voice, and liked to sing it slowly, with no regular pulse or beat. I started singing it up north, and out west. In '58 I even had a chance to sing it at Highlander. Zilphia had died, only forty-five years old. Myles Horton wrote me, "Can you come to Highlander for our 25th reunion? Without Zilphia, we need others to lead songs." It was there I met young Dr. King and his colleague Rev. Ralph Abernathy. Anne Braden (one of the courageous southern whites who openly helped the fledgling civil rights movement) was driving them next day to another speaking engagement, and she remembers King in the back seat saying, "We shall overcome. That song really sticks with you, doesn't it?"

But the song really got around in the spring of 1960, when Guy, aged thirty-two at the time, organized and helped run a South-wide workshop at Highlander on songs for the civil rights movement. And three weeks later some of those who had attended the workshop sang the song with Guy at the founding convention of SNCC in Raleigh, North Carolina, for several hundred black and white students. Within a few months it was known as the unofficial theme song of the movement. And it was those young people who added the rhythmical deep pulse, the "soul beat," popular on so many Motown records. The melody is still slow, but each beat now has a feeling of three short beats within it. This rock-steady rhythm does not falter till the last note of the song.

We print this song in C, but tenors and sopranos will prefer it in D or E. Altos and basses will prefer it in A or G. In my Hudson Valley home I accompanied Gretchen Reed, a fine gospel singer, at the annual Martin Luther King celebration, and to my amazement, she said she wanted to do it in F. "Who will be able to sing it that low?" I said to myself. To my surprise, the crowd started on the high C, and in order to hit the high F and G six measures later, they had to belt it out. I had never heard the song sung so spiritedly. This was in January 1988. Gov. Mario Cuomo was in the crowd, with his wife and other New York State officials. The crowd crossed their arms, right over left, and swayed slowly in time. I shouted out the lines one by one, to give them the words, and Gretchen kept it going for eight or nine verses.

The European tradition says, Here are the notes; play it this way. The African tradition says, Here are the notes; use them as a base to improvise.

It is a tremendous cultural victory that no two song leaders today choose exactly the same verses, nor sing exactly the same notes. You, the reader, must now choose which of the words given here, or others, you'll sing, shout, harmonize, change. The future of the world will not be scripted. All we can do is plan for improvisation. Politicians, engineers, economists, lawyers: *plan for improvisation.*

—*Peter Seeger*

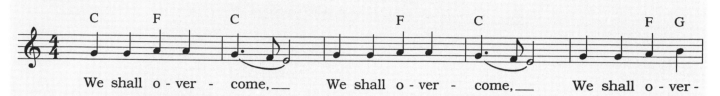

We shall o - ver - come, __ We shall o - ver - come, __ We shall o - ver -

come   some   day. _____   Oh __ deep   in   my   heart

I   do   be - lieve   oh ___   We shall o - ver - come   some   day.

We'll walk hand in hand . . . (some day)

We shall live in peace . . .

The truth shall make us free . . .

We are not afraid . . . (today)

Black and white together . . . (now!)

The whole wide world around . . . (some day)

Whatever verses you choose, you should end with:

WE SHALL OVERCOME . . .

Selma Singers, Alabama, 1963.
© Danny Lyon / Magnum

OVERLEAF. Mississippi sharecropper shacks, 1958.
Courtesy Highlander Center

NEXT OVERLEAF. Pamphlet,
Council of Reconciliation,
1957.
Courtesy University of Mississippi

PART ONE

THE WALL

From the late nineteenth century on, segregation was a part of the American way of life. . . . Black men and women lived behind a seemingly impenetrable wall of segregation. . . . It was apparent on trolleys and trains and buses. There were Negro and white waiting rooms everywhere. There were Negro and white schools, Negro and white communities, Negro cemeteries, Negro jobs, Negro motels, Negro balconies. Sometimes there were separate entrances for Negroes. Sometimes there was no entrance at all, only a wall. . . . Beginning softly, then more and more insistently, men and women began to beat against the wall. Finally, in the mid-1950s, the wall began to crack.

VINCENT HARDING,
SPEECH TO THE
MISSISSIPPI VOLUNTEERS, 1964

MARTIN LUTHER KING
AND
THE MONTGOMERY STORY
10c
HOW 50,000 NEGROES FOUND A NEW WAY TO END RACIAL DISCRIMINATION.
WASHINGTON PARK
DECEMBER 5, 1955
WALK TO FREEDOM
DECEMBER 21, 1956
VICTORY FOR JUSTICE

I

1955

Montgomery, Alabama
"The Morning the Black Man Was Reborn"

Montgomery, Alabama, 1955. The city had been divided for years: White against black. Black against black. Old against young. To the white establishment, it was a "quiet town, where nigras know their place." It seemed the last place on earth for the rebirth of the civil rights movement. But beneath the surface, fire smoldered.

Dorothy Cotton: *We had apartheid. . . . A professor in Cornell tells me I should call it petty apartheid because it wasn't quite as bad as South Africa. It sure felt as bad. When a woman got beat up and her nose broken because she wanted to use the white ladies' room, that was apartheid. At the movies, when we had to sit up in the highest balcony—we called it the buzzards'— that sure was apartheid. While we were up there we talked about throwing things down on the white kids in the orchestra. Made us feel a little better.*

In those days when a black person from another country, from Africa, visited the U.S., they said they could recognize when a black person had grown up under our system, because they always walked with a little bit of a stoop, a little bit of shame. That was apartheid.

E. D. Nixon, a Pullman porter and a long-time activist in the NAACP, had been trying to unite the black population of his city to fight Jim Crow. One afternoon he got a call in his office that Rosa Parks, a respected Montgomery seamstress and a member of the NAACP, had just been arrested for refusing to give up her seat on the bus to a white man.

The Montgomery segregation laws said that white people sat in the front of the bus, black people sat in the back, and if whites were standing, the blacks sitting nearest the front had to give up their seats. Rosa Parks, a gentle, quiet woman, had been to the Highlander Center earlier in the year. There, for the first time in her life, she saw white and black people eating and talking together as equals. She saw the possibility of a new kind of life. So that December afternoon, when the bus driver told her to give her seat to a white man, she simply told him No. Within hours she found herself in jail, charged with violation of the municipal segregation laws. She used her one phone call to dial E. D. Nixon at the NAACP office.

Nixon put down the phone. "This is it," he said to himself. "Everybody knows Rosa Parks. This is the issue that could unify our whole community."

He called the NAACP in Washington. "Oh, this is very interesting," they said. "We'll discuss it at our meeting next week."

"Next week!? We've got to move today!"

He hung up, called his old friend A. Philip Randolph, who had been president of Nixon's union, the Brotherhood of Sleeping Car Porters. "You're absolutely right!" said Randolph. "Don't waste a minute. Have you a pencil?"

Nixon listened carefully to Randolph's advice. He hung up and called the pastor of a conservative local church. He asked if he could hold a meeting at the church.

"Well, Mr. Nixon, I'll have to check with my deacons. Can you call me back in two hours?" Two hours later Nixon called again. The answer now was Yes.

"Reverend King, I'm so glad you said that, because I've just told two hundred people we are meeting at your church at eight o'clock."

Nixon arranged the details on the phone. He didn't know King, but had heard him speak six months earlier for the NAACP. If this divided community was ever to be united, he thought, it would be with the help of this "idealistic young man with the impeccable reputation." As Nixon explained later: "After I heard that speech, I remember turning to my friend J. E. Pierce, 'That guy made a heck of a speech!' 'Sure did,' said Pierce. 'You know something,' I said, 'I don't know how I'm going to do it, but someday I'm going to hang him to the stars.' "

Meanwhile, Jo Ann Robinson, a teacher at Alabama State College, met with the other leaders of the Montgomery Women's Political Council. They decided that they would pour all of their efforts into a one-day bus boycott.

E. D. Nixon recalled: "I told my wife about it and I said, 'We can beat this thing— we're gonna boycott the buses.' 'Cold as it is?' she said. I said, 'Yeah.' She said, 'I doubt it.' I said, 'If you keep 'em off when it's cold, you won't have any trouble keeping 'em off when it's hot.'

"My wife just shook her head. 'My husband! If headaches were selling for a dollar a dozen, my husband would be just the one to say "Gimme a dozen headaches." ' "

All weekend word spread about the planned boycott. Jo Ann Robinson and her organization mobilized dozens of teachers and students to mimeograph and distribute 35,000 leaflets throughout the city. On Sunday, preachers spread the word from their pulpits. "Tomorrow morning Rosa Parks will go on trial. Do not ride the buses." Montgomery's 120 black-owned taxis agreed to transport people to work.

Nixon called the *Montgomery Advertiser* and told them that the black community was meeting to plan a bus boycott. He read them the leaflet that he was circulating in black neighborhoods. The newspaper ran the story as a front-page exposé about the NAACP. They quoted the leaflet: "Don't ride the buses. . . . Another Negro woman has been arrested. . . . Come to a mass meeting Monday at 7 pm at the Hold Street Baptist Church. . . ." Without realizing it, the paper helped get the contents of that broadside into nearly every black home in Montgomery.

On Monday morning rain threatened. Coretta King looked out of her front window, and shouted, "Martin, Martin, come quickly!" Martin Luther King never forgot the moment. "As I approached the front window Coretta pointed joyfully to a slowly moving bus: 'Darling, it's empty!' . . . I knew that the South Jackson line, which ran past our house, carried more Negro passengers than any other line in Montgomery." Another bus passed the house—empty. The boycott was going to work. A torn piece of cardboard flapped from the bus shelter downtown: DON'T RIDE THE BUSES TODAY. DON'T RIDE IT FOR FREEDOM.

Downtown they found Rosa Parks guilty. "In twenty years I seldom saw another black man around the court, unless he was being tried," said E. D. Nixon, "but when we got outside, police were standing with sawed-off shotguns, and the people were up and down the street from sidewalk to sidewalk. . . . I bet there was over a thousand black people out there. . . . The morning of December 5, 1955, the black man was reborn."

That night, over five thousand people and local black leaders, including Rev. Ralph Abernathy, Rev. H. H. Hubbard, Rev. E. N. French, and Rev. Martin Luther King, created the Montgomery Improvement Association. Its president—Martin Luther King: "We are here this evening because we are tired now. . . . We are not advocating violence. Don't let anybody . . . compare our actions to the Ku Klux Klan or the White Citizens Council. There will be no crosses burned at any bus stops in Montgomery. There will be no white persons pulled out of their homes and taken out on some distant road and murdered. . . . If we protest courageously and with dignity . . . future generations of historians will pause and say, 'There lived a great people, a black people, who injected new meaning and dignity into the veins of civilization.' That is our challenge and our overwhelming responsibility."

Without a single dissent, the assembly voted to extend the boycott until the law that convicted Rosa Parks was gone. The Montgomery chief of police and several officers even applauded the speeches. "A bus boycott in December!" one joked afterward. "It won't last a week!"

But the boycott continued month after month. The Improvement Association arranged for special taxis to take people to work for ten cents a ride. The town fathers fought back by stopping the special taxis. "Unfair competition to the city's other taxis," they said. So, the boycott committee asked citizens to volunteer and drive people to and from work. One hundred and fifty volunteered—black people, white people, rich people and poor people, old people and college students.

We Are Moving on to Vict'ry

(Optional words for the song leader are in italics.)

We are mov - ing on to Vic - t'ry,_ We are mov - ing on to Vic - t'ry, We are mov - ing on to Vic - t'ry,_ With hope and dig - ni-ty. We know love is the watch - word, *(Sing it)* We know love is the watch - word, *(Once more)_* We know love is the watch - word, For peace and li - ber - ty._ _ *(We are mov - ing)* We are mov - ing on to Vic - t'ry, We are mov - ing on to Vic - t'ry,_ We are mov - ing on to_ Vic - t'ry, With hope and dig - ni - ty.

We shall all stand together . . .
Till everyone is free.

We know love is the watchword . . .
For peace and liberty.

   Whatever verses you choose, you should end with:

We are moving on to vict'ry . . .
And we know the time ain't long.

Black and white, brothers and sisters . . .
To live in harmony.

Yancey Martin, a college freshman driving one of the free "taxis": *At a meeting at the Day Street Church, Martin was talking to this old lady. "Now listen," he said, "you have been with us all along, now you go on and start back to riding the bus. You're too old to keep walking."*

"Oh no," she said, "I'm going to walk as long as everybody else walks. I'm going to walk till it's over."

So he said, "But aren't your feet tired?"

She said, "Yes my feet is tired, but my soul is rested."

The boycott took money to operate. So, at the almost nightly mass meetings, people contributed dimes and quarters. The churches contributed free public transportation—"rolling churches," taxis with the names of churches on the sides. There were also contributions from the Montgomery Jewish community and from sympathetic middle-class whites.

Week after week went by. The city's segregationists demanded that the boycott be crushed. On January 30, King's home was fire-bombed. On February 1, E. D. Nixon's home was bombed. That month several hundred KKK members paraded through Montgomery's black section in an attempt to strike fear into the community. "We told everyone to put on their Sunday clothes, stand on their steps, and when the Ku Kluxers come, applaud them. Well, they came, marched three blocks, and left. They could not comprehend the new thing. They were no longer able to engender fear," said Bayard Rustin.

"One feels history is being made these days. It is hard to imagine a vision so

Mass meeting, Montgomery,
Alabama. © 1980 Dan Budnik /
Woodfin Camp & Associates

blinded and provincial as not to be awed with admiration at the quiet dignity, disci-
pline and dedication with which the Negroes have conducted the boycott," wrote
white librarian Juliette Morgan.

Intimidation didn't work, so the city turned to arrest. Black people always feared
arrest, the authorities reasoned. They would arrest and humiliate the leaders. The
grand jury convicted King and twenty-four other leaders for "conspiring to boycott."

Walk Together Children

This song is a traditional spiritual.

Instead of cringing with shame, the ministers stood prouder than ever. The whole country would know what was going on. "There will be no stopping us now."

Bayard Rustin: *Martin made going to jail like receiving a Ph.D.*

For thirteen months the boycott continued, characterized by increased violence from the segregationists, and more restraint from the protesters.

Joe Azbell, white reporter for the *Montgomery Advertiser: They were on fire for*

We Are Soldiers in the Army

One person singing this song alone—with no other singers around to help out—would sing the bottom staff of the chorus. If two or more sing, the leader would take the top line. If a group likes to harmonize, it should be easy to add alto, tenor, and bass parts.

freedom. There was a spirit there that no one could capture again. . . . It was so powerful. . . . This was the beginning of a flame that would go across America.

Meanwhile, a group of the ministers kept meeting at a local luncheonette. Rev. Joseph Lowery remembers that "we were all preachers, exchanging ideas, discussing strategies as to how we could support each other. . . . We agreed we needed some kind of organizing force, a 'southern leadership conference.' Later on the name

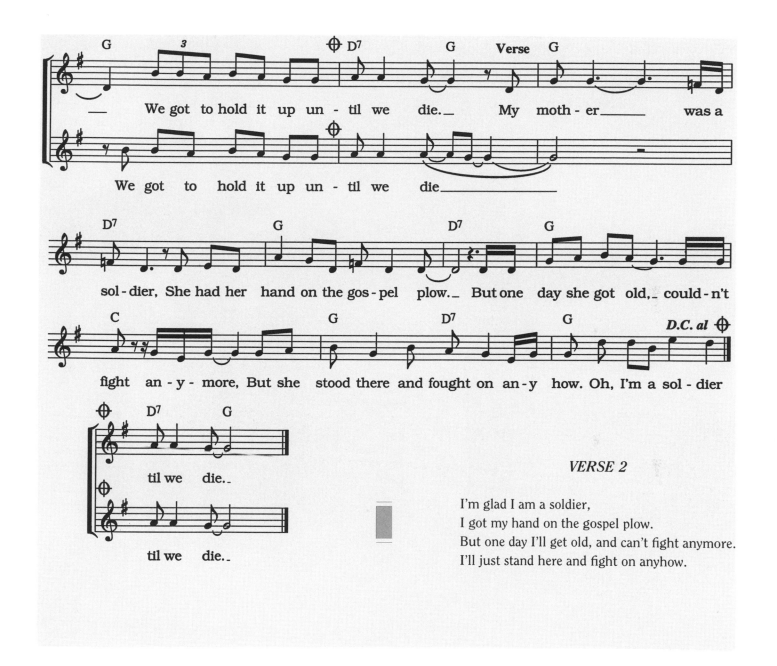

VERSE 2

I'm glad I am a soldier,
I got my hand on the gospel plow.
But one day I'll get old, and can't fight anymore.
I'll just stand here and fight on anyhow.

'Christian' was added. . . . See, the black preacher in the South always saw Jesus as a liberator. . . . When they sang *Steal Away Jesus,* they were singing at night that the Underground Railway was at work and Jesus was the symbol of freedom. . . . With the coming of the SCLC, the struggle was put in the moral arena. That's what got people marching. . . . It opened up people's eyes for the first time to how ugly and immoral segregation was."

Profile: ROSA PARKS

OPPOSITE. Rosa Parks, Montgomery, Alabama. UPI / Schulke Archives

The following is from a November 1980 interview by Cynthia Stokes Brown. She begins by introducing Rosa Parks.

"Mrs Parks astonished me. She was no confident assertive heroine. On the contrary, she was a petite quiet woman who avoided the limelight—just the sort of person I had always thought one would have to stop being if one were ever to have any effect on the world. . . .

"In the restroom, where she went to straighten up, she pulled out a few hairpins, and her braids fell below her waist in a cascade of thick wavy hair. . . . When Mrs Parks saw the astonishment on my face she chuckled softly, 'Well, many of my ancestors were Indians. . . .'

"It was dawning on me that people of different races were getting together here, long before the Civil Rights movement. . . . Racial purity was a fiction of southern legislators. The heroine of the black struggle for civil rights was herself partly native American. . . ."

Rosa Parks: *I noticed* [at Highlander in 1954] *how Septima Clark could organize and hold things together in this very informal setting of interracial living. I had to admire this great woman. I was just the opposite. I was tense, and I was nervous, and I was upset most of the time. . . . I felt that I had been destroyed long ago. But I had the hope that young people could be benefited by equal education. . . .*

Myles Horton just washed away a lot of my hostility and prejudice and feeling of bitterness toward white people, because he had such a wonderful sense of humor. I often thought about many of the things he said and how he could strip the white segregationists of their hardcore attitudes and how he could confuse them. There was a great thing about black and white people sitting down to the same table eating. But Myles managed it, and these reporters were asking him, "How do you get the races to eat together?" And he says, "First the food is prepared. Second, it's put on the table. Third, we ring the bell." I found myself laughing when I hadn't been able to laugh in a long time.

I actually did not think in terms of non-violence and Christian love in connection with the Movement—we didn't call it a movement in those days, we just called it survival—until Dr. Martin Luther King came to Montgomery and I heard him speak. But it was a long time before I could feel the philosophy he was teaching, just as it was a while before I could realize where Myles Horton was coming from and what his dedication meant. I had a hard lesson to learn, that I could not help others free their hearts and minds of racial prejudice unless I would do all I could within myself to straighten out my own thinking and to feel and respond to kindness, to goodwill from wherever it came, whether it was the southerner, northerner, or any race.

Sit-in, Jackson, Mississippi.
Fred Blackwell, Jackson Daily
News / *Wide World Photos*

II

1960

The Sit-ins

February 1, 1960—Greensboro, North Carolina. Four black college freshmen from North Carolina Agricultural and Technical College—Joe McNeil, Frank McCain, Dave Richmond, and Ezell Blair—had spent the night before, in the college dorm, talking about how they could help the civil rights movement in their own town.

The segregation practices in Greensboro were the same as in most of the South. In movie theaters black people sat upstairs, white people sat downstairs. Whites went to white-only bathrooms, blacks to black-only bathrooms. Whites drank at white-only water fountains, black people at black-only water fountains. It was as if there were two distinct kinds of human beings inhabiting the town, and the well-kept condition of white facilities and the run-down black facilities made it clear whom the town fathers and businessmen considered the superior kind of human. Some of the most humiliating segregation practices were in dime stores, where black people could spend their money for toothbrushes and shoelaces, but could not sit down for a cup of coffee. The lunch counter was for "whites only." The four young men wondered if they could make a step toward breaking the race line at downtown lunch counters.

That morning, they go into Woolworth's. It is one of those old stores, with streaky yellow light and huge mahogany display cases. It smells of disinfectant and chewing gum. Old ladies with blue hair are moving up the aisles with their colored maids in tow. "I'd like some of those pins, Jemima, and that fabric—isn't it lovely . . ." Books under their arms, they wander around nervously. Joe McNeil buys a tube of toothpaste, Frank McCain buys a pack of notebook paper. Finally, they look toward one another—it is time. Without a word, all four sit down at the lunch counter.

At first the white waitress pays no attention to them. McCain asks for a hot dog and coffee. The confused waitress runs over to the manager. After a moment she returns, "Sorry, I can't serve you. We don't serve colored here." "But you do have hot dogs and coffee," says McNeil. He can see white customers eating that same food farther down the counter. "I can't serve you!" insists the frightened waitress, and she walks away. A black woman washing dishes walks over to them and mutters, "Why don't you boys go out and stop making trouble?"

All afternoon the students stay at the counter. A white policeman walks in from the street. "He paced up and down the aisle," McCain recalled later, "with this club in his hand, just sort of knocking it into his hand and looking mean and red and a little bit disgusted. You had this feeling he didn't know what the hell to do. See, we haven't provoked him outwardly enough for him to resort to violence. And I think it's just killing him."

A couple of older white women also come by. They pat the boys on the back. "It's a good thing I think you're doing," they say.

The school newspaper prints an account of the sit-in. Amazingly, the next day there are twenty-seven students, sitting quietly, textbooks in their hands, waiting for service. The Greensboro newspaper picks up the story. Local white toughs come in to taunt the students, but they sit quietly, refusing to move and refusing to lose their composure. By the next day, white students from North Carolina Women's College join them, occupying stools and refusing to eat until the black students are also served. When the TV cameras pick up the sight of the jeering, foul-mouthed whites, and the quiet, dignified students, something in the South stirs. "Gad!" exclaims James Kilpatrick, editor of the conservative *Richmond News Leader*. "It gives one pause!"

The story flies across the South. Other students, at other universities, see the sit-ins and decide that they want to help. Sit-ins everywhere. The police begin to break up the demonstrations, arresting the students, dragging them away with their notebooks and pencils and slide rules flying. One policeman in Orangeburg, South Carolina, picks up a dropped slide rule. He slides the center scale out at one end. He slides it out at the other. He holds up the rule. "Damnedest switchblade I ever saw," he says finally.

Nowhere else did the sit-ins create as much electricity as they did in Nashville. Fisk University, the American Baptist Seminary, Tennessee A. and I., and Meharry Medical College had an incredibly talented group of young black students, including Marion Barry, James Bevel, John Lewis, Diane Nash, and Bernard LaFayette. For several months Rev. James Lawson, who had studied Gandhi's methods in India, had been holding workshops on nonviolence for these students. "We had begun preparing for sit-ins in Nashville in the fall of 1959," explained Diane Nash, a student at Fisk. "When word came of the North Carolina sit-ins, we began sitting in at Nashville outlets of the same chain stores."

Candie Anderson (later Candie Carawan), a white exchange student at Fisk, was

I'm Gonna Sit at the Welcome Table

I remember, we were at a meeting and song-swap at Highlander when Ernie Martin suggested that *I'm Gonna Sit at the Welcome Table* would make a great lunch-counter song. All we had to do was change a few words. So right then and there, we all changed it. People testing out verses, throwing them in. —*Guy Carawan*

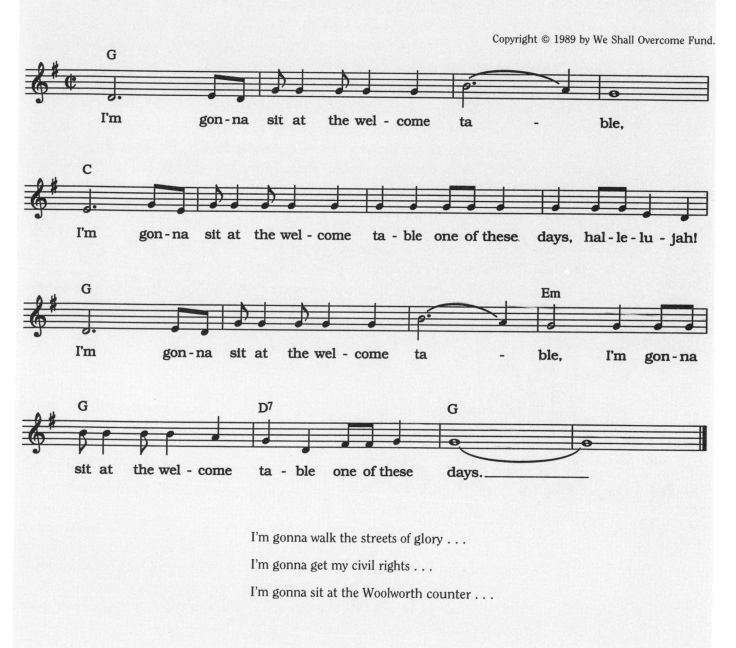

I'm gonna walk the streets of glory . . .

I'm gonna get my civil rights . . .

I'm gonna sit at the Woolworth counter . . .

another regular at Jim Lawson's workshops. "I didn't know whether, as a white person, I was just horning in on someone else's cause," she said. "But the group felt that it was important to show that this was an integrated movement. Also, we had a specific role in the sit-ins. If the stores were on the lookout for black students, white students would go in and take the seats at the lunch counter and then turn them over to blacks."

On February 18, two hundred Nashville students marched downtown and sat at the lunch counters. Miraculously, the sit-in went without incident.

Diane Nash: *The waitresses were nervous. They must have dropped two thousand dollars' worth of dishes. It was almost like a cartoon. We all worked very hard not to laugh, even though I was wall-to-wall terrified.*

Candie Carawan: *We felt like we were going to move a whole society!*

John Lewis: *I had the feeling we were involved in something like a crusade. . . . To redeem the city, like Dr. King said, to redeem the soul of America. You put on your Sunday clothes, and we took our books and papers to the lunch counter, and we did our homework, trying to be as dignified as possible. I drew up these rules, like: "Show yourself friendly at the counter at all times. Sit up and face the counter. Don't strike back or curse back if attacked. Don't laugh out. Don't block entrances." And it ended with something like "Remember the teachings of Jesus, Gandhi, Martin Luther King. God bless you all."*

On Saturday, February 27, violence came.

Bernard LaFayette: *We got word from downtown that the police were going to arrest us. Also, we heard that some people were going to beat us up. On top of that it was cold and it was snowing. This was going to be a showdown. Unfortunately, there weren't many people going out on this demonstration. We debated and we debated, and finally we decided we couldn't let a threat of violence deter us. Well, we went.*

Candie Carawan: *About eighty of us went down to the lunch counter that day, fifty girls and about thirty boys. Two girls and three boys were white. I still remember how neatly we all dressed. The idea was to go just as well dressed, as dignified, as you could. The girls in their white blouses and pleated skirts, and the boys with their suits; some of them even had a Bible under their arms. There were fourteen seats at the lunch counter. Fourteen of us sat down.*

Right away the toughs started throwing things over us and pouring catsup in our hair; putting out cigarette butts on our backs. I've got to say that didn't surprise me. What did surprise me was that when the police came they just watched. Finally they turned to the students at the lunch counter: "OK, you-all nigras, get up from the lunch counter or we're going to arrest you." When nobody moved, they just peeled those people, with their neat dresses and their Bibles, right off their seats and carried them out to the paddy wagons. Before they were out of the store, another fourteen

of us took their places at the counter. They got peeled off, and another fourteen sat down. By the end, eighty of us got arrested. Boy, it was something!

Bernard LaFayette: I was not supposed to be arrested. My job was to help coordinate the sit-ins: if the students were being arrested in one place, my job was to let people know at another location, so they could come and help. The more the merrier in terms of being arrested.

Well, at one place, they had some trouble, so the police asked the demonstrators to leave. The police grabbed a white student and started to pull him out. Well, the black students filed out after the policeman because they were sure they were being arrested also. But the police pushed this white fellow into the paddy wagon and locked the door behind him. They ignored the black students. Then, they locked the door to the department store so no one could go back in.

We waited around very inconspicuously. As soon as one of the customers came out of the door, the students rushed inside. But one of the young ladies pulled me inside. I wasn't supposed to go, but she pulled me. I was literally pulled into the

Everybody Says Freedom

There were parents and grandparents bringing us sandwiches and coffee; there were high-school students marching with us; there were mass meetings, and fund raising; I had never seen a whole community come together like that. When we came to trial a crowd of 2,500 gathered around the courthouse. Mostly, they were people who simply wanted to show by their presence that they were behind the students. As we waited to go inside we sang:

> Everybody says Freedom, Freedom, Freedom, Free*dom*, Free*dom*,

and

> Everybody says Civil Rights, Civil Rights. . . .

I looked out at the curb, where the police were patrolling, and I saw one burly cop leaning back against his car, singing away: "Civil rights! Civil rights . . ." He saw me watching him, stopped abruptly, and walked to the other side of the car.

—Candie Carawan

This old spiritual has been adapted many times. It is perfectly suited for improvising new phrases which overlap the singing of the larger group. Harmony, high and low, can be easily added by the group.

The song can go on as long as any member of the group can think of phrases to throw in. Here are a few of the many hundred we have heard:

> All across the South . . .
>
> In Mississippi . . .
>
> In spite of Ross Barnett . . .
>
> Gain the victory . . .

This might be a good time for a word about endings. Some folk-song traditions call for ending a song abruptly, unpretentiously, on a low note. Other traditions call for the singer to end on a high note, arms wide open. The African American traditions to which most of these songs belong call for not slowing down the rhythm until the last two or three notes. Then, if a song has been sung over and over, till everyone has had a chance to "get into it" or add a verse, it may end rather softly, as though the participants have given their "all," and the last note can be held quite long, but quite softly.

movement. I remember her name—Angela Butler. I told one of the students to get someone else to coordinate because my role had ended.

By April, the Nashville Movement had reached into the whole community.

The movement touched the North. Bob Moses, a mathematics teacher at the Horace Mann School in the Bronx, New York, saw a picture of the Greensboro sit-inners: "The students in the picture had a certain look in their faces—determined. Before, the Negro in the South had always looked on the defensive. This time they were taking the initiative. They were kids my age, and I knew this had something to do with my life." Soon Moses would go south to join the movement.

By early spring, students all across the South were marching and protesting and sitting in. A whole new generation had entered the civil rights movement. The annual meeting of activist southern students at Highlander changed its topic to "The New Generation Fights for Equality." Eighty-two college students showed up. They came from Nashville, Knoxville, North and South Carolina. Forty-seven of them were black, thirty-five were white.

Candie Carawan: *I remember one workshop we had on tactics. The subject worked its way around to going to jail. What good was it, what did it accomplish? Myles [Horton] was playing devil's advocate. That's how he worked—he didn't try to push any idea, he just kept asking questions, making us clarify our thinking. By the end of the discussion we came to the conclusion that if we wanted to make jail part of our tactic, we'd have to be willing to stay in. Otherwise, we'd just be draining our resources in bail money, without tying up the opposition at all. That's the tactic the whole movement used after that. After the freedom rides, and in Mississippi—everywhere!*

The other thing I remember was the music. There was the Nashville Quartet and Bernard LaFayette and his friends and songs from all over the place. That was the first time I heard We Shall Overcome. What a perfect song—it pulled us together with such power, it had such quiet strength. We knew we were going to take it back to Nashville.

Bernard LaFayette: *Myles Horton loved to play devil's advocate. . . . He was arguing the whole question of why do black and white have to be together. He was saying things like "Why don't you do something for yourself? Why do you have to be with white people?" I had never heard a white man say those things to my face, and he was supposed to be a friend. I got madder and madder. Of course, he was trying to force us to be very clear about what we wanted. I knew what he was doing, but it made me furious. He was always pushing you further; you think you have come to some conclusion about something, and there he is, pushing out the walls, and you have to reach out and grab something. That's what a good teacher does—keeps making you rearrange the blankets to make room for broader ideas.*

Student strategy discussion, 1960. Courtesy Highlander Center

I Love Everybody

Don't be confused by singing this song in minor while accompanying it with major chords. This is standard practice in much African American music, and in the blues also.

I love ev-ery-bo-dy, I love ev-ery-bo-dy,

I love ev-ery-bo-dy, in my heart.

I love ev-ery-bo-dy, I love ev-ery-bo-dy,

SNCC button.
Courtesy Avon Rollins

Ella J. Baker, the executive secretary of the SCLC, wanted an expanded version of this meeting—a conference among all the student civil rights groups. She believed that if you could bring people face to face, to share ideas, to work out their problems, to build their own organization, you could unleash a wonderful power. During Easter recess three hundred students gathered at Shaw University, in Raleigh, North Carolina, to discuss the future of their movement. There were people like Diane Nash, who had participated in countless lunch-counter sit-ins, and active white students from the North, like Tom Hayden.

Jane Stembridge: *The most inspiring moment was the first time I heard We Shall Overcome. It was hot that night upstairs in the auditorium. Students had just come in from all over the South, meeting for the first time. There was no SNCC, no funds, just people releasing their common vision in that song. . . .*

The students decided to form their own organization to coordinate sit-ins and nonviolent activities, the Student Non-Violent Coordinating Committee. The first acronym suggested was SNVCC (pronounced "snivick"). But since that made them

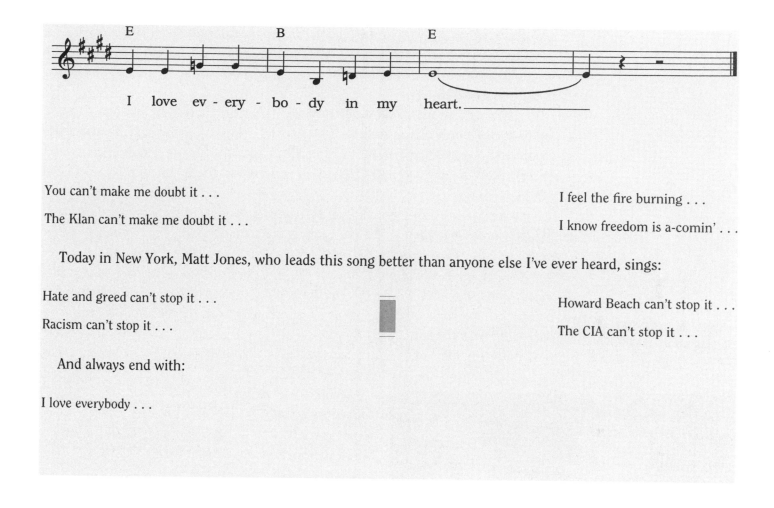

I love ev-ery-bo-dy in my heart.

You can't make me doubt it . . .

The Klan can't make me doubt it . . .

I feel the fire burning . . .

I know freedom is a-comin' . . .

Today in New York, Matt Jones, who leads this song better than anyone else I've ever heard, sings:

Hate and greed can't stop it . . .

Racism can't stop it . . .

Howard Beach can't stop it . . .

The CIA can't stop it . . .

And always end with:

I love everybody . . .

sound like some agency of the KGB, the delegates decided on SNCC (pronounced "snick"). Marion Barry became the first chairperson. Jane Stembridge became their executive secretary, their sole paid staff person.

Profile: GUY AND CANDIE CARAWAN

Guy sits in the study / living room of the home that he and his wife Candie built just outside of Knoxville. Musical instruments, books, and recordings line the wall. Full of energy he moves around, pulling out papers and old photos they have collected during their thirty years on the cultural staff of Highlander. Candie is on the porch placing new strips onto the bottom of a split-oak chair; she's never done it before, but that's part of the fun—learning something new.

Guy: *My father was born in North Carolina, my mother in South Carolina. But I grew up in California. I knew I was part southerner. Sometimes, when my mother* and father would get into an argument, she would call him "poor white trash." He was a poor farm boy and she was a Charlestonian blue blood. I always itched to know more about my roots. Every time I'd hear a recording of a five-string banjo, something in me stirred.

In 1952 Guy heard Pete Seeger play the five-string banjo in Topanga Canyon, fifteen miles north of Los Angeles, and decided to go back and find his roots. He visited the South, then toured the U.S., Europe, and China as a folk singer. After hearing Martin Luther King in 1958, Guy returned to the South to be part of what was happening.

I called Myles; I'd met him before. He said Highlander needed a musical director. My job would be to help get people singing and sharing their songs. When someone began to sing, I'd back them up softly on my guitar so they'd get courage and keep going. Sometimes in sharing a song, people find bonds between themselves that they never knew they had. I can't tell you how many pictures I have of myself standing behind other people, accompanying them on my guitar. I took the job, just for a year—that was thirty years ago.

Amanda Bowens (Purdew) and Guy Carawan. © Joe Alper, courtesy Jackie Gibson Alper

Candie, a native of California, had studied at Pomona College before becoming an exchange student at Fisk.

Candie: *I was raised as a Unitarian; I was taught to believe in equality. Here was my first chance to do something about it. I probably had the most educational semester of my college career. I learned about southern black people, racism, nonviolence, police, jail, southern courts; I met brilliant people like James Lawson who planned these campaigns. On that first day we targeted a few lunch counters and started walking to downtown. My stomach hurt. It always would hurt before a sit-in. I had this cartoon view of southern bigots in my head, and I was sure they would attack us. But no one did.*

After about two weeks of sitting in every day I got arrested. We were pretty sure it would happen. The worst thing was that in jail they isolated the two white women. All the other women were together in one cell. It was really wrenching! The only connection we had with the others was the music—we could hear the women in one cell and the men in the other cell exchanging jokes and swapping songs, making up verses. Then they called down to us and shouted, "Hey, don't you know any songs?" It was a lifeline.

Guy: *Songs were a real lifeline. In 1959, when I came down here, I knew about the old labor-movement tradition of changing an old song into something new, with words for the moment. Solidarity Forever came from The Battle Hymn of the Republic. But the songs that everyone in the South knew, the spirituals and hymns, weren't really being used that way.*

So, at our workshops, when people were looking for appropriate songs, I suggested adapting some of the spirituals and hymns. Some people were offended at first—these were very personal songs about salvation. But sometimes people would be suddenly moved to change a word—like Bernice Johnson Reagon did when she changed "over my head I see trouble in the air" to "FREEDOM in the air"—and something happened. People realized that these were their songs and they could change them to express what they were feeling.

The songs could take on so many meanings. They could be jubilant, or they could be a lament because someone had gotten killed. They could help people gather their determination, or they could be funny and satirical. You could dance to some of the songs, anything to help people get through all this. The music became a part of everything—you couldn't tell who was singer and who was an organizer, because the organizers sang and the singers organized.

This is a culture where everybody sings. So people swapped the songs and the words anytime they got together. Luckily, I got to travel around and hear some of the songs that people created. In the Georgia Sea Islands I had heard Alice Wine, one of the people in our literacy program, sing her great version of the song Keep Your Eyes on the Prize, and I helped spread it around.

Candie: *I was really lucky—my mother and father were out of the country. So I didn't have to deal with worried parents. But my cell mate in Nashville wasn't so lucky. Her parents found her a local white lawyer. Then when he got her out, they whisked her back home. It was a shame. We were kids—we needed our parents' understanding.*

It was just as bad for the black kids—their parents worried that they had spent their lives earning enough to send their children to a good college, and here the kids were, blowing it all. But most parents were supportive.

Guy: *The biggest song-spreading I did was teaching people We Shall Overcome, first at that Highlander meeting in March—that's where I met Candie—and then at the founding convention for SNCC a couple of weeks later. People just heard that song and knew it was theirs—it expressed exactly what they felt.*

That weekend at Highlander was incredibly important. There were eighty people from Nashville and Atlanta and Orangeburg. Most of them had never met before— maybe they had just spoken to one another on the telephone. Some of them were pretty well known already in the movement, like Marion Barry and Diane Nash. Most of the action was right in the center room, where we had the seminars: people sitting around in a big circle and talking about tactics and strategy and goals—nonviolence and civil disobedience, whether to stay in jail or go out on bail, whether or not there should be northerners in the movement and white students, all the big questions. If we were sitting too long, or all talked out, or if someone just got the impulse, we'd sing. Sometimes Bernard LaFayette and James Bevel and a few others and myself would go off into another room, just to jam for a while—they loved hillbilly music! Sometimes, I might jump in with a song I had learned, like *Eyes on the Prize, We Shall Not be Moved,* or *I'm Gonna Sit at the Welcome Table.*

It was a great weekend. But none of us had any idea that this was the beginning of a movement so large.

Candie: *I was also very naive. I was sure that we would have just a few sit-ins, point out to the nation that there was something wrong, and the world would change. It took a while till we saw how deep the roots of racism ran. Quite wonderfully, we did end lunch-counter segregation in Nashville within a few months. But by then we knew that this was just the beginning.*

After the semester, I went back to Pomona in California to finish my senior year. Not because I was in love with college, but because I had to tell people what I had seen. There was an art-history teacher who had always scared me to death, a very— er—forceful person. I told her what I had seen, and she got involved in the movement herself. She went on the Selma march a couple of years later. Another teacher invited me to talk to the Republican Club. On the other hand, the ROTC decided I was subversive, and whenever they did a security check on someone, they asked whether the person knew me. It was one thing to have lived through something extraordinary. How do you communicate that to people?

The songs communicated. Guy came out and brought his music and his documentary tapes, and that really hit people. We even organized a local protest at the Greyhound station in support of the freedom riders. [For the freedom rides, see chapter III.]

Guy: *I think the freedom rides gave the biggest boost there was to the spread of freedom songs. See, after the rides reached Jackson, everybody got arrested and thrown in jail for forty days; the idea of nonviolence is that you don't do violence, but you don't submit to it—you keep coming and coming, and so the freedom riders kept coming and coming. Finally, there were four hundred of them from all around the country. So they held meetings and strategy sessions and religious services, and they sang—the Nashville students sang their songs, and the North Carolina people and the Washington people and the New York people, and the CORE people and the SNCC people. There was even a rhythm-and-blues trio with James Bevel and Bernard LaFayette and Joseph Carter singing things like My Dog Loves Your Dog. After forty days everyone knew all the songs.*

When they were finally released there were so many good new songs and song leaders that they didn't really need me to go around and teach songs. What they really needed was somebody to document all this, to record it, to write it down, because the people in the thick of the action were not going to have time.

Candie: *So, we took our Ampex tape recorder and traveled to Albany and Birmingham and Greenwood—and we went to jail like everyone else. You couldn't be in the movement very long without going to jail.*

Guy: *In 1980 Bernice Reagon brought together about fifty of us from the movement for a reunion. Everybody had a chance to get together and talk about what they did and what they were doing. Charles Sherrod got up and said, "I'm lonely." I knew just what he meant. We were so close to one another back then. We were all living a life that was so close to the bone. Now we've got families and jobs. The movement got people to use the best that was in them, their greatest skills; now, people use their abilities, but with a fraction of the intensity and passion we had then. I was lucky to be a part of it.*

Candie: *What I'll always take with me is the feeling of being a part of this "beloved community." Nonviolence gave us a way to fight for change without hurting anyone, without doing violence to someone else. Whenever I meet people I knew from the movement I can see how they've kept that spirit alive, how they're trying to apply it to their own lives. You really can confront evil, you really can overcome it, and you don't have to fire a single shot. But you can't do it alone. With a community you can celebrate together, sing together, cry together. So many young people in this country today feel so cynical and alone. I think it comes from believing that you just can't change anything, that you're powerless, that you better look out for number one.*

In a place like Nicaragua, where people feel like they are in an endless war against this giant to the north, the United States, there is still a spirit that they can overcome, there is a community, songs, a pulling together. I know something will re-awaken that in our young people. I just don't know when.

Since 1966 Guy and Candie have written four books about the music and the people that they love both in Appalachia and the Deep South. They have also produced a number of documentary albums and videotapes and organized numerous cultural workshops at Highlander. They continue to bring together people and their music and to include the music of people's struggles in their concerts.

Freedom bus outside of Annis-
ton, Alabama. Schulke Archives

III

1961
The Freedom Rides

*W*ith the new energy in the movement, events moved ahead faster than ever. The sit-ins showed the value of publicity, of deliberate, orchestrated nonviolent resistance. How could the energy of the local sit-in movements be moved onto the national stage?

James Farmer, the new head of CORE, hit on an idea. Back in 1947, under CORE's leadership, an interracial group had traveled across the South on interstate buses to test the new law banning discrimination in interstate travel. They called their effort the "journey of reconciliation," but there had been no reconciliation. By the time they reached North Carolina, the bus riders had all been arrested, and the government had not made a move to protect them. The new law was toothless.

In 1961 Farmer and several other movement people decided to have a new journey, not just for reconciliation, but for freedom. They would call it the "freedom ride."

At the end of April, a group of thirteen volunteers arrived in Washington, D.C., for a week of training in nonviolence. The group included Dr. Walter Bergman, a sixty-year-old white professor, and his wife, Francis; James Peck, a white veteran of the earlier journey of reconciliation; Rev. B. Elton Cox, a black minister; Hank Thomas, a student from Howard University; Charlotte DeVries, a white writer from New York; Jim McDonald, a singer; and several others.

For a week, the group planned the fourteen-day trip through the South. At training sessions they learned what to do when arrested, what to do when attacked. They role-played, with some members acting as freedom riders, and others as white toughs. In these little plays, people got thrown off bus seats and lunch-counter stools, got clubbed, got jailed. They tried to anticipate every contingency and then play it out, and then talk about it, then reverse roles and play it out again.

On May 3 they gathered in a Chinese restaurant for what one member called "our last supper." The next day, the riders split into two groups—six boarded a Greyhound bus, and seven a Trailways bus.

Their first destination was Richmond, Virginia; their final destination was New Orleans, and they planned to arrive on May 17, the anniversary of the Supreme Court school desegregation decision.

For a week, the ride continued through Virginia, North Carolina, South Carolina, and Georgia. Then, at the start of the second week, they entered Alabama, the Deep South. Bus 1, the Trailways, stopped at the state line. "A half dozen white toughs got on board. You could see their weapons," said one freedom rider. "They had pieces of chain and brass knuckles and blackjacks and pistols." The bus driver pulled over to the side of the road. "I ain't moving until the niggers get into the back of the bus where they belong." Nobody moved. The thugs started to move back through the bus, yanking black riders from their seats and shoving them toward the rear.

Two of the older freedom riders, Jim Peck and Dr. Bergman, tried to intervene. "Stop that. These men haven't done anything to you." One white grabbed Peck by the collar and swung at him with an uppercut that lifted him into the air. He hit the

Dog, Dog

I lived next door to a man and he had a lot of children, and so did my dad, but we weren't allowed to play together because they were white. But we had two dogs. He had a dog and we had a dog. Our dogs would always play together. . . . So we wrote this song for our group, the Nashville Quartet.

—James Bevel

Guy Carawan accompanying Bernard LaFayette and James Bevel, 1960. Courtesy Highlander Center

Repeat throughout tenor solo

C
Lead (Tenor solo)

1. black dog
2. white dog
3. rab-bit dog
4. coon dog

I'm talk - in' 'bout a   all 'em dogs

all __ 'em dogs   All 'em dogs, Lord, Lord, all __ 'em

No change in tempo

dogs   a love - a my   dog   and then - a   why   can't

dog   a love - a my   dog   and then - a   why   can't

eat this bone! Dog dog Dog dog well then - a

Dog dog (ti - kaw - ka ti-ka) Dog dog, well then a -

why can't we sit un - der the ap - ple tree.

why can't we sit un - der the ap - ple tree.

Repeat B then A very fast; use the following variation for the soloist.

Ⓐ

My dog a - love - a your dog and - a your dog . . . . (drop out)

Falsetto

dog

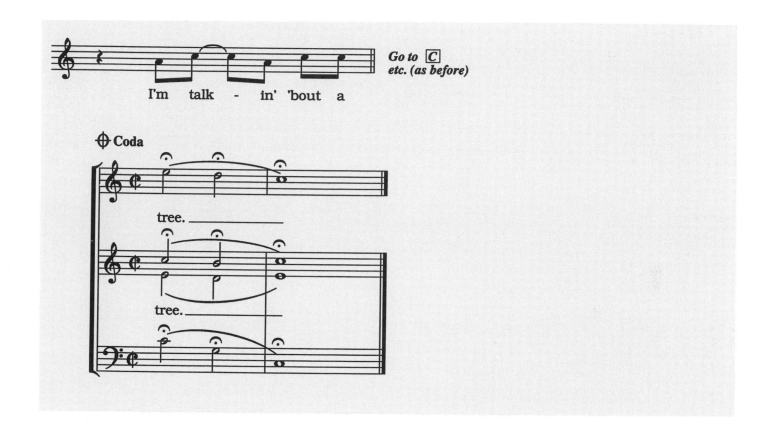

Go to [C]
etc. (as before)

floor unconscious. They knocked Bergman onto the floor next to him and began to kick him again and again in the head. The cerebral hemorrhage that they caused left him in a wheelchair for the rest of his life. A young woman boarding at the next stop looked down at the pools of blood on the bus floor. "Doggone," she said, "has there been a hog killing on this bus?" The bus driver and one of the hoodlums snickered.

The ordeal for bus 1 wasn't over. In Birmingham, a mob of whites was waiting for the freedom riders. Bull Connor, the commissioner of public safety, had refused to post any officers at the terminal because of the Mother's Day holiday. The riders stepped into the terminal. As usual, the whites walked to the black facilities, the blacks walked to the white facilities. The mob ran at them. Jim Peck, who was white, walked toward the black waiting room. A group of local whites jumped on him, threw him on the ground, and began kicking at his head. They left him lying unconscious in a pool of his blood. The ride of bus 1 was over.

Bus 2, the Greyhound, escaped trouble at the border. It got as far as Anniston, Alabama, where a crowd of over two hundred waited at the terminal. The riders decided to stay on board. The driver started the motor, preparing to move on to the next stop. Suddenly, the mob moved forward, slashing at the bus tires with knives and ice picks. Here, a few officers had been assigned, but they stayed in the crowd, shouting and joking with attackers. The bus started to move. The townspeople jumped into their cars and pursued, shouting and throwing bottles and bricks.

Just outside of Anniston, one of the slashed tires blew. The bus stopped. The crowd moved closer. The riders inside were debating whether to stay in the relative safety of the bus or risk getting out. "Guess they're going to stay inside!" shouted a skinny teen-aged boy. "Then let's keep them inside!" shouted someone up close to the bus. At that the crowd moved closer, blocking all the doors so they could not be opened.

There was the sound of smashing glass, and then a puff. Someone had broken a rear window and thrown a fire bomb into the bus. People inside started screaming. Albert Bigelow, a freedom rider who had been a navy captain, got the emergency door open and started evacuating the passengers—possible death at the hands of the mob was better than burning to death in the bus. The driver went out first, then the freedom riders stumbled out, choking on the smoke of burning metal and horsehair upholstery. They threw themselves, retching, onto the ground. Just seconds after Bigelow jumped to safety, the bus exploded. "That's probably what saved our lives. The crowd didn't want to get burned," said one of the riders afterward.

The next day, the riders tried to regroup at the Birmingham bus station. Almost all who could still walk wanted to go on. But the bus driver would not take them. They argued and pleaded, but the company refused. Finally, the toll of their exhaustion and injuries began to tell, and most of the group decided to fly on to New Orleans, their scheduled destination. It seemed like the ride had stopped cold.

But by now it had attracted eyes all over the nation. Diane Nash called up James Farmer and pleaded with him to let the ride continue. She said she had a group of SNCC volunteers who would go on in place of the injured riders.

"You know that may be suicide," Farmer answered.

"We know that," she answered, "but if we let them stop us with violence, the movement is dead! Every time we start a drive, they will just roll in the violence. Your troops have been badly battered. Let us pick up the baton and run with it."

The new freedom riders arrived in Birmingham by the afternoon of May 17. That night Bull Connor arrested them, threw them into cars, and sent them 120 miles to the Tennessee state line. They sat by the road for a while, the students and a couple of the original group who were still physically sound enough to travel, then found a nearby house and called the office in Nashville. Two hours later, a car driven by Les Lillard picked them up and took them 120 miles back to Birmingham. The next evening the group, augmented with ten more volunteers from Nashville, stepped out of the white waiting room and walked toward the Birmingham–Montgomery bus.

The driver took one look at them, got up out of the driver's seat and left the bus.

Bernard LaFayette: *"How many of you from CORE?" he said. Nobody said anything. "How many from the NAACP?" Nobody said anything. He had never heard of*

SNCC. So he said, "Well I have one life to give, and I'm not going to give it to the NAACP or CORE."

So we stayed there. Went into the white waiting room and waited for the next bus to Birmingham. That's a principle of nonviolence. Wherever you're stopped, that's where you stay—until you get some results. Well, they stopped all buses going to Montgomery. They knew we'd be on the next one.

This was my first time coming in contact with the Ku Klux Klan. They spent the night with us in the white waiting room. In fact, Robert Shelton, the Imperial Wizard, was there. He was this small guy. He was a Baptist minister wearing this black robe, this beautiful black satin robe with this huge serpent on the back of it. A gorgeous thing—almost oriental. Then there were the lower ranks—these guys with these bed sheets on, they looked sloppy and had coffee stains on their sheets and their hoods were all falling down. They didn't look impressive at all. So, all night, while we tried to sleep, they didn't have anything to do but walk around and step on our feet. And they were drinking these sodas with ice and when they finished their drinks, they'd drop the ice on us.

There were Birmingham police there. They had these long night sticks. They were nodding off too. They were probably working overtime. Every once in a while, you'd hear this clank on this ceramic tile floor and it would echo throughout the bus station, off of the high ceiling; it was like an echo chamber. You'd know a policeman had dozed off and dropped his night stick. And you'd always know who dropped it, because he had to lean down to pick it up. Another thing is, if you had to go to the bathroom, the policemen weren't going to follow you to protect you. If you went in by yourself, the Klan would probably follow you in. So we had to go in a group. When one man had to go, every man went. We made such a large group, the Klan couldn't even get in.

By now, the eyes of the Kennedy White House focused on Birmingham. Every moment that the riders stayed in town, the potential for violence grew. The president had an upcoming summit conference with Khrushchev and did not want pictures of American riots in every newspaper. While the riders sat around the bus station, phone calls and threats, recriminations and vows, flew from Washington to the Alabama state house.

Finally, the state promised to protect the riders from the time they left Birmingham to the time they arrived at Montgomery, ninety miles away—a two-hour bus ride.

Bernard LaFayette: *A news reporter came and told us, "They're making arrangements for you. They're getting a bus." But then we found out they were going to put us on a special bus that would take us straight through to New Orleans—no stops. That was against everything we'd been trying to do. We were trying to go stop by stop, as ordinary passengers, desegregating the local facilities and meeting with the people in each city as we went. Zipping us straight through to New Orleans in a few hours would have accomplished nothing. We tried to explain that, but Kennedy and the reporters didn't quite get it. They didn't understand that the goal was to desegregate as we went along. They thought the goal was to get to New Orleans. They probably started agreeing with the governor saying these kids are just trying to get killed. It is not always easy to communicate.*

Anyhow, what we did was buy one-way tickets to Montgomery. That way they couldn't whisk us straight to New Orleans without kidnapping us. They would have to take us to Montgomery.

By dawn on Saturday morning, May 20, eighteen students sat on the platform of the Birmingham bus terminal. The bus stood abandoned. Finally, after three hours, a bus driver appeared at the platform. It was the same one who had earlier refused to give his life for the NAACP. Without a word, he began to collect tickets. Only this time some bus-company officials also boarded the bus. "It looked like the driver had made a deal—he would put his life on the line if his bosses would do the same," said LaFayette.

As the bus pulled from the station, the riders could see the elaborate arrangements made for them. A plane flew overhead, and police and troopers lined the road. The riders sat back and read magazines. Maybe this wouldn't be too bad. But as the bus approached Montgomery, the plane veered off, the state troopers disappeared, and the patrol cars drove away. The city was stone quiet as the bus turned in and out through the streets. Strange for any downtown to be so silent, even on a Saturday afternoon. Finally, as the bus turned into the terminal, every living person seemed to disappear.

Bernard LaFayette: *We learned later that they had blocked off the streets around the terminal. Meantime, hiding inside the terminal were all these white farmers dressed in overalls, and others in khaki and blue jeans and plaid shirts. There were also a few women sprinkled in the group. They held axe handles, lead pipes, pitchforks, and baseball bats. I can still see the mean pinched looks on their faces.*

The media was waiting for us outside the terminal. We were preparing to get off the bus. Then the terminal doors busted wide open and the mob started to pour out. I told everyone, "Listen, I want each of you to hold hands with your partner, the person sitting next to you. You're responsible for that person. Whatever happens to that person, you stick with them." That way nobody would be alone.

Fred Leonard: *And then, all of a sudden, just like magic, white people were everywhere, sticks and bricks. "Nigger," they were shouting, "kill the niggers!!!" I was thinking, if we got off the back of the bus, like they wanted, maybe they wouldn't kill us. Then I decided, No! I'll get off the front and take what's coming!*

Bernard LaFayette: *The first thing, the mob ran after the reporters, started busting cameras and knocking them to the ground. Clearly they were trying to smash the camera lenses, to blind the eyes of the press. One reporter had a special metal camera with lead all over it. They smashed it right in his face. It was awful, and that was still white on white. We were gonna be next—and we were clearly freedom riders, black and white.*

We decided that the ones of us who survived would regroup that evening at the First Baptist Church, where there was a scheduled meeting.

While the mob was busy attacking the press, the freedom riders made their way off the bus.

Bernard LaFayette: *We tried to get the women into the cabs. There were a few black-run cabs at the terminal. But as soon as the white women got in a cab, the black driver would get out. This was the Deep-South; the drivers were brave enough to drive the freedom riders, but there was a taboo—a black man couldn't drive a white woman.*

So then we tried to put the black women into the cabs, but they wouldn't go. "How are we going to look—the black men stay and the white men stay and the white women stay, but the black women leave." I think that's when I really started to respect women's power.

But now we were trapped, nowhere to go. Our only hope was to stay together. We joined hands in a circle and started singing We Shall Overcome. The song has different meanings at different times. Sometimes you're singing about the problems all over the world—"We shall overcome"; sometimes you're singing about problems in the local community—"We shall overcome." But in that bus station it was a prayer—a song of hope that we would survive and that even if we in that group did not survive, then we as a people would overcome.

Then the mob broke into the circle and grabbed Jim Zwerg, a student from Appleton, Wisconsin. They all stomped on him and made him the victim because he was white.

John Lewis was right next to me when they swung a metal bat at him. Then I saw them grab William Barbee, a student at American Baptist Seminary in Nashville, and throw him down onto the pavement. They had a foot on his neck and they tried to force a lead pipe down his ear.

They began to chase Bernard LaFayette and Fred Leonard. They trapped the two men at a railing overlooking a parking lot fifteen feet below.

Bernard LaFayette: *After I had taken a few punches in the chest, which cracked my ribs, it was a question of whether or not we should jump off now or let them push us. We decided to jump. We saw we were in the back parking lot for a federal building—we figured we'd be safe there, and we ran for it.* It was the post office. The two men ran past the clerks and the mail sorters, pursued by this screaming mob, while piles of letters and postcards flew everywhere.

Meanwhile, John Seigenthaler, the representative of the Justice Department who

I'm on My Way

In 1942, I sang with a group in New York called the Almanac Singers. One of the others in the group, Arthur Stern, heard a black woman singing:

> I'm on my way to Canaan Land,
> I'm on my way to Canaan Land,
> I'm on my way to Canaan Land,
> I'm on my way, praise God, I'm on my way.

He changed only two words, and the Almanacs sang it and got many crowds of white and black people to sing it with us. After I got out of the army, I sang it around the U.S.A. for fifteen years, and was deeply moved when I heard it being sung by the freedom movement in 1960. We are all links in a chain.

A note about overlapping voices: One of the loveliest African traditions is for the solo or bass voice to hold a long note while others come in on top, or vice versa. Sometimes it can sound confusing as two different sets of words are being sung simultaneously. But as a group of singers become acquainted with a song and with themselves, they will enjoy this "answerback" singing. European musicians call it antiphony. (Needless to say, the soloist can vary notes, the group response can add harmony.)

—Pete Seeger

I asked my brother to come with me . . .
I'm on my way, great God, I'm on my way.

If he can't go, I'm gonna go anyhow . . .
I'm on my way, great God, I'm on my way.

If you can't go, don't hinder me . . .
I'm on my way, great God, I'm on my way.

If you can't go, let your children go . . .
I'm on my way, great God, I'm on my way.

was there at the president's orders, lay unconscious just outside the bus terminal, victim of a blow with an iron pipe.

The battered riders sat in the street or lay on the bus platform, dazed, blood pouring down their shirt fronts, as the crowd moved away. Jim Zwerg sat in a parked car, trying to staunch the blood flowing from his nose and his face. A black woman who had seen the beatings called an ambulance. A black ambulance came for Barbee, who was completely unconscious. But no help came for Zwerg. A reporter asked Police Commissioner Sullivan if they could get an ambulance for Zwerg. The commissioner shook his head: "He hasn't asked for one." Finally, a local black minister took him to the hospital by car.

Bernard LaFayette: *I saw Barbee in the hospital later; his face was all bashed in—on the side—all smashed, and he had tubes in his nose and everyplace else. One of his pet phrases had always been "good brother," he called everybody "good brother." And he said to me, "Good brother, when are we going again?" I could see he was in no shape to go, but I didn't say anything. He was ready.* Barbee never recovered from the beating. He remained partially paralyzed until he died in 1986.

Bernard LaFayette: *That night the police were waiting for us at the First Baptist Church. They were all through the church, with our pictures and warrants in their hands. As soon as they saw us, they were going to arrest us. We came in through the back of the church. We saw these choir robes. We put them on, kept our faces covered, and walked on up to the choir stand. We had been singing together for a long time, since Nashville, so we sounded good. We had harmony, we knew the words. We sang away. John Lewis had a patch on his head—we put him in the back, so they couldn't recognize him. We could see plain-clothes men out there in the congregation, looking up at the balcony, looking around the room. They never recognized any of us.*

The freedom riders slept in the homes of Rev. Fred Shuttlesworth and several of the black parishioners of the First Baptist Church. The next day, a big meeting was going to take place at the church, in honor of the freedom riders. On the way to the church with James Farmer of CORE, the reverend noticed that something was wrong.

James Farmer: *The streets were full of roving bands of short-sleeved white men, shouting obscenities. . . . The crowds grew thicker as we approached the church. . . . As we got close, they clogged every roadway, waving Confederate flags and shouting rebel yells. . . . As we stopped, the crowds grabbed hold of the car and began rocking it back and forth. We shoved the car into reverse, heavy-footed the accelerator and zoomed backwards. . . . The only approach to the church was through a graveyard, but we were too late, the mob was already there, blocking the entrances to the church. Shuttlesworth just plowed in, elbowing the hysterical white men aside. . . . "Out of my way," he said. "Let me through." The mob obeyed. . . . Looking back, I can only*

First Baptist Church, Montgomery, Alabama. © Joe Alper, courtesy Jackie Gibson Alper

guess it was an example of the "crazy nigger" syndrome—"Man, that nigger is crazy; leave him alone, don't mess with him."

The inside of the church was a fort under siege. Twelve hundred people jammed together, "three or four times as many as the church was supposed to hold, and it was hot and it was uncomfortable," according to Frank Holloway, a student from Atlanta who had come to join the freedom riders. "Some were trying to sleep, but there was no room even to turn around. But it was a relief, like a haven, to be among friends."

"Everybody say Freedom!" came a shout from the platform. "Freedom!" responded the group. "Say it again!!" "Freedom!!" even louder. "Freedom . . . Freedom. . . . Freedom Freedom Freedom!!!" like a locomotive gathering speed, twelve hundred voices chanting louder and louder.

By afternoon, Martin Luther King and Ralph Abernathy had arrived from Chicago. They were moving through the aisles, chatting with people—some old friends from the movement, some who had never seen King before. Suddenly, someone came running from the church office. There was a phone call for King. A few minutes later, he reappeared in the church, and found James Farmer: "The attorney general wants to stop the freedom rides. He wants a cooling-off period, so you can work things out." "Let me check with Diane," said Farmer. He elbowed his way through the crowd to find the freedom riders. They were sitting with the choir near the pulpit, bandages around some of their heads. He told them about Robert Kennedy's proposal. Diane Nash looked at the other riders. They shook their heads. "No," she said. "We can't stop now, not right after we've been clobbered." Farmer nodded, and went to find King: "Tell the attorney general that we've been cooling off for 350 years. If we cool off anymore we'll be in deep freeze." King smiled: "I understand."

While he returned to the phone, the meeting began. "Ain't but one chain a man can stand, that's the chain of a hand in a hand." The voices of little Diane Nash and Ruby Smith from Atlanta, of John Lewis with his head in bandages, and the other freedom riders, rose from the platform. Jim Zwerg and William Barbee were still in the hospital from their beatings. "Keep your eyes on the prize, hold on, hold on, hold on!" The voices of hundreds rose from the heat and the sweat. A woman in the back, in a purple and pink flowered dress, lifted her head; her voice rose high, weaving harmonies over the group.

Outside, the mob grew in the darkness. Two or three thousand, shouting at the church, "Hey, come on out!" Suddenly there was a roar from the back of the church. A group of locals had found a passage to the basement. The mob surged toward the back door. They began kicking at it: "If you ain't comin' out, nigger, we're comin' in!" They threw themselves against the door. It creaked. Inside, a group of parishioners started to build a barricade. They put chairs and desks against the door. They leaned their weight against the weakening plywood. Again the crowd threw themselves at it. There was a splintering crack. The door started to split. They were coming in!

Upstairs in the auditorium, King was starting to speak. People could hear the shouts from the floor below. His voice rose over the sound: "The first thing we must do tonight is decide we are not going to become panicky; we are going to be calm, and we are going to continue to stand up for what we know is right. . . . Alabama will have to face the fact that we are determined to be free!" The audience had grown quiet now. The only sound came from the mob downstairs. "Where the hell are those marshals?" shouted someone below. King continued, "We have come too far to turn back. We are not afraid, and we shall overcome."

From down below, they heard the screaming: "They're inside!" There were thumps and groans as the mob started to move in. At any moment they would be rushing up into the sanctuary. Suddenly, as if out of nowhere, a group of two hundred U.S. marshals and a division of the Alabama National Guard appeared and moved into position outside the door. The crowd retreated, throwing bottles as they went.

Two days later, two buses of freedom riders left Montgomery for their next stop—Jackson, capital of the most segregationist state in the South, Mississippi. There were twenty-seven now, including Farmer himself. As they crossed the line, they saw the famous sign WELCOME TO THE MAGNOLIA STATE.

James Farmer: *Our hearts jumped to our mouth. The Mississippi National Guard flanked the highway, their guns pointed toward the forest on both sides of the road. One of the riders broke out singing, and we all picked it up. I remember the words:*

> *I'm taking a ride on the Greyhound bus line*
> *I'm riding the front seat to Jackson this time*
> *Hallelujah I'm a-traveling*
> *Hallelujah ain't it fine*
> *Hallelujah I'm a-traveling*
> *Down freedom's main line.*

Courtesy Ed King Collection, Tougaloo College

No mob greeted the riders in Jackson—only the local police. As each freedom rider stepped off the bus, an officer stepped to his side. As the rider walked into the all-white or all-black waiting room, the policeman would take out his gun and say, "Keep moving."

Outside, the riders found themselves herded into wagons and driven to jail. This time the federal government did not help.

Cordell Reagon: *We were in the Hinds County jail, and we were fasting and singing all the time. We were in separate cells, but we could sing to each other so it wasn't bad. Suddenly one morning, very early, they come for us and they say, "Get dressed. You're leaving." This was Jackson, Mississippi, in 1961. Well—I knew I was going to die. All I saw was these people taking us out in a field and shooting us. I prayed and gave up my life in my mind.*

They threw us into these big old trucks, really high up, the bed of the truck as high as your head. And we were in there, all thrown together, and it was dark, no ventilation, and we all knew that we were going to get killed. They could kill every black man and black woman among us and it wouldn't even make the papers.

Hallelujah, I'm A-Traveling

In a New York City radical newspaper in 1946 I read about the trial in Columbia, Tennessee, of some black people accused of "fomenting racial unrest." One verse of the song was quoted. I wrote to Harry Raymond, the newspaper reporter, and got the rest of the verses. He said the author was a farmer who asked to be anonymous. We printed the song in our little folk-music bulletin, *People's Songs.* I sang it in schools and camps throughout the U.S.A. in the 1950s. The freedom riders added new verses. If the farmer near Columbia is still alive, or any of his family, I hope they will know how this song helped make history.

—*Pete Seeger*

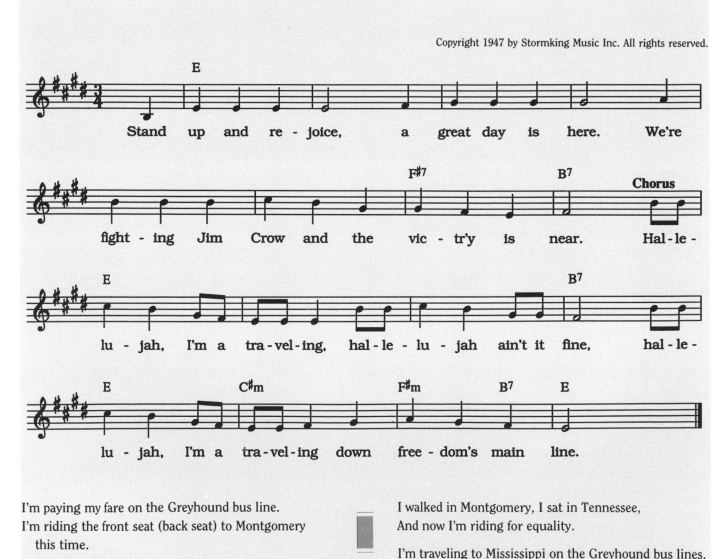

Stand up and re-joice, a great day is here. We're fight-ing Jim Crow and the vic-tr'y is near. Hal-le-lu-jah, I'm a tra-vel-ing, hal-le-lu-jah ain't it fine, hal-le-lu-jah, I'm a tra-vel-ing down free-dom's main line.

I'm paying my fare on the Greyhound bus line.
I'm riding the front seat (back seat) to Montgomery this time.

In Nashville, Tennessee, I can order a coke.
The waitress at Woolworth's knows it's no joke.

I walked in Montgomery, I sat in Tennessee,
And now I'm riding for equality.

I'm traveling to Mississippi on the Greyhound bus lines.
Hallelujah, I'm a-riding the front seat (back seat) this time.

THE EARLIER VERSES, FROM 1946

I read in the news the Supreme Court has said,
Listen here, Mr. Jim Crow, it's time you was dead.

The judges declared in Washington town,
You white folks must take that old Jim Crow sign down.

Columbia's the gem of the ocean they say.
We're fighting Jim Crow in Columbia today.

Well, I hate Jim Crow and Jim Crow hates me.
That's why I'm fighting for my liberty.

I felt so helpless, I became furious. Despite all my nonviolent training, that was when my rage became solid inside me.

We end up at Parchman penitentiary. It is six in the morning now, and they start taking us off. Two white men are with us. They are real committed pacifists. They decide to be noncooperative. So they wouldn't get off the truck. The police just dragged them off. They hit the ground like sacks. Then they put these cuffs on them, the kind with tongs on the inside that stick into your skin, and they drag them, while another guard walks behind them and keeps walking on their feet.

We get inside—and there two rows of cells facing each other across a long corridor. The men are on one side and the women are on the other. The guards yell for us to undress. But these cats land in the middle of the corridor because they are not cooperating.

The guards start yelling at the guys, "Git up! Goddamned nigger lover!" and kicking them, and we're not doing anything. They tell them, "Take off your clothes." These guys don't move.

So, the guards bring over some cattle prods—electric cattle prods—and they start sticking them. They take these cow prods and they start up and down these cat's bodies. These guys are just laying on the floor, their bodies twitching and jerking with the electric shocks, but they don't even make a sound. Finally, they just cut the clothes off these guys and took them away.

I'd been through a lot—having cigarettes put out on me, and been hit and bashed— but this day, watching these two men, I lost my fear. It happened to all of us in that jail. We realized we could say to them, "Kill me—I'm going to love you anyhow. But I am not going to cooperate with you."

We all realized that we were much more powerful than them. That's when we all became noncooperative. We took the mattresses off of our beds, and stood them up against the wall, and slept on a half-inch piece of steel. We fasted and everything.

The rednecks did everything they could. Every time they tried to bogart us—they would bash our heads against the wall, everything they could—and we would just keep singing and praying. They could not understand the stuff."

The buses continued to come, and the jails grew full—fifty riders, a hundred riders. Over the summer, hundreds of freedom riders traveled through the South. Arrest after arrest. But the people continued to ride, month after month, till the jails swelled near to bursting. By July there were three hundred freedom riders in Parchman alone. Quakers from New York and students from Nashville and teachers from Detroit

Which Side Are You On?

In 1932 this song was written as a union song by Florence Reece, a Kentucky miner's wife. In 1941 it was recorded by the Almanac Singers in New York City in the album *Talking Union* (still distributed by Folkways). From person to person the song has spread through the English-speaking world; in 1986 it was recorded in England with new verses by Billy Bragg. In 1961 one of the most exciting reincarnations came with the verses written by James Farmer and the freedom riders.
—*Pete Seeger*

While I was in the Hinds County jail, myself and some of the freedom riders were speculating about the attitude of local Negroes. We learned through the trustees at the jail that most local Negroes were with us, but afraid to do anything because of fear of reprisals. They told us that, of course, there were a lot of Uncle Toms around and it was hard to tell who was with us and who was not. That's when I rewrote the old labor song *Which Side Are You On?* right there on the spur of the moment.
—*James Farmer*

(Optional words for the song leader are in italics.)

Come all you free-dom lo-vers and lis-ten while I tell Of how the free-dom ri-ders__ came to Jack-son__ to

and old people from Knoxville and merchants and janitors shouted and sang and prayed and joked from cell to cell. They changed the prison, and most of all they changed one another.

"There were lot of little movements going into Parchman, but one big one coming out," said one freedom rider.

For all the coming years of the movement, the title freedom rider became a synonym for civil rights worker, the highest compliment, a testament to a person's courage and tenacity and selflessness.

dwell. *(Tell me now)* Which side are you on *(Oh won't you tell me)* Which side are you on? *(Sing it o-ver now)* Which side are you on *(Once more now)* Which side are you on?

My daddy fought for freedom and I'm a freedom's son.
I'll stick right with this struggle until the battle's won.

Don't Tom for Uncle Charlie, don't listen to his lies,
'Cause black folks haven't got a chance unless we
   organize.

They say that in Hinds County, no neutrals have they met.
You're either for the freedom ride, or a Tom for Ross
   Barnett.

Oh people can you stand it, oh tell me how you can.
Will you be an Uncle Tom or will you be a man?

VERSES BY LEN CHANDLER

Come all you northern liberals with all that excess fat,
A few days on the picket line will sure get rid of that.

Come all you high-tone college girls, pronounce your
   final *g*'s,
But don't forget your grandma, she's still scrubbing
   on her knees.

ABOVE AND OPPOSITE. *Danville,
Virginia, 1963.* © Danny Lyon /
Magnum

Profile: BERNARD LAFAYETTE

It is 1988. Bernard sits in the minister's office at a Brooklyn church. A lively, friendly man, he is visiting from Nashville, where he is vice president of the American Baptist College (formerly the American Baptist Seminary, which he attended as a student). He is in the North as a consultant for the New York State Martin Luther King Commission, teaching the techniques and philosophy of nonviolent protest.

In about 1950, I was a kid living in the ghetto in North Philadelphia, Pennsylvania. There was a boycott going on against a local baking company called Tasty Bread because they had refused to hire any blacks. Tasty Bread also made Tasty pies—deep filled pies and they were just great. But we kids got together and decided that we

were going to boycott not only Tasty bread but Tasty pies, too. That was a big sacrifice for a ten-year-old boy!

Nine years later, as a student at the American Baptist Seminary in Nashville, Bernard began to attend nonviolent workshops with his roommate John Lewis and his friend James Bevel. This became the center for the Nashville sit-in movement, and for the fledgling new student organization SNCC.

[In the winter of 1961] *I heard about the freedom rides which CORE was putting together. John Lewis, my roommate, was going to go. I wanted to go. But you see, I was still twenty. I needed parental permission. So I sent the permission form to my parents. Not only would it have been dangerous, but it would have meant dropping out of school in May, before exams. My parents said, "Do you think we're signing your death warrant? You're staying in school!" So I didn't go. I kept in communication with John, who went on to Washington, D.C., to join the other riders.*

You know, they were attacked in Birmingham and a bus was burned outside of Anniston. People were in the hospital for broken bones and smoke inhalation. Governor Patterson of Alabama said he couldn't give protection and Attorney General Kennedy said he had no jurisdiction, so the rides stopped for what they called a cooling-off period.

In Nashville we had just finished desegregating the movie theaters. That had been our project for 1961. We had fourteen nights of demonstrations, very well planned, spreading out the hundred selected students over five movie theaters in the downtown area. They attacked us every night, and we responded persistently but nonviolently and we won. We were well-trained, experienced, nonviolent Green Berets. We were like troops waiting for another war. We had experienced lots of violence, so we couldn't understand why they were stopping the rides. So we decided that we were the ones to continue the freedom rides.

CORE didn't want our blood on their hands. But we were determined. We felt that we had to continue. The movement was at stake. If you allow a show of violence to stop your movement, then you'll only encourage a violent response every time you do something. A principle was at stake here. Also, we were outraged. They had done such dastardly things to the freedom riders, and the whole nation, from the attorney general on down, seemed paralyzed.

It was a very serious decision—my parents were furious—this was the first time we really felt like we were facing death. But what we started to realize was that we weren't too young to face death. We might have been drafted to die in a war, like many of our fellow students who were killed in Vietnam. We could have died senselessly in a car accident. The whole question of life and its fullness and its limitations and its value came up. Life is so tenuous. We felt an urgency of making a contribution; we felt like we had been very fortunate to be black and to have been in good colleges in the South, and we felt we wanted to give something back; we owed a debt to leave things better than we found them.

On the other hand, if we didn't make our contribution then, while we were in college, we'd be in the working world raising families and buying homes. Very soon we'd have too many obligations. This was the time to make a contribution.

After his release from Parchman State Prison, Bernard asked to go to Selma, Alabama, the city of Sheriff Jim Clark.

I went to Selma in 1962 to get the lay of the land, to see if a movement was possible there. We had already been told that it was hopeless; between Jim Clark's crazy posse and the apathy, there wasn't any sense in starting anything there. But we figured if the place was so bad, it could only get one way—better. There were good people there—Marie Foster and Mrs. Boynton and Attorney Chestnut—and they wanted to get a voter-registration campaign going. So my wife and I went back in '63 and stayed. There was no great expectation that Selma was a major campaign, so I could spend time, without pressure, building an organization, a movement, in my own style. Basically, what we did was weld together relationships between the people who had leadership potential. That's the key to building a movement. You can always get people to come together to make a coalition for one march, but the next week everyone goes his own direction—everyone has his own cause. But a movement happens when a group of leaders can stay together for a sustained period of time. And it worked. That group sustained itself and grew, and two and a half years later came the Selma march.

Singing was one of the greatest joys in the movement. We had a group—Jim Bevel, Joseph Carter, Sam Collier, and myself—the Nashville Quartet. We made up a lot of songs—funny songs, hillbilly songs. We sang around the country. We went up to New York and got a chance to sing with Pete Seeger and Guy Carawan and the Montgomery Trio. It was fun! It also meant that people thought all the stuff we were doing was important! Then we went down to the Gaslight Pub in Greenwich Village and there was this woman singing there, and Guy Carawan took us over to meet her—she was an old folk-singing friend of his. We got up and sang songs with her— This Little Light of Mine. Her name was Mary Travers—of Peter, Paul, and Mary.

What I miss is the way people worked together and stayed together to change things. Now I'm training people for community action, for organizing their own nonviolent movements. Today you have movements around strikes like the Hormel plant. You have a movement against capital punishment. You have a very strong peace movement. But it's not coordinated yet.

I would like to see some of the energy that goes into commemorative marches and reminiscences turned into active movements for the present. The best way to honor Martin Luther King is to follow in his footsteps, not necessarily in the line of march, but in the line of protest. Martin Luther King said the movement (civil rights, human rights, people's rights—all of the nonviolent movements) doesn't move in a straight line; it goes through watersheds, it comes in stages. Now we are between stages. But the largest stage in the nonviolent movement is yet to come.

Night march, Albany, Georgia.
Courtesy Highlander Center

IV

1961–1962
Albany, Georgia
"Ain't Gonna Let Nobody Turn Me 'Round"

*T*he Albany Movement officially began one rainy late-autumn afternoon. On November 22, five students sat down at the lunch counter at the Trailways bus terminal in Albany, Georgia, to test the new federal ruling prohibiting segregation in interstate bus and train stations. A sleazy bus-station lunchroom. The terrified white waitress looking at a half dozen black freedom riders at the counter. Grease and grits on the grill, plastic castings of women with huge breasts at the cashier's station, and outside, the stirrings of a coming storm. Suddenly, the storm breaks, and amid the crashes of thunder, twenty-five yellow-slickered troopers run in waving their clubs. The five students go to jail. Three years of upheaval have begun.

Before it was over, Martin Luther King and Ralph Abernathy would make it a major campaign. The attention of the entire nation would focus on this little southern city of fifty thousand. And it would become the forge to toughen a generation of young people who would lead the civil rights movement in the coming years.

In September 1961, Cordell Reagon and Charles Sherrod, two early SNCC field secretaries, had come to Albany to help organize a local movement. Sherrod was twenty-two, and Reagon was nineteen.

Cordell Reagon: *When we first went to Albany people would cross the street to avoid us. We were followed by the police everywhere we went. We had no money. We slept in people's homes, or on the floor. A couple of times we even slept in an abandoned car. Sometimes, Charles and me might slip into the Albany State College dormitory late at night, and sleep there. When the community saw that we weren't dead and that the college students were speaking to us and listening to us, they started to pay*

If You Miss Me at the Back of the Bus

In 1962 there was a campaign to desegregate the municipal swimming pool in Cairo, Illinois, and some of the demonstrators were put on trial. At just that time, the brother of a civil rights worker was drowned while swimming in the nearby Mississippi River, the only place where local black people could swim; the last verse given here was actually the first one written by Chico Neblett. Soon verses were added by him and others in Cairo, all sung to the tune of *Come On Up to Bright Glory* (same melody as *Oh, Mary, Don't You Weep*). This high-spirited song was never sung twice the same way, as new verses were improvised—"Come on over to the State House, I'll be governor there," and so on.

This transcription is by Ethel Raim.

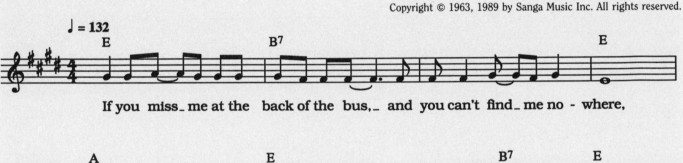

If you miss me at the back of the bus, and you can't find me no - where,

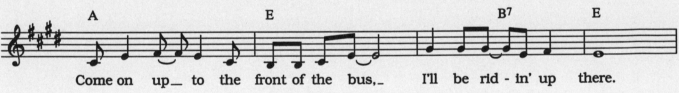

Come on up to the front of the bus, I'll be rid - in' up there.

us more attention. Then the middle-class leaders—the teachers and the small business people—accepted us, and finally, when they saw it was safe, the preachers began to speak to us. That was the beginning of the Albany Movement.

Three days after the November 22 arrests, the movement held its first mass meeting. In a church the arrested students, out on bail now, spoke to the assembled four hundred people and introduced a new song to them.

Goldie Jackson, secretary to the Albany Movement: *It was Saturday night at the Mount Zion Baptist Church. So many came, there was no room for some to sit. That night we sang We Shall Overcome for the first time. . . . People stayed there all night that first night, singing and praying.* Songs had been at the heart of the movement

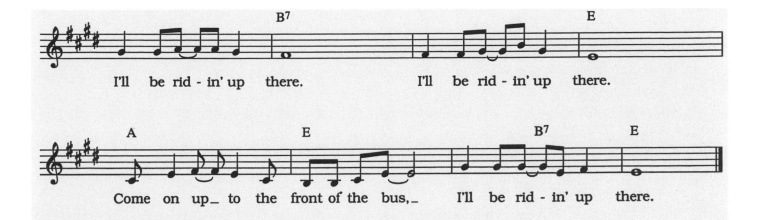

I'll be rid-in' up there. I'll be rid-in' up there.

Come on up to the front of the bus, I'll be rid-in' up there.

If you miss me at the front of the bus, and you can't find me nowhere,
Come on up to the driver's seat, I'll be drivin' up there.
I'll be drivin' up there, I'll be drivin' up there,
Come on up to the driver's seat, I'll be drivin' up there.

If you miss me at Jackson State, and you can't find me nowhere,
Come on over to Ole Miss, I'll be studyin' over there . . .

If you miss me from knockin' on doors, and you can't find me nowhere,
Come on down to the registrar's room, I'll be the registrar there . . .

If you miss me in the cotton field, and you can't find me nowhere,
Come on down to the courthouse, I'll be voting right there . . .

If you miss me on the picket line, and you can't find me nowhere,
Come on down to the jailhouse, I'll be rooming down there . . .

If you miss me in the Mississippi River, and you can't find me nowhere,
Come on down to the city pool, I'll be swimming in there . . .

since Montgomery, down through the sit-ins and the freedom rides, but here in the rich musical soil of Albany, they flowered as never before.

Bernice Johnson Reagon: *The mass meetings always started with these freedom songs. Most of the meeting was singing. Songs were the bed of everything, and I'd never seen or felt songs do that before.*

On December 10, a group of black freedom riders entered the white waiting room of the Albany railway terminal, and a group of whites entered the black waiting room. They were arrested, and the Albany Movement became a national event; the press arrived.

Ain't Gonna Let Nobody Turn Me 'Round

This old spiritual (its last line slightly changed) was first introduced in Albany by Rev. Ralph Abernathy during the summer of 1962 when mass arrests and demonstrations erupted for the second time. He taught it one night to a mass meeting at Mount Zion Baptist Church. It immediately caught on and became widely used in the demonstrations. A nationally televised CBS documentary showed spirited students rhythmically clapping and singing "Ain't gonna let Chief Pritchett turn me 'round" while the policemen picked them up, two to a student, and carried them into the paddy wagons.

—Guy Carawan

". . . anybody who thinks this town is going to settle back and be the same as it was, has got to be deaf, blind, and dumb."

—A black woman in Albany, Georgia

This transcription is by Ethel Raim.

Ain't gonna let Chief Pritchett turn me 'round, turn
 me 'round, turn me 'round,
Ain't gonna let Chief Pritchett turn me 'round,
I'm gonna keep on a-walkin', keep on a-talkin',
Marching up to freedom land.

Aint' gonna let no police dogs . . .

Ain't gonna let Nervous Nellie . . .

Ain't gonna let no Uncle Tom . . .

Ain't gonna let segregation . . .

Ain't gonna let Mayor Kelley . . .

Ain't gonna let no fire hose . . .

Ain't gonna let no jailhouse . . .

Ain't gonna let no injunction . . . (after a federal
    injunction prohibiting further demonstrations)

Whatever verses you choose, you should end with:

Ain't gonna let nobody . . .

Tuesday: A total of 267 students from Albany State College and Albany High School marched on the train station. Police Chief Laurie Pritchett roared over his bullhorn, "Get off the street or you will be under arrest. You are blocking traffic." They kept on walking. Two hundred went to jail.

Wednesday: Lines of people, over two hundred, poured from the churches, singing and praying and kneeling on the sidewalk, asking for the release of the arrested freedom riders. The police moved in. Said Marian King," We didn't expect to be jailed for praying. We were terrified."

By the middle of December almost five hundred demonstrators were in prison. The jailhouses bulged and still the movement continued.

The demonstrations continued that day, and the next and the next. Before and after each demonstration—a prayer meeting. Pat Watters, a southern white reporter, drawn into the movement after hearing the freedom riders singing on a passing bus, sat in back of the Shiloh Baptist Church and listened:

A quietly spoken prayer begins:

> *Guide them, Lord*
> *Guide our white brothers*
> *Guide them, Lord . . .*
> *Make them conscious of the fact*
> *That men are all equal*
> *That color does not matter*
> *To the Lord*
> *But purity of heart.*
> *We love freedom*
> *We love freedom*
> *We love freedom.*

The congregation has joined in, repeating with the preacher: We love freedom. Four little girls, one with pigtails, are on the front row between their father . . . and their mother.

Watters returned again and again:

This has become a nightly thing, sitting like this in the mass meeting at the church, sitting limp, my head back, giving myself to the sweating, the heat, seeing through sweat-blurred eyes back through the crowd the many black faces, arms, wet, too, with sweat, cardboard fans in soft motion in the heat, in the crowd. They are singing the unaccompanied, hand-clapping music of the movement, and I give myself to . . . the music.

Cordell Reagon: *Charles [Sherrod] and I brought with us the music we had been doing on the freedom rides, and when it mixed with that rich Baptist and African tradition in Albany, something happened. Before we came, the kids might have been* singing the Negro National Anthem—we brought something to them and they gave something to us, a spirit, a power that made us less afraid. Together we all made something unbelievable, a total spiritual experience.

Take two churches directly across the street from one another, filled to the rafters with people—people hanging out of windows—I'm talking about people eighty or ninety years old, and young kids and babies, and nobody is speaking. You could sit in the heat and feel the energy. Anybody that felt the spirit move them might start moaning, or somebody might go to the front of the church and get down on their knees and start praying. Not these mild-mannered prayers you would get out of a book, but something that was folklore with its language and its images and its rhythms, something that was music in itself. Then two thousand people would join in—

It was what we called common-meter hymns. The preacher might just say, "Line it out!" He might say, "Thank you, Jesus," and someone else might say," I hear you brother." And then you go into "Ahhhhhhhhhh." And two thousand voices say "Ummmmmm."

See, it's not about words, it's about spirit. These people might not know each other. The kids probably made fun of their parents for going to church and singing this old stuff. But now the kids were caught in the grip of the movement, and without ever having done it before, the spirit caught them, and as natural as daylight it comes out of the spirit and their soul.

Finally somebody would get up and say, "It's time to go. Let's just line on up and keep on singing." Then we would line up and march out of the church and singing and singing, and that music kept us together, and kept us less afraid. It's like an angel watching over you. You know you are in trouble, you know you are going to get your butt beaten, you know you are probably going to jail, you know you might even get killed, but the sound, the power of the community was watching over you and keeping you safe.

I like to think that Sherrod and I were responsible for bringing movement music to Albany, and then having the sense to leave the music alone and let it grow in its own way.

Bernice Johnson Reagon: *There was a woman at Shiloh Baptist Church who would sing one song for an hour. It is not a song anymore. People are clapping, feet are going, you can hear her three blocks away. Your ears are not enough, your eyes are not enough, your body is not enough. The only way to survive the singing is to open up and let go and be moved by it to another place. . . . The voice I have now I got . . . after I got out of jail, I did the song Over My Head I See Freedom in the Air, but I had never heard that voice before, I had never been that me before. . . . A transformation had taken place in all of us.*

Friday night Martin Luther King arrived. The next night in the Shiloh Baptist Church, the congregation was singing "Everybody says Freedom, Everybody says

Boys in a park.
© *Robert S. Reiser*

Over My Head I See Freedom in the Air

The power of this song comes through when it is sung with no accompaniment, and disarming simplicity. People heard Bernice Johnson Reagon sing it in the early sixties, and their lives were changed. Now I urge readers of this book to listen carefully to this woman, and read what she writes. She is one of the wisest people I know. Her work as a scholar, teacher, singer, songwriter, and organizer of the singing group Sweet Honey in the Rock is just becoming known worldwide; in 1989 she received a MacArthur fellowship.

—*Pete Seeger*

Slowly – freely, unaccompanied

O-ver my head_____ I see free-dom in the air, O-ver my head,___ oh Lord,_____ I see free-dom in the air, O-ver my head_____ I see free-dom in___ the air, There must be a God_____some-where.

Over my head there is singing in the air . . .

Over my head there is glory in the air . . .

Over my head I hear praying in the air . . .

Over my head I see victory in the air . . .

Freedom, Freedom, *Free-dom.*" Suddenly, silence—King spoke. At the end of his sermon, he said, "Don't stop now, keep moving. Walk together, children. Don't get weary." In the following silence, *We Shall Overcome* rolled forth verse after verse, toothless old men, schoolteachers in glasses, children, young men, pouring the passion from their bellies and hearts into the words. King decided to stay.

Pat Watters: *His entire career was turned in the happenstance of the hour. . . . the people in the church that night so caught Dr. King in their fervor that he could not leave them.*

The next day a hundred followed him and Abernathy to jail. Total jailed—six hundred.

A fifteen-year-old girl: *We marched around the courthouse first. Nothing happened. We decided to go again and got to the corner, and a policeman said we were under arrest. They pushed us into the alley and took our names. . . . Then they loaded us on a bus. It was a regular city transit bus. . . . [At the jailhouse] they told us not to sing and pray. But we did pray. Everybody prayed real soft. We kneeled and prayed during the night.*

In the streets, in the jails, in the churches, they sang, while the grim and red-faced segregationists solemnly saw the end of society and swore undying hatred against the black integrationists.

Every day, the march to the bus terminal, or to the courthouse, and every afternoon the arrests:

From the diary of one march participant: *Reverend Wells and a 13 year old boy led today's march, behind them several hundred—the song, Ain't Nobody Gonna Turn Me Around. . . . Round the block, turn left toward the crumbling Jefferson St. Trailways station. Police and angry local whites line the route. A policeman steps forward—"Have you a parade permit?" "No I don't" answers the reverend, and he kneels, "This is the time to pray," he cries. "Every man is created equal, every man is created free, regardless of the race and to the kind. Oh Lord do not leave us alone in this struggle. . . . They think they are going to kill all of us. How many are they going to kill? They can't kill us all."* The police bring over the paddy wagon, and as the prayer continues, they carry off the marchers one by one on stretchers, carry them to jail.

And every night, the meetings—"in the packed-in, ecstatic heat" Pat Watters described.

Ralph Abernathy: "We don't want to be the white man's brother-in-law. . . . All we want to be is his brother. . . . it appears to us as we look around this audience tonight that it is he who tried to be our brother-in-law. . . . I drove to the office of my church yesterday and just as I started to put the key in the door, a white insurance agent came down the street. . . . He was real fat and it was real hot. I was sweatin' and he was sweatin' and there sat a Negro woman on the porch as she always does, right across from the rear of my church office. And he passed by and he says, ah, 'Good mornin', Auntie' . . . and I looked at him and said, 'When did she get to be your auntie?' The Negro does not want to be his brother-in-law, his cousin, his aunt or uncle or BOY. All he wants to be is his brother!"

Martin Luther King: "The Albany Movement is a great movement. . . . It breaks all academic lines. The Ph.D's and the No-D's have joined together. It breaks all denominational lines—the Baptists, the Methodists, the Presbyterians, the Holy Rollers, the Church of God in Christ, the Church of Christ in God. . . . It breaks all age barriers. It is not a youth movement; it is not an adult movement; it is not a middle-age movement; it's not an old-age movement. . . . this is something remarkable.

"[Gandhi told the Indian people], 'Now we're just gonna march. If you're hit, don't hit back. They may curse you. Don't curse back. They may beat you . . . but just keep goin' . . .'

"Just a few men started out, but when they got down to that sea more than a million people had joined in that march . . . and Gandhi and those people reached down in the sea and got a little salt in their hands and broke that law, and the minute that happened it seemed I could hear the boys at Number Ten Downing Street in London, England, say: 'It's all over now.'

"There is nothing in this world more powerful than the power of the human soul, and if we will mobilize this soul force right here in Albany, Georgia, we will be able to transform this community."

"Freedom—not at high noon, but NOW!" shouted the preacher, and the people echoed back, "Now! Now!" and with a clapping foot-stamping rhythm that grew faster and faster like a locomotive, "Freedom! Now! Freedom! Now! Freedom Now Freedom Now Freedom Freedom!"

After three years, there was only partial integration in Albany. A. C. Searles, editor of the *Southwest Georgian,* a black newspaper, said, "What did we win? We won self-respect. It changed all my attitudes. This movement made me demand a semblance of first-class citizenship."

© *Diana Davies / Insight*

We'll Never Turn Back

If you cannot sing a congregational song at full power, you cannot fight in any struggle. . . . It is something you learn.

In congregational singing you don't sing a song—you raise it. By offering the first line, the song leader just offers the possibility, and it is up to you, individually, whether you pick it up or not. . . . It is a big personal risk because you will put everything into the song. It is like stepping off into space. A mini-revolution takes place inside of you. Your body gets flushed, you tremble, you're tempted to turn off the circuits. But that's when you have to turn up the burner and commit yourself to follow that song wherever it leads. This transformation in yourself that you create is exactly what happens when you join a movement. You are taking a risk—you are committing yourself and there is no turning back. . . .

Bernice Johnson Reagon.
© *Robert S. Reiser*

Organizing is not gentle. When you organize somebody, you create great anxiety in that person because you are telling them to risk everything. Put yourself in the place of a woman getting by as a hairdresser. You spend your day curling and frying hair, curling and frying. Somebody asks you to put up some civil rights workers in your home. You have to imagine what is going to happen: there may be people shooting up your home; you have to picture the check you get, the car you drive, everything you own, going on the block. You decide to take that risk because this is important enough. . . .

When you get together at a mass meeting you sing the songs which symbolize transformation, which make that revolution of courage inside you. . . . You raise a freedom song. —*Bernice Johnson Reagon*

We've been 'buked and we've been scorned. We've been talked a-bout sure's you're born._ But we'll nev-er____ turn_ back, no we'll nev-er turn____ back,____ un-til we've all____ been_ free and we have e-qual-i-ty____ ty.____

We have walked through the shadows of death.
We've had to walk all by ourself.

We have served our time in jail
With no money for to go our bail.

(DOUBLE VERSE)
We have hung our heads and cried,
Cried for those like Lee who died,
Died for you and died for me,
Died for the cause of equality.

8 3

Profile: CORDELL REAGON

A thin man forty-four years old, sitting in the kitchen of his loft apartment in Westbeth, in New York's Greenwich Village. Boxes are all over. He is going to Tennessee to sing with a gospel group for a year—a year of "musical and spiritual renewal." We sit next to a large open window looking out onto the street. Twilight deepens as we talk, until I can barely see him in the darkness.

As a child I always loved music. I come from a musical family. At a family reunion, we have three hundred or four hundred members—we have entire gospel groups and boogie-woogie groups. It's a mixed family—we even have redneck crackers playing banjos and telling stories. One man, a stone-cold cracker raised in Tennessee, insists on coming to this reunion. "This is my family," he says, and he plays his banjo and winds out the most incredible stories about our family—teaching us things about ourselves that most of us had never known. For years I resented this white part of my family, and now I'm finding I love them.

I grew up in Nashville with fourteen brothers and sisters. I was going to be a gospel singer. Then, as a teen-ager, I was going to be a rock-and-roll singer. I would hang around the clubs, drink beer, and sing till four in the morning, and get whipped like a dog by my mother and brothers when I came sneaking in so late.

Cordell Reagon.
© Robert S. Reiser

Then came the sit-ins. Nashville became a real center for activity. But I was unconscious. I was still into my rock and roll. I was a high-school student. My high school was just down the street from Fisk University. And every day I would sit in school, and see all these college students marching downtown, right past our school. Well, we didn't really respect them. First of all, we all considered the Fisk students the children of the black intellectual elite. Snobs, in other words. They looked down on us, too. Anytime we'd try to work with them, they'd say we high-school students were "too undisciplined."

One day they came by, and just on impulse I got some friends together and said, "Let's go." We weren't committed to the cause or anything. We just wanted to see what they were up to—it looked exciting. And we hated being left out. So, about five or six friends and myself just walked out of school that day. We cut school, and joined onto the tail end of that march.

They were marching to the jail, where Diane Nash, one of the main student leaders in the movement, was being kept. We go down to the jail, and we're all singing. There up in the jail cell we could see Diane. And everyone is shouting and waving. And I'm just looking. There is something amazing—a black woman only a couple of years older than me, up in this cell. There was some spirit, some power there, I had never seen before. Suddenly, I realized that everyone had marched down the street, and I was all alone staring at the cell. I ran down and caught up with the end of the march. But, I figured then I better not let these people go. There is some power here that I had never experienced before.

Part of the draw had to be the music. I had never really heard such music. After I joined the marches in Nashville, I met Guy and Candie Carawan. I thought they were the strangest people I had ever seen—white guy with his guitar trying to sing black spirituals, and this girl, his wife, singing along. They were trying to sing this black gospel music with a twang. Thing is I didn't know anything about protest music. After I got in, and was on the bus rides, I had learned how to recreate old songs with new words. I saw other people do it and then I did it—natural evolution. I loved music, and music was what held the movement together. It was like we were made for each other.

There was music in everything we did. If you had a staff meeting, or if we were just around the office, somebody would just come out with a song. Or if there were bad feeling, a painful discussion, tension, anybody, not a singer or anything, just anybody at the meeting or in the office, would open up with a line of a song, and somebody else would take it over, and somebody else would add a verse, and by the end, everybody would be hugging each other and loving each other. You can't have a movement without that.

So I stayed with them. I went on the sit-ins. I got disciplined—I went to the nonviolent workshops. I listened to talks on nonviolence. I learned how to be non-cooperative. I went to Mississippi to work with Bob Moses. By the time I joined the freedom rides, I was a committed pacifist. I couldn't believe all this was happening. I couldn't believe I could just sit at a lunch counter and let people spit in my face, and spit up your nose and put cigarettes out on my back, and not respond.

I don't know if I still could be such a pacifist. I'm too angry—God put me here for some purpose, I am not an accident, and I am not going to let someone mess with me or just take away my life before I am ready. If I give up my life it will be in a struggle that I choose. My love doesn't carry as far as it did then.

The music doesn't change governments. Some bureaucrat or some politician isn't going to be changed by some music he hears. But we can change people—individual people. The people can change governments.

Selma, Alabama, 1965.
© Joe Alper, courtesy Jackie
Gibson Alper

Interlude
Telling the Story

Whatever small protection we had came through news reports that brought our actions to the attention of the nation and broke the cover of secrecy. . . . Whenever a field secretary was jailed or a church mass-meeting bombed. . . . whenever a local leader's home was shot into, Julian Bond and I went into high gear.   —*MARY KING, SNCC PUBLIC RELATIONS*

Even if somebody got hit in the head with a rock, it didn't mean a goddamned thing unless you got a picture of it.   —*DANNY LYON, SNCC PHOTOGRAPHER*

You needed everybody. You needed Marion Barry in the office writing press releases, you needed Stokely [Carmichael] in the field inspiring people, you needed Matt Jones singing the songs. It was painful for Matt to pick up the paper and read about what we're doing in Birmingham and Danville, and he's in Columbus, Ohio, doing a concert to raise money. But we needed everybody doing what they were doing.   —*AVON ROLLINS, SNCC EXECUTIVE BOARD*

*B*ehind the front lines of the movement, behind the field secretaries, behind the marchers, behind the shock troops of the movement, were thousands of people who made it possible for the movement to continue. They spread the word, they took the pictures, they paid the bail. You can't have a spear with just a point—you need a handle as well.

Avon Rollins: *So little credit has been given to the black women who made up a huge part of the movement. They not only marched and got beaten, but they did the baking and the cooking and brought the food to the mass meetings. They cared for the youngsters who came from all over the country and let them stay in their homes.*

There were women who suffered the most terrible physical brutality—pushed down stairs and kicked by police. I developed a whole new respect for the women in the movement.

Violence is a fearful thing. You don't know what is going to happen. People don't realize how frightened you get. I remember when I had to take a stand, where the words wouldn't come out of my mouth, where my teeth were just crushing together, chattering because the fear was in me so strong, not knowing what was going to happen. Then I'd see these black females out there, and I knew I couldn't let them take the beating, and the words would come out and I would make my stand.

We never give credit to those who gave their money or their homes or the love and support to the young people who were in the movement.

Profile: DOTTIE ZELLNER

Dottie, now living in New York and working for the Center for Constitutional Rights, was secretary and assistant director of public relations for SNCC under the direction of Julian Bond, between 1961 and 1963.

I grew up in the fifties. Nothing was happening. Adults acted impotent. Suddenly, here was an opportunity to be right where history was being made. It wasn't always wonderful. A lot of times we felt like we were butting our heads against a stone wall. But you knew what you were doing made a difference.

I hung around the SNCC office just to see if I could help. I didn't get any salary for almost a year. I was a fast typist. Fast, with a lot of errors. So Forman asked me to work at night, typing up affidavits from the field secretaries when they came back to Atlanta. They would sit next to me and talk about what happened when they took people to the courthouse in Liberty, Mississippi, or wherever. Here were people three–four years younger than me, kids; and what they had done was so brave. You would listen to the stories and try to be nonchalant, but inside you couldn't.

On the other hand, these were the people you worked with every day. They were on the phone, they sat in the office, you couldn't lie down and die every time you saw them—they were your co-workers. Sometimes they'd tell these terrible stories and they would be funny. People would laugh.

I don't like to tell heroic stories—I am philosophically against it. In fact, when we wrote our press releases they were completely understated. Julian [Bond] and I never sent out a release that wasn't strictly factual. I think that was what made them so devastating to people. And when people would talk in the office and tell us their stories, they were very quiet, very understated—I remember how Hollis [Watkins] would just quietly tell me, "We were walking up the steps to the courthouse and suddenly this guy came out of nowhere and you're not going to believe what he was swinging from his hand!"

The stress was incredible. A very well known psychiatrist who lived in Atlanta volunteered his services to help out. He was fascinated by what made these people able to do what they did. So, whenever they were in town, field secretaries would drop in and talk to him. He wrote a paper about what makes heroes tick. He said, far from being neurotic as some psychiatrists claimed, these were extremely solid, well-integrated personalities.

The payback came when we went north and met the movie stars and the celebrities and they were in awe of us—they hung on everything that someone like Bob Moses or Bob Zellner would say. We were their movie stars. Then of course we'd go back south where we were treated like dirt.

These were some truly incredible people. If you had a SNCC meeting in 1964, sitting in that room were the most creative, intelligent young people, black and white, of their generation. To me they were just friends.

At one point the Freedom Singers were using the office to practice. You couldn't work. The music was fantastic. They would go on for hours. One song like This Little Light of Mine could go on for a half hour. They sang like nothing I've ever heard. But most of the time we were too busy to sing—I remember cranking the mimeograph machine, and Forman's running around trying to get a lead on raising some money, and Julian's on the phone trying to find out who has been arrested. We didn't have much time to sing.

Now, in the context of twenty years, what I remember most are the personalities. Bob Moses—quiet, thoughtful. He never ever raised his voice. He could sit and listen at a meeting for hours without saying a word. But when he spoke, everyone listened. Stokely was a really extroverted, outgoing type. McDew was hysterically funny. Danny Lyon was a funny man too.

I was very lucky to have the sense to join the movement and throw myself into the middle of it. What I miss is being part of something so vast—to know that tens or hundreds of thousands of people are with you. We don't realize how many people made the movement possible. It was millions—having millions of people working together to make things better. It's there today, but it's not focused. There is an incredible energy out there. People don't realize the power they have. I pray that kids today find a cause and can feel like we did then.

Profile: MATT JONES

Matt, a small, energetic African American man of about fifty, sits drinking tea. He wears a stocking cap over his gray hair. Even while we talk acquaintances drop into the snack bar to speak to him. Right now he is running a community coffeehouse that features political music. "It is a place for people who usually don't get a chance to sing to come and share their songs."

Matt was an organizing secretary and a Freedom Singer for SNCC from 1963 to 1965.

When I was about five years old I lived in a town called Lewiston, North Carolina, right down the road from a woman called Ella Baker. I didn't know who she was at the time, but everyone knew she was doing something important for our people.

My father, a principal in the elementary school, wrote an article for the Raleigh News and Observer talking about the bad conditions in the black schools—windows with no glass, no heat for the students, and so forth. Well, this was the early forties, so the Klan came after him.

A white man who was a real segregationist came to my father and warned him to leave town. He said the Klan was out to get him. Sure enough, that night the Klan surrounded the house, shining their lights at us, and they asked for him. But he had already gone. We were scared to death that they would take it out on us, but they left the family alone. We left the next day. Later on my father told us it was a white man who warned the Klan to stay away from the family. Dad always kept the man's picture on our mantel place.

There is a tradition in our family. We had always been literate. My great-great-grandfather taught his master how to read. He designed the master's colonial house. My cousin Chance, some years older than us, was the one who fought segregation on railroad dining cars and took the case all the way to the Supreme Court. That was the branch of the family with Paul Robeson—of course, respectable families didn't talk about Paul in those days. He was not respectable. When people mentioned his name, we'd just look around like it was some stranger they were mentioning. But we all knew he was family.

So, there was this activist strain in my background, but I never got involved while I was growing up. I was going to finish my graduate degrees and maybe become an educator like my father.

But when I was a student at Tennessee State in Nashville, all hell started to break loose—the sit-ins were spreading. A group of students from Fisk University were sitting in on the Nashville stores, and it was getting nationwide attention. But I still didn't do anything. I had faith that the elders, the teachers and the ministers, would show us the wisest course. Besides, unlike Fisk, Tenn State wasn't a very politically minded school—our main preoccupation was with our football team, which kept winning games in spite of second-rate equipment and broken-down buses.

One day Dr. W. S. Davis, president of the school, called us into the auditorium and spoke: "Governor Buford Ellington of the state of Tennessee has promised us two new thirty-thousand-dollar buses with water fountains for our football team." Everyone cheered, naturally. "However, we must all agree to take no part in the demonstrations going on in Nashville."

I was furious. I said to myself, "The elders have been bought—they are not going to help. You're going to have to do this yourself." So I went right down to Fisk and spoke to Reverend C. T. Vivian, who was coordinating student sit-ins, and I said, "I want to help."

He sent me out on my first demonstration. I was arrested in four hours at a place called Cain-Sloan's, a five-and-dime. I'll never forget the first time I just stood. They came up to hit me, and I just stood.

Well, I was married at the time and trying to earn a decent living, so I went to Macon, Georgia, to teach mathematics and music in junior high school. I tried to keep silent, just do my job. But one day, I was in a bus, and it was full of black people, and it went through a white neighborhood, and white people started getting in. The bus driver yells out to me, "Move to the back of the bus." Automatically I got up and moved back. Then I started to think, and I got madder and madder, and finally I *walked up to the bus driver and I told him, "You asked me to move to the back of the bus, and I did it this time—but I'm never going to do it again."*

I was humiliated. So, I started talking in school to my students. This was just around the time they were organizing the Macon bus boycott. The principal warned me to stay out of it. But some people asked me to speak at a demonstration. The principal told me, "No speech!" "Can I sing?" I asked. "All right," he said. So I wrote a song for the occasion. I stood up in front of everyone and started to sing:

> *What is this road we travel on, it looks so dark and gloomy?*
> *We chose this road because we know it leads us to equality.*
> *Yes, this is freedom road that Jesus trod, so I am told.*
> *Haste, haste, along this path, although this walk may be our last.*
> *God has brought strong and violent men,*
> *Many are placed in front of them.*
> *Now this road through Macon goes,*
> *Where it'll stop, nobody knows.*

It was my first freedom song.

Matt had to leave his job. He returned to Knoxville, where he met Avon Rollins, then a young activist in SNCC. He joined the SNCC staff in 1963 to help in the Danville campaign.*

When I got there, I saw they needed somebody to work with the local youth, to train them how to demonstrate and how to protect themselves. Being a teacher, it was a natural job for me.

Jim Forman had taught us early that the way you change people is one on one. That's how I worked with the kids, one on one. I trained them to be ready and to move with fifteen minutes' notice. There were demonstrations, boycotts, actions going on all over town; and we couldn't let the word get out where we were going to be. In the morning I would call maybe four or five of the kids and tell them to get ready. I'd call another five or six and tell them to stay by their phones in case they were needed. I wouldn't tell them where we were going. The kids would come down with their dungarees and their toothbrush—dungarees so they wouldn't get their good clothes torn if they got dragged by the police, and the toothbrush if they had to spend the night in jail. They were nonviolent guerrillas.

Then, at the request of James Forman, he joined the Freedom Singers, the group

---

*Danville, Virginia, was the site of one of the bloodiest and least-known campaigns of the civil rights movement. Night after night, the police attacked protesters with sticks and dogs and hoses, as Avon Rollins described it, "rolling the children like leaves down the street with their hoses." On one horrible night a thousand people were chased through the streets, beaten so badly that hundreds had to be hospitalized. But by harassing and arresting reporters as well as demonstrators, the city achieved an almost complete press blackout, and little news of what was happening reached the outside world.

that Bernice Johnson Reagon, Rutha Harris, Cordell Reagon, and Charles Neblett had started in Albany, Georgia.

Freedom Singers.
© Joe Alper, courtesy Jackie Gibson Alper

It turned out to be one of our best fund raisers. Some weeks we sent back four or five thousand dollars. People always look down at fund raising, but it is what keeps an organization alive. We did see action. In Yellow Springs, Ohio, Antioch College was having a protest, and so help me, when the town reacted, I thought I was back in Mississippi—they gassed us and beat us, burned crosses on the lawn during our concert. I couldn't believe I was up in the liberal North.

We still considered ourselves field secretaries, and I would work doing organizing in Mississippi and Atlanta. But the Freedom Singers took up more and more time. Others would taunt us, "Why don't you join us in the field?" People tend to look down on fund raising. But I made a choice. SNCC couldn't live without money.

After leaving the movement in the late sixties, Matt went through a difficult time.

We couldn't get jobs. Soon as you applied, they would look at your record—see you spent all this time in jail and had the FBI on you. They didn't want any part of you. Most of us had stopped our education short to get into the movement. Most of us were going on for master degrees and doctorates—we would have been lawyers and doctors and ministers. I was slated to go on to grad school. That's how it was in our family. Some of us went back to school; but the ones of us who were in the field never really went back. We had given too much—seen too much—felt too much. Who knows.

The kids look at us now, they say, "Oh, he never did anything."

I've kept on writing. I want to make songs that will move and change people. I've done music for Northern Ireland and southern Africa. In London I did music with Bob Marley. I guess I'm a singer-organizer.

I never really took a job since then—not one that felt like a job. I tell people I've only had but one job that felt like a job in my life—that was field secretary for SNCC. Everything else I've done has been like second nature. At a reunion a couple of years ago, everyone was singing Oh Freedom. So I sang a verse, "No more job over me." I looked around and I was singing all alone! No help on that verse. They all had legitimate jobs or were in politics. But I feel if the world is in the condition it is, what other job can I have than what I do?

Demonstrating G.I.

I was in solitary in Danville—they didn't want anyone associating with me. This soldier was thrown in with me. I couldn't figure out why. So he told me his story. He dared to demonstrate with his uniform on. So the Secretary of Defense McNamara told him that he couldn't do that anymore. But he did. So they threw him in jail—they had to keep him isolated until the army figured out what to do with him. In solitary you don't get books and papers, so I wrote the song out on toilet paper.

—*Matt Jones*

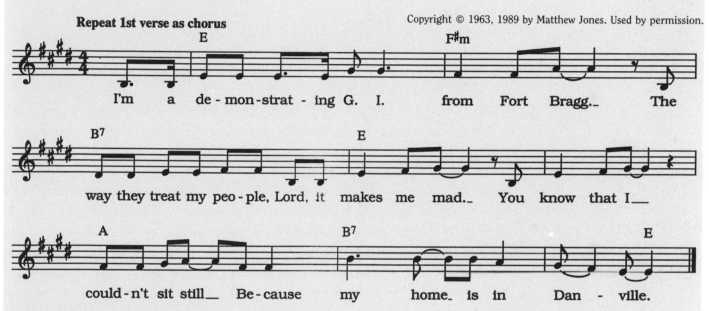

Repeat 1st verse as chorus

I'm a de-mon-strat-ing G. I. from Fort Bragg._ The way they treat my peo-ple, Lord, it makes me mad._ You know that I_ could-n't sit still_ Be-cause my home_ is in Dan - ville.

I came home one Friday night,
I saw my sister fighting for her rights.
I said, "Keep on Sis, and I'll be back,
Standing tall in my boots so black."

Sitting in camp I read the paper,
I said to my sergeant, "I'll see you later."
I caught the bus and came on home.
"I told you Sis, you wouldn't be alone."

I got arrested on a Sunday eve.
The policeman said, "You've been overseas,
But don't you forget one simple fact,
That your skin is still black."

I was bound in jail for over a week,
All I got was some beans to eat.
On a rusty tray, I was fed
And I slept on an iron bed.

Secretary of Defense McNamara
Said, "Come on Boy, what's the matter?
I don't care if you fight for freedom,
But please take off your uniform."

I said, "Well I'm an American fighting man,
And I'll defend my country as long as I can,
But if I can defend it overseas,
Why can't you set my people free?"

Come on army, air force and navy,
Come on you soldiers, and don't be lazy.
If you want to integrate,
Come on down here and demonstrate.

Profile: DANNY LYON

Danny sits on a battered couch in his studio, part of an old barn near his home up in New York's apple country. The walls are covered with his prints, some dating back twenty years to his days in the movement, some as recent as last month. He is now putting together *Merci Gonaives,* a book of photos tracing Haiti's recent turmoil and its reaching toward democracy.

Danny joined the movement during the summer break after his junior year at the University of Chicago, when he hitchhiked down to Cairo, Illinois, with his Leica camera in his pocket.

The first morning there was a meeting in a church—it was one of the first times I had ever been in a church. John Lewis spoke. In his own way John was as great a speaker as Martin Luther King, and he was my age. He was maybe twenty-one years old. I can still hear his Alabama voice.

Then something happened that changed me for the rest of my life. It was a fundamental break with anything that had ever happened to me before. In Chicago I had been with people who sang folk songs and held meetings—people speaking out against the Korean War, against the government; people with all kinds of ideas about what the world should be like. They could talk about it till two in the morning. They'd blow smoke in your face and argue and talk and talk and talk. But they never did anything about it. When John finished talking, he got up and marched out the door to begin the sit-in, and the people went with him. It was the first time I'd ever seen somebody put action where their mouth was.

I went right along with my camera. We marched two or three blocks to the white part of town to a swimming pool which wouldn't allow blacks. There were white people there shouting and heckling. And John and the group knelt down in front of the pool and prayed. I took pictures of John and Chico Neblett [Charles Neblett's brother] and a young girl praying.

Then a truck came through, down the street, pushing into the crowd to try to break it up. But they wouldn't budge. It hit the girl—she wasn't hurt badly. At the end of the day, how could I not be part of the civil rights movement?

The next fall, Danny was asked to cover voter registration in Mississippi.

I got to Greenwood [Mississippi] looking really scruffy. I hadn't slept or washed, and I had an address, No phone number, just an address. I didn't want to take a cab, so I started walking—I was walking and walking and finally got to a door and knocked on it. This white person opened. I showed them the address I was looking for—they said, "Why, that's the other part of town. That's North Magnolia Street, the black end of town. How come you want to go there?" I was already in trouble. I walked back the other way. By now lots of people had seen me. I knew I was in trouble.

I finally got to the right address. I walked up to the door—I told them who I was.

They asked me to sit down. I sat down in the kitchen. Bob Moses was there and Sam Block and a bunch of others. It was early morning, so some of them were still in their pajamas. I took some pictures. We talked. There was no press. There were no photographers. There were not even SNCC people taking out Instamatics.

Up in Ruleville I followed along with a group of canvassers. They would walk from shack to shack out in the country, and talk to the people, and ask them about their problems. I had never been in the rural South before. It was beautiful. The delta and its fields are beautiful. People posed with cotton sacks—men in battered-down hats, beautiful teen-age girls with no shoes on and cotton sacks over their back.

After four–five days going out with the canvassers and taking pictures, I was standing in front of the freedom house in Greenwood and a squad car pulls up. I didn't like it at all. The guy took me downtown and a gray-haired man who was somewhat polite to me went through a book and read me an ordinance that said the town required a thousand-dollar bond from anyone engaging in the profession of photography. If I wanted to take pictures I'd have to pay them a thousand dollars. I asked if they would take a check. The guy laughed—at least we were keeping a sense of humor. Anyhow, I told him I'd get the money, and I left the office.

I didn't get very far because the policeman who had picked me up in the squad car was standing in the parking lot, and he was shaking. The first thing he said to me was he was going to blow my brains out. I tried to talk coolly, even though my heart was pounding really hard. "What for?" I said. "Because you're messing with the black

John Lewis and Chico Neblett kneel at swimming pool in Cairo, Illinois; 1962.
© Danny Lyon / Magnum

people," he said. "White people stay in the white part of town." So I said I was colored. This was not as crazy as it sounds. In the South, if you grew up black, in a black neighborhood, it didn't matter what color you were or what origin you were, you were considered colored. If you grew up white, you could have quarts of black blood in your veins and you were considered white. That's how segregation worked.

But then I made a mistake. I said my father was black. He started screaming. You see, if you say your mother was black, then she was raped or was a prostitute or a white man's mistress. That was OK. But if it was on your father's side, that meant your black father slept with a white woman. He screamed, "If I see you again, I'm gonna kill you!" He was very agitated. The next day I got out of town. I mean I had a pocketful of rolls of film. If I was dead or in jail or the film got confiscated, what good was I to myself or to SNCC? That was my first trip to Mississippi. At least I got the pictures.

Even after that year, Danny still felt like an outsider in the movement.

SNCC was a bare-bones organization. It didn't have photographers. It had organizers, that's all. Everybody considered themselves an organizer. They were very reluctant to hire me—a northern white boy who was just there to take pictures. But Forman fought for me.

Forman asked him to come south again. He arrived in time to record the terrible brutality in Danville, Virginia.

For the next few weeks, me and Dottie Zellner and Forman and Julian Bond worked on getting the news out on what was happening. Those marches kept coming up, candlelight marches, beatings, fire hoses throwing people's bodies around. Because I was white, I could photograph things no black person could. Jim Forman was like the general—we respected him. He was ten years older than us—he was thirty-one and we were twenty-one—and he'd say, "Danny, you go downtown. There's a colored-only water fountain. I want you to get a picture of it." I'd go, and I'd take the picture. I could sneak in, get the photos and sneak out, like a spy. I really got into that. I had all these stealthy maneuvers.

Once Forman told me to go up to the newspaper office and get pictures of the violence from their files. I went up to the newspaper office. "I'm from Chicago," I said. "They really admire the way you're handling the niggers here. I think if they see this back home, they'll really learn something." So they let me go through their files. It might seem funny to some people, pretending to be a racist. But I wasn't being nice to these segregationists for the fun of it—that's where the photos were. If I wanted pictures of Alabama state troopers, I had to spend time with them.

I can still picture the SNCC freedom house where we stayed in Danville. It was just a big old house in the black section where somebody had enough room to take us in. I can still see us crammed together trying to use the bathroom at the same time. I'm shaving and Jim Forman is on the toilet and Julian is trying to take a bath.

Later that summer, things changed.

Americus, Georgia, ten miles from Plains, home of Jimmy Carter. We got reports that there were kids being kept in jail. So, I went down to where they were having this meeting—in a funeral home. You know, the only blacks down there that had any power in the community were ministers and funeral directors. Probably because white people didn't want to bury black people. I found out what was going on—most of the high-school girls were in this prison with no charges against them. They had been there for weeks. We were talking about what I could do—

This kid about fifteen says to me, "I'll drive you out there. We'll get the pictures. You hide in the back of the car and I'll drive." Only he really didn't know how to drive. He said, "There's an old guard at the prison called Pops. I'll talk to him. While I talk to him in the front, you go in back and make pictures." It was an insane idea. But I did it.

I lay in the back of the car and waited while he went and talked to Pops. I snuck around to the back of the prison. The girls were all being kept in one open stockade. They had a toilet that didn't flush. It had piles of shit on it. The whole place stank. It was covered with flies. They had no facilities for anything. The girls were astounded. Here I was with curly hair and Jewish, and the girls liked me right away. They were saying "Freedom" and reaching through the bars. It was a very emotional kind of thing. I think the best picture was the first one, when the girls were just standing there shocked.

I remember sneaking back to the car, and lying in the back. There was this big hump from the transmission. The guy gets in and starts to drive. Only he can't drive a stick shift. This was supposed to be the big escape, the getaway, and we're going kachunk ka-chunk ka-chunk and I'm trying to tell him how to do it.

I got back to Atlanta, and found a place to process the film immediately. The very next day a congressman who was a friend of SNCC's made a speech about this and put the picture into the Congressional Record. When the news got back to Georgia the girls got released. After that SNCC accepted me. Even the people who said, "What do we need a white boy taking our pictures? We'll take them ourselves," changed their mind. It was because I actually did something. I changed something.

People talk about the movement leaders—Martin Luther King, Ralph Abernathy, Forman, Carmichael. The movement didn't have leaders. King didn't lead the movement. SNCC didn't lead the movement. At best, the leaders scrambled to catch up with the people in the streets and in the churches—usually high-school students, people who are completely anonymous, whose names you've never heard. I have pictures of them—like this woman in Selma, Alabama, with the most magnificent voice I'd ever heard. I have her picture, but I don't know her name. Those people made the movement. They belong on the posters and the stamps. But today they are completely forgotten.

Women in Leesburg Stockade, Georgia, 1963. © Danny Lyon / Magnum

March,
Washington,
D.C., 1963.
© 1963 Flip
Schulke

PART TWO

BREAKING
THE WALL

With fervent determination they
continued to beat at the wall. Sometimes
the price was jail, sometimes it was
broken skulls, sometimes it was
murder. . . . The wall was high and
hard. . . but the cracks grew into fissures
and chunks of masonry began to fall.

VINCENT HARDING

Reverend Fred Shuttlesworth, Birmingham, Alabama. © Dan Budnik / Woodfin Camp & Associates

V

1963
The Birmingham Movement

*I*n the heart of the Deep South stood Birmingham, Alabama's largest city. Eighteen bombings in black neighborhoods within six years—no arrests. In 1957 a crowd chain-whipped Rev. Fred Shuttlesworth and stabbed his wife for seeking to enroll their children in a "white" school—no arrests. In 1958 a black man was dragged from the street, taken to a shack, and castrated—no arrests. In 1961 a mob attacked and beat a group of freedom riders almost to death—no arrests. Birmingham, "the magic city," home of segregationist police commissioner Bull Connor. "Bombingham," where dynamite from the mines was as available as firecrackers—"the Johannesburg of America." Here the tide would turn. Out of a year of defeats would come the movement's greatest victory to date.

In the black community, passion for justice had been growing.

Rev. Ed Gardener: *But any man that attempted to lead out here in Birmingham, he was put out of business. . . . The city would take his license, and the Klan would come in and the police would harass him. If he was in his car, they'd charge him with running a red light when there was no red light. . . . Then we got Fred Shuttlesworth.*

Shuttlesworth seemed afraid of nothing. In 1956 a bomb exploded in his home while he lay in bed.

Fred Shuttlesworth: *The bomb went off right behind my head. Immediately I knew they knew where I would be and where I rested my head . . . and I also knew I wouldn't get killed. . . . The dynamite went off and the lights went out and the floor was blown from under the bed. We never did find the springs. The front wall was blown out into the street and all I was lying on was the bed. . . .*

I knew we had to challenge. . . . Segregation wasn't just going to die away. . . . Then I realized we needed a different type of confrontation. Here, with Bull Connor being the epitome of segregation, the SCLC should meet him with our epitome.

And so Shuttlesworth invited SCLC co-member Martin Luther King to come to Birmingham.

Fearing the national attention that King would bring with him, several downtown merchants voluntarily desegregated their facilities. Bull Connor would not allow it. The stores were ordered to restore "Whites Only" signs on their facilities, fountains, and lunch counters or close down for "violations of the sanitary code." Desperate to protect their city's image and keep King away, some Birmingham whites called for an election to replace Connor.

In January 1963, King and the SCLC staff held a three-day retreat in Georgia. They decided that Birmingham was, indeed, the epitome of segregation. This could be the most important challenge yet—if they could confront segregation in its stronghold, they could confront it anywhere. So was born Plan "C" (for "Confrontation"). To avoid a stalemate like the one in Albany, Georgia, they would plan every step carefully.

Andrew Young: *First we had to unite everybody, black business people, leaders, anyone who felt that they were a leader, young people, old people.*

In a series of small and large meetings, King pulled together the black community: "This is the most segregated city in America. We have to stick together if we ever want to change its ways. We have come to help you break down its walls."

Second, the nightly mass meetings began, moving from church to church throughout the city. "Through these meetings we were able to generate the power and depth which finally galvanized the entire Negro community," wrote King. The mass meeting became a news center, a rallying center, a learning center.

Bernice Johnson Reagon: *The Birmingham Movement Choir, sixty voices, would begin. "Five, ten, fifteen won't do. Twenty, twenty-five, thirty won't do." With a quickening tempo the choir would continue to "Ninety-nine and a half won't do."*

Ninety-nine and a Half Won't Do

The variety of singing to be heard at mass meetings in Birmingham probably wasn't matched in any other movement in the South. Starting off with an old-time prayer service in which the older people sang and lined out the old-time spirituals and "Dr. Watts" hymns in a style which went back to slavery days, the meetings were then turned over to the songs of the movement's sixty-voice gospel choir accompanied by the organ playing of its leader. After the church had rocked and spirits were jubilant, it was time to hear from their leader, Reverend Fred Shuttlesworth.

—*Guy Carawan*

This transcription is by Ethel Raim from an arrangement by Carlton Reese and the Birmingham Movement Choir.

Then came the crescendo, when the choir, and audience shouted. "One hundred percent will do!" The song articulated commitment to completing a task—to total involvement.

The drama itself began quietly on April 3 with an attempt to integrate the public facilities at the courthouse and the bus station. The police responded by locking up all facilities and turning off the water fountains and locking the toilets.

Fred Shuttlesworth: "This morning there were a lot of people in misery at the courthouse, and not necessarily just because there was a lot of injustice being cast out under the guise of justice.

"I have always seen the Negro fountains dry. But this morning both the black and white fountains was dry. And all the toilets was locked up. . . .

"Segregation is a silly thing. . . . Rather than for you to get water out of the fountain marked WHITE, they will close the White and the Black fountains, so nobody drinks. Before we got here God had put the water down here. HERE WE ARE ARGUIN' OVER SOMETHING THAT'S FREE! Maybe the segregationists . . . might try to segregate the air for a while. . . ."

On April 6, Shuttlesworth led 45 demonstrators to city hall to kneel on the steps and pray. They were arrested. The next day 65 demonstrators led by Rev. A. D. King, Martin Luther King's brother, knelt on the steps. This time the police attacked. On the third day, 85 demonstrators marched and went to jail. On the fourth day, 130. Every day, the numbers grew. The "drama of Birmingham" was building.

The third phase called for a boycott of all the segregated downtown stores—right in the midst of the Easter shopping season. The store owners screamed. But Connor would not allow them to take down their "Whites Only" signs. Instead, he obtained a court injunction forbidding King and most of the other civil rights leaders from participating in the protest.

Without King and Abernathy and the others willing to lead the marchers, the momentum of the movement might begin to fade. On the other hand, if they did defy the injunction, they would most certainly go to jail. The whole plan was in danger.

On the morning of Good Friday, King met with his staff.

Andrew Young: *We already had many people in jail, but all the money was gone and we couldn't get people out. . . . The black business community and some clergy were pressuring us to call off the demonstrations. We didn't know what to do. King sat and didn't say anything. He listened to people talk for about two hours. . . . Then he left the room. . . . He came out of the bedroom after a while. He turned to us. He said, "Look, I don't know what to do. I know that something has to change in Birmingham. I don't know if I can raise money to get people out of jail. I do know I can go to jail with them. . . ." Not knowing how it was going to work out, he walked out of the room, went down to the church, and went to jail. That was, I think, the beginning of King's true leadership.*

From jail King wrote to the black religious leaders who had urged him to "go slow":

"For years now I have heard the word 'Wait!' It rings in the ear of every Negro with piercing familiarity. This 'Wait' has almost always meant 'Never.' . . .

"The nations of Asia and Africa are moving with jetlike speed toward gaining political independence, but we still creep at horse-and-buggy pace toward gaining a cup of coffee at a lunch counter. . . . when you have seen vicious mobs lynch your mothers and fathers at will and drown your sisters and brothers at whim; when you have seen hate-filled policemen curse, kick and even kill your black brothers and sisters; when you see the vast majority of your twenty million Negro brothers smothering in an airtight cage of poverty in the midst of an affluent society; . . . when you have to concoct an answer for a five-year-old son who is asking: 'Daddy, why do white people treat colored people so mean?'; . . . when your first name becomes 'nigger,' your middle name becomes 'boy' (however old you are) and your last name becomes 'John,' and your wife and mother are never given the respected title 'Mrs.' . . .—then you will understand why we find it difficult to wait. There comes a time when the cup of endurance runs over. . . ."

Martin Luther King in Birmingham jail, 1963. Wyatt Tee Walker / Schulke Archives

The bail money was gone. Hundreds of people were still in jail. The marchers realized that if they were arrested, they'd have to stay in jail. Most people could not afford to lose the income. The demonstrations dwindled in size. The press started to leave. The Birmingham campaign ground to a halt.

Rev. James Bevel, one of the founders of SNCC, and now on the SCLC staff, had an inspiration: Let the children march. "Most adults have bills to pay—rent, utility bills—but the young people are not hooked. A boy from high school can put the same pressure on the city as his father, yet there is no economic threat to the family, because the father is still on the job," explained Bevel.

During the weeks that followed, Bevel, Diane Nash, Dorothy Cotton (SCLC director of education), Andrew Young, and others trained the youngsters in nonviolence, and on May 2 they marched.

Len Holt, movement lawyer: *From inside the Sixteenth Street Baptist Church came the sound of three thousand voices singing We Shall Overcome and Ain't Gonna Let Nobody Turn Me 'Round.*

Keep Your Eyes on the Prize

The old spiritual said,

> Got my hand on the gospel plow.
> Wouldn't take nothin' for my journey now.
> Keep your hand on the plow, hold on.

But in the mid-fifties Alice Wine of South Carolina thought of the new last line. It caught on like wildfire, along with many new verses.

A technical note about the flatted seventh note of the scale (the word "on" in "hold on"). It clashes with the accompaniment. African tradition tends to do this. It also lowers the third, and raises the fourth. This makes problems for musicians trying to accompany the songs on keyboard instruments or fretted instruments. But keep in mind that most of these songs were composed and usually sung without accompaniment. The blues tradition solved it by singing the flatted, minor notes but accompanying the song with major chords. Likewise, the black folk singer Huddie Ledbetter accompanied many "minor" melodies with major chords on his twelve-string guitar. But this song is usually accompanied in minor, although it tends to overemphasize the flatted notes.

And a reminder: no two singers sing this song alike, and you, the reader, should make the decision—if you want to try singing the song—exactly what notes you want to sing or slide around.

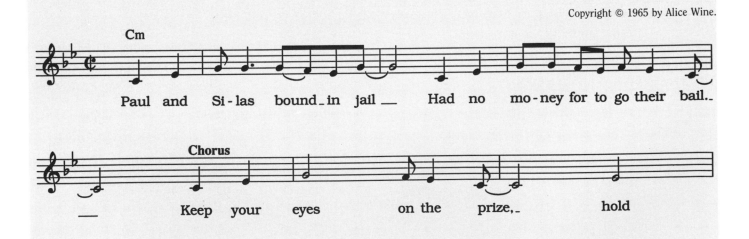

110

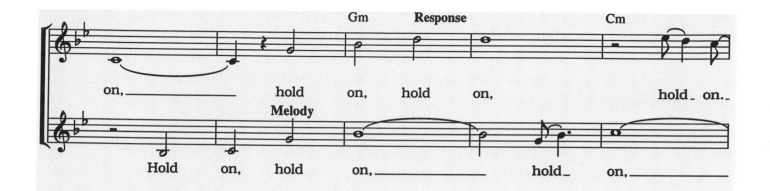

Ain't but one chain a man can stand,
That's the chain of a hand in a hand.

Freedom's name is mighty sweet,
Black and white are gonna meet.

The following two popular verses were used in more than one song:

Ain't but one thing we did wrong,
Was staying in the wilderness too long.

Only thing that we did right
Was to organize and fight.

Ain't A-Scared of Your Jail

They started singing a new song that summer. It went to the tune of *The Old Gray Mare*. There wasn't only a song; there was a dance that went with it—sort of a hesitation step with a twist and a step forward and a step backward. The singers would use it like this: Rev. Fred Shuttlesworth would be lecturing everyone in the church, explaining all about nonresistance. "It's to be a silent demonstration," he would say. "No songs, no slogans, no replies to obscenities." Everyone would nod. "However," the reverend would add, "when you're arrested, sing your hearts out."

So, all the young people would file out of church, solemn as deacons, quiet as mice. Then a cop would come along and shout, "You're all under arrest!" That was the cue. Suddenly there were five hundred bodies moving at once, their voice shouting out:

> Ain't a-scared of your jail cause I want my freedom
> I want my freedom
> I want my freedom
> I want my freedom . . .
>
> —*Len Holt*

Ain't a - scared of your jail, 'cause I want my free-dom, I
want my free-dom, I want my free-dom. Ain't a - scared of your jail, 'cause I
want my free-dom, I want my free-dom now!

Ain't a-scared of your dogs, 'cause . . .

Ain't a-scared of your hose, 'cause . . .

Birmingham, Alabama, school children, 1963. © Charles Moore / Black Star

The temperature hit ninety degrees. Everyone was sweating. "Freedom! Freedom!" A roar arose from the church. [Outside,] officers unleashed clubs from their belts. The faces of those I could see had turned crimson. Jeremiah X, a Muslim minister standing near me, commented, "At any moment, they expect three hundred years of hate to spew forth from that church." . . .

Sixty demonstrators were on their way, marching two abreast. . . . Dick Gregory, the night-club comedian, was leading the group. At a signal, forty policemen converged, sticks in hand. "Do you have a permit to parade?" asked the police captain. "No," replied Gregory. "No, what?" asked the captain in what seemed to be a reminder to Gregory that he had not used a "sir." "No, no a thousand times no," Gregory replied. The captain said, "I hereby place you under arrest. . . ."

For the next two hours the scene was repeated over and over as group after group of students strutted out of the church to the cheers of the spectators, the freedom chants of those being carried away . . . a cacophony of freedom.

One thousand students went to jail that day.

Day after day the marches continued. Connor and his men ran about the streets, grabbing eleven- and twelve-year-old demonstrators. The children used decoy tactics, a small group leading the police astray while the main column of marchers took another street to downtown.

A policeman ran up to an eight-year-old child walking with her mother, and screamed, "What do you want?" The little girl looked up at the policeman. "Freedom," she said.

An unidentified police captain said, "Ten, fifteen years from now, we'll look back on this and say, 'How stupid could we have been!?' "

Within days Bull Connor's prisons were full of children.

Tuesday, May 7, before 10:00 A.M., before police lines and fire hoses went into place, the students set up pickets in front of eight department stores.

Len Holt: *I was standing near a police motorcycle, could hear the pandemonium at police headquarters. . . . Over the police radio, I heard Bull Connor's voice. He was mad. He had been betrayed. Never before had the students demonstrated before 1 P.M. . . .*

Nearly four thousand persons returned to the church from the victory march. While they joyously sang inside, preparations were being made outside. Cars with dogs drove up. About three hundred police officers surrounded the church and park area. Fire hoses were set up.

As soon as the people emerged from the church, they found themselves surrounded by Connor's police. Squad cars pulled up in front of the church, blocking any chance to retreat to safety. "Let 'em have it," cried Connor. With TV cameras and newsmen watching, the firemen turned on their hoses. Columns of water crashed into children and adults, knocking them down, ripping their clothes, smashing them into the sides of buildings. From the other side of the park, Connor unmuzzled the German shepherds. The dogs lunged into the black ranks, biting the running children.

Len Holt: *On one side, the students were confronted by clubs; on the other, by powerful streams of water. The firemen used the hoses to knock down the students. As the streams hit the trees, bark was ripped off; bricks were torn loose from the walls. . . . A stream of water slammed Rev. Fred Shuttlesworth against the church wall, causing internal injuries. Mrs. Colia LaFayette, twenty-five-year-old SNCC field secretary from Selma, was knocked down, two hoses brought to bear on her to wash her along the sidewalk.*

At that moment, while Commissioner Connor laughed "Look at them niggers run," A. G. Gaston, a black businessman who opposed the demonstrations, looked from his window. "My God," he cried to the person on the other end of the phone, "they've turned the fire hoses on a black girl. They're rolling that little girl right down the middle of the street. I can't talk to you now." The black community was one.

Glen Evans, Birmingham police officer: *I was standing there by the fire hose when they put the hose right on Reverend Shuttlesworth. His feet were knocked out from under him. I had the thought at the time, What's the purpose of this? . . . What does it accomplish? What do we hope to do by doing these things?*

The nation woke up to the movement.

Dorothy Cotton: *If it hadn't been for television nobody would have ever believed they turned the dogs on us and turned the fire hoses on our children.*

Danny Lyon: *That's when the press discovered the movement. Until then, maybe you'd get one story a year about civil rights. A burning bus in Alabama on the cover of Life Magazine, then nothing for a year. Martin Luther King and hundreds, thousands, of people getting arrested in Albany, and then nothing. Nobody covered the movement. Now, the press was really excited. They decided that fire hoses and dogs made good newsreels. They realized this was good material.*

May 10, with three thousand people in jail, with what King called "the boil of segregation opened to the air and light," the black citizens of Birmingham and the white businessmen's association, reached an accord. In return for an end to the

Firemen turn hoses on demonstrators, Birmingham, Alabama, 1963. © Charles Moore / Black Star

demonstrations and boycott, the merchants agreed to desegregate lunch counters and hire blacks for clerical and sales positions.

But the drama was not over. Late Saturday night, May 12, bombs exploded at SCLC headquarters and at the home of Rev. A. D. King, Martin Luther King's brother. The black citizens, who had not been goaded to anger by the police dogs or fire hoses, were finally driven too far—they milled about downtown throwing bricks, 2,500 people. A taxicab was set on fire. Movement leaders circulated through a mob urging restraint. The crowds began to quiet. Suddenly, Col. Al Lingo and his state troopers arrived. Despite pleas by the Birmingham police to let the situation alone, the troopers began to clear the streets with shotguns, rifles, and clubs.

Hundreds were jailed, including Guy and Candie Carawan, who were arrested for trying to join a mass meeting at a black church.

Guy Carawan: *The jails were really crowded by now—the fairgrounds were full of youngsters. They put Candie upstairs and me downstairs, and they told me that upstairs the prisoners were beating up Candie, and they told Candie that downstairs the prisoners were roughing up me. Nobody hit anybody.*

We were all squeezed into one cell, drunks and pickpockets and me. I slept on a plain spring that night. Or I tried to sleep. But more and more people kept gettting shoved into the cell. I remember hearing one drunk come in swearing and "looking for that damned freedom rider."

Really late I heard this remarkable sound—from outside the jail window I could hear hundreds and hundreds of voices singing freedom songs. People had marched over from the mass meeting to the jailhouse, just to let all those in jail know that everyone was thinking of them.

On September 15, 1963, came the last and most horrible act in opposition to the Birmingham movement. It was Sunday. At the Sixteenth Street Baptist Church, Sunday school was just over. Four little girls stood in the back of the church, putting on choir robes. A stick of dynamite exploded—debris, plaster, glass, wood, flew about with tattered remains of the dead children's Bible lessons. Seventeen others were injured. Awaiting what they were sure would be the most horrible black retribution, the town called in troops and marshals.

Pat Watters: *Police and press alike, in the strange quiet of the afternoon, as grief-stricken people walked numbly about the Negro section, expected God knows what retributive horror that night. And as the hot afternoon wore on, violence, like a mad dog loose, continued—white violence. White youths shot to death a Negro boy on a bicycle. Police shot a Negro youth to death, claiming he ran when ordered to halt.*
But the black retribution did not come. Still America waited. The expectation of violence hung like a still unfulfilled prophecy over the whites, especially in the South.

The drama was done. At terrible cost the movement had breached Birmingham, segregation's fortress. The rest of the Deep South lay ahead.

Birmingham Sunday

In the mid-sixties, large numbers of white people who had until then been on the sidelines became drawn into the civil rights movement. They realized, as do the authors of this book, that its victories were their victories as well. Popular singing groups like Peter, Paul, and Mary sang songs which made oblique references to the freedom struggle:

> How many roads must a man walk down
> Before you call him a man?
> . . .
> The answer, my friend, is blowin' in the wind,
> The answer is blowin' in the wind.

The following song was widely sung by Joan Baez and others. The melody Richard Fariña set his words to is one of the great English ballad melodies. Though now this song would be accompanied by guitar, in ancient times such songs were usually sung unaccompanied, with an "imperiodic rhythm"—that is, a free cadence—rather than a measurable rhythm of any sort. In any verse an unexpected note might be held a long time, or a note usually held might be cut short. The song would end unpretentiously, often spoken, as though to say, "This is the end of the song." It is a quite different tradition from that of the opera soloist, ending on a high note, or the black church singer, holding out the final note as though with a sigh.

Sixteenth Street Baptist Church, Birmingham, Alabama, after bombing. © *Danny Lyon / Magnum*

Slowly

Come 'round by my side and I'll sing you a

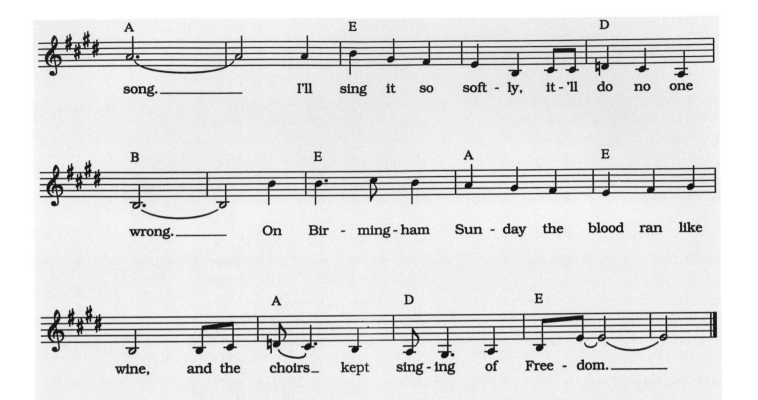

song. _____ I'll sing it so soft-ly, it-'ll do no one

wrong. _____ On Bir-ming-ham Sun-day the blood ran like

wine, and the choirs_ kept sing-ing of Free-dom. _____

That cold autumn morning no eyes saw the sun,
And Addie Mae Collins, her number was one.
At an old Baptist church there was no need to run.
And the choirs kept singing of Freedom.

The clouds they were gray and the autumn winds blew,
And Denise McNair brought the number to two.
The falcon of death was a creature they knew,
And the choirs kept singing of Freedom.

The church it was crowded, but no one could see
That Cynthia Wesley's dark number was three.
Her prayers and her feelings would shame you and me.
And the choirs kept singing of Freedom.

Young Carol Robertson entered the door
And the number her killers had given was four.
She asked for a blessing but asked for no more,
And the choirs kept singing of Freedom.

On Birmingham Sunday a noise shook the ground.
And people all over the earth turned around.
For no one recalled a more cowardly sound.
And the choirs kept singing of Freedom.

The men in the forest they once asked of me,
How many black berries grew in the Blue Sea.
And I asked them right back with a tear in my eye.
How many dark ships in the forest?

The Sunday has come and the Sunday has gone.
And I can't do much more than to sing you a song.
I'll sing it so softly, I'll do no one wrong.
And the choirs keep singing of Freedom.

Profile: DOROTHY COTTON

A compact, energetic women, Dorothy Cotton stands before an audience of black and white, students and old people. Remembering an African tradition that the spirits do not descend until people have sung together, she will not speak until she has brought the audience to full-throated song, to "invoke the spirit—God or whatever, to come down and be among us."

When I was a high schooler in Goldsboro, North Carolina, when we said the pledge and we had to say "liberty and justice for all," something inside me wouldn't let me say that. I would say "liberty and justice for white people." . . .

My perspective began to change in my last year in high school: I heard Mary McLeod Bethune say that when she was a child with no bottoms in her shoes, she would dig her toes through the holes in her shoes and would say, "One day I am going to help my people." And she did. This woman who came from a slave environment achieved entree to the Roosevelt White House and made real changes for black people. That's when I began to flash on the fact that what I wanted to do was help my people.

I got my chance in 1963, when Reverend Wyatt T. Walker, pastor of Gilfield Baptist Church in Petersburg, Virginia, decided to go to Atlanta to help Dr. King and work for the SCLC. He asked me to go with him. I thought it would be for six months. I stayed for twenty-three years.

I'll tell you about my assignment with the Southern Christian Leadership Conference. There was a citizenship school program that Myles Horton and Septima Clark and others at Highlander School had developed in the islands off the coast of Charleston, South Carolina—a poor area, almost entirely black, where there was a high degree of illiteracy. This education program brought together these people from these islands and helped them give voice to the churning that was inside of them. They gave this wonderful program to the SCLC to continue and develop. That program was my responsibility.

We would bring together people who had already started to become leaders in their communities. Some people think the movement happened because Martin Luther King or Stokely Carmichael stood up and said, "Let's march," and everybody marched. Not true. People were working for months and sometimes years in small ways in their communities, learning about citizenship and its responsibilities, and teaching it to their neighbors.

We in SCLC would bring in these people, these new community leaders, to a building that was once a little schoolhouse we had in Hinesville, Georgia, a little town south of Savannah. They would come by school bus and train to our little school, and they would go home to start citizenship schools in their own towns— helping others learn what they had learned.

These workshops were something special. They were intellectual and emotional at the same time. We encouraged people to express themselves—their emotions as well as their ideas. Intellect and brain and academics are fine, but we also have a heart and soul, and we realized it is OK to use all aspects of ourselves.

We would start a session by saying, "We're going to talk about the Constitution today, but first why don't you tell us about what's going on where you came from."

And Mrs. Fannie Lou Hamer would stand up and say, "Let me tell you about where I come from." And she'd talk about the field holler: "You know what a field holler is?" she'd say. "In the cotton patch you'd have to sing a message to someone down at the end of your row. You might sing about how hard it was to get to the end of your row. You know, back in slavery times, if you didn't get to the end of your row, you'd get lashes on your back. So you might sing:

Freedom School, South Carolina. Courtesy Highlander Center

Oh Lord, I can't make out my row.
Lord, I can't make out my row and the sun is going down!

And that singing would lighten you, and give you that extra bit of energy so you could get down and get to the end of your row!"

Then Mrs. Hamer would lead us in a song, so we could lighten ourselves and give ourselves that extra boost of energy. Before we started talking about the Constitution, we would sing together, we would invoke the spirit. We would sing about anything we felt. We would sing about why we sing. We would sing, "The reason I sing this song, Lord, I don't want to be lost." We would sing about the abuses we suffered, like not being allowed to vote. We would sing songs of sorrow and songs of hope.

Then the people would speak. They would unburden themselves, talk about what they had lost, about what they wanted, about how they had come to be there. And, in talking we would unburden ourselves and set some goals. One woman said, "The cobwebs are moving from my brain." That's how it felt to all of us—the cobwebs were moving from our brains! The last hope was reclaimed.

Then we'd say, "OK folks, let's talk now about what is a citizen!" People would say many things. They'd say, "Well, if you obey the law and you're a good child of God, you're a citizen." But suddenly someone would flash on another reality. "Isn't there a law that makes us all citizens?" someone would say. Then the discussion would open up and we could talk about the Constitution and what rights it guaranteed. And we'd learn to spell the word, C-I-T-I-Z-E-N.

They recalled hearing about people taking the Fifth, so we'd talk about amendments. What is an amendment? A-M-E-N-D-M-E-N-T. We'd learn about the First Amendment and the Fourteenth—about our right to assemble peacefully to petition the government for redress of our grievances! I learned more about being a citizen and citizenship teaching those classes than I did in years at college.

The civil rights movement that rearranged the social order in this country did not emanate from the halls of the Harvards and the Princetons and Cornells. It came from simple unlettered people who learned that they had the right to stand tall and that nobody can ride a back that isn't bent. That was a phrase Dr. King used a lot. They learned that maybe the Constitution hadn't meant them when it was written, but by God, they were going to appropriate it for themselves.

Voter-registration education became the base of the civil rights movement—affirming that you are a citizen, that government is for you and by you, and that you can hold anyone you elect accountable to you is what people came to know. That's why some folks got killed, black and white! When that happened, we knew we had to continue; we must be on the right track if they are willing to kill to stop us.

The next step, after deciding to vote, was deciding to run for office. You could be a tax assessor or a mayor. When people complained about their officials, others would ask, "Why aren't you the mayor?"

People stayed in these workshops just five days and returned home doing things they had never dreamt they would do. I remember Ms. Topsy Eubanks from Macon, Georgia, a sixty-year-old woman with a bandanna on her head, saying as she left the workshop, "When I left, I felt like I had been born again!"

We all felt like that. All the time we kept singing, "Do what the spirit say do!" We sang joyous songs—Freedom Is A-Comin', glorious songs affirming the joy of coming alive, of becoming new persons.

I dreamt once the movement would be done and over. But I see the face of hate in Howard Beach, and see a white boy saying out loud, "They can't live where we live." That is overt hatred and ignorance and the basis for our own brand of apartheid. As Dr. King said in his last book, Where Do We Go from Here? Chaos or Community, we will either have community, or we will have chaos. I hope for community, a community where all can be affirmed and no one derives a sense of worth from putting down another.

Lone civil rights marcher on Alabama highway. Dan Budnik / Woodfin Camp & Associates

VI

May 1963
The Freedom March

During the last half of April 1963, William Moore, a white postman from Baltimore and a long-time member of CORE, began a personal freedom march through the South. He wore a sandwich sign. On the front it said EAT AT JOE'S—BLACK & WHITE, and on the back, EQUAL RIGHTS FOR ALL. MISSISSIPPI OR BUST! The last leg of his trip was to take him from Chattanooga, Tennessee, to Jackson, Mississippi, where he would deliver a message of brotherhood to segregationist governor Ross Barnett. On April 24, he was walking alone on a road just outside of Attalla, Alabama. An old man waved at him. Moore waved back and turned the bend in the road. Minutes later a car with no license plates roared around the same corner.

The next day Moore was found lying in the bushes, bullets in his head and neck, his placards scattered, a hole blasted into the sign he was wearing.

On May 1, a group of black and white members of SNCC and CORE began to retrace William Moore's steps. Equipped with boots and camping equipment they intended to follow Moore's route to Jackson, and there to deliver Moore's message of brotherhood to Governor Ross Barnett. The idea was to show the people along the way that they were human—not violent, but not afraid. On foot like this, they could talk to people, explain their goals, and, maybe, start to turn the community around.

"This will not, of itself, open a lunch counter, integrate a school, or add a single Negro voter to the list of the nation's registered voters. But it affords a magnificent occasion for the people of the towns and cities through which we pass to participate. . . . They can do so simply by giving their quiet consent to our passage," explained the group before they left.

Carry It On

Gil Turner, who wrote this song, was a theology student, then briefly a Baptist preacher, then made a living as a folk singer.

It's interesting that a number of songs sung by the freedom movement were originally put together by white people. In the singing of them, the songs might be said to have been Africanized. I have heard the last eight measures, with harmony and overlapping responses, repeated over and over for ten minutes, while people got up and danced in a ring. Gil Turner died young, but his song keeps on going. —*Pete Seeger*

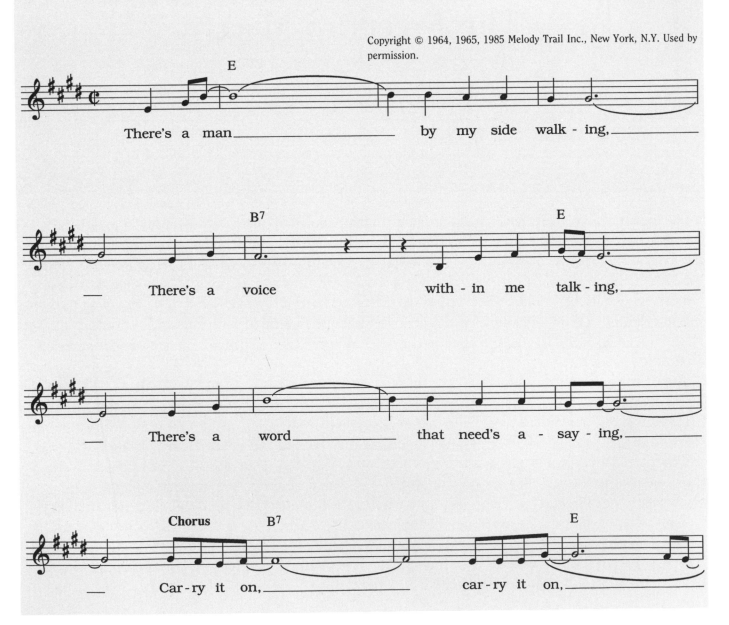

There's a man _____ by my side walk-ing, _____

_ There's a voice with-in me talk-ing, _____

_ There's a word _____ that need's a - say - ing, _____

Chorus _ Car-ry it on, _____ car-ry it on, _____

car-ry it on,_____ car-ry it on,_____

VERSES ADDED BY THE CIVIL RIGHTS MOVEMENT

They will tell their lying stories,
Send their dogs to bite our bodies,
They will lock us into prison,
Carry it on . . .

All their lies will be forgotten
All their dogs will lie there rotting
All their prison walls will crumble
Carry it on . . .

If you can't go on any longer
Take the hand held by your brother
Every victory gonna bring another
Carry it on . . .

In the 1980s, in these days of women's consciousness, new verses have been added:

Sister to sister, brother to brother,
Every victory leads to another
Every action brings a teaching,
Carry it on . . .

Two beautiful new verses were added by singer Marion Wade in 1985:

For the dream never ending,
You can hear the voices blending,
Loud and clear their echo sending,
Carry it on . . .

Through the air the song is winging,
Down the years, hope keeps springing.
No more tears! We're still singing,
Carry it on . . .

CIVIL RIGHTS' FIGHTER MURDERED!

Tuesday, April 23, 1963, William Moore of Baltimore, Maryland enroute to Jackson, Mississippi was MURDERED near Gadsden, Alabama while engaged in a peaceful protest against segregation. He carried the sign: EQUAL RIGHTS FOR ALL! He DIED FOR FREEDOM! Can you not live and ACT?

THEN:

1. Send telegrams and letters of appeal to

   The President of The United States of America
   The Governor of Alabama

2. Join the Silent March of Protest to the Federal Courthouse Building as an appeal to the Federal Government:

   When----Friday, April 26, 1963
   Time----   9:00 A. M.
   Where---A & I Students meet in front of the"I"Building
           Fisk Students meet in front of Fisk Chapel
           High School Students meet in front of Fisk Chapel
           Scarritt Students meet in front of Fisk Chapel
           Meharry Students meet in front of Fisk Chapel
           All Others meet in front of Fisk Chapel

                              Nashville Christian Leadership
                              Student Nonviolent Movement

They set out from the Chattanooga Greyhound terminal at 8 A.M., two weeks after Moore had started from this same spot. But Moore had gone alone. With the group of ten are reporters from the AP and UP and Time-Life. There are well-wishers and cordons of police, and there are crowds shouting, gawking. A white woman in a blue-wool coat shouts, "We all gonna have to die anyhow. What counts if we gonna die for what's right! Ask God to be with ye on the road, will you. . . . Oh, glooory hallelujah!"

A twenty-year-old white Alabamian named Sam Shirah wears Moore's "Eat at Joe's" sign. As they start to move, he begins softly singing "Ain't gonna let nobody turn me 'round, turn me 'round, turn me 'round." The other marchers pick up the song, louder and louder as they wind through Chattanooga's skid row, through the traffic of downtown, and finally out of the city, trailing their caravan of reporters and police and hecklers.

The first day of the march holds promise. The air in the mountains outside of town is cool and sweet. Most of those on the roadside either watch and stare, or cheer them. A teen-aged white girl runs up and down the thin line of marchers getting autographs. "I'd like to know who they are. They are doing a great service for the South!"

About five miles out of town the road grows steeper as it climbs Lookout Mountain. They stop by a stream to eat sandwiches and rest. A white mountain man also sits beside the stream. He tells the marchers that he knows that sign they're carrying.

He had talked to Moore when he came through. "Whether I agree with him or you agree, he meant deep down in his heart to be doing the right thing."

Billy Sol Estes, awaiting trial for an illegal commodities deal, stops his car, and walks among the marchers, wishing them well.

At another rest stop, a group of teen-agers park nearby. They watch from their cars for a long time, muttering among themselves. Finally, a couple of the marchers—Eric Weinberger, a lanky white youth who had worked with sharecroppers in Tennessee, and Winston Lockett, a black member of CORE—walk up to the cars. The whites jump out, defensive, on guard.

"What'll y'all do when ye get to Alabama?"

"Just keep going."

"Them folks have other plans. Maybe you'll end up like the other feller. . . . What do you want anyhow?"

"I want people to be united. Segregation separates people."

"Oh yeah?" exclaimed the shortest one of the local group in a nasal mountain accent. "Who discovered this country? Christopher Columbus did! Christopher Columbus was white!"

"Black people was on his ship. . . ."

"On the same boat? Hell! It ain't right black and white should mix!"

"I'm in favor of everyone mixing."

"Why do nigras have to go to school with whites?" said a lanky farm boy with a gap between his front teeth.

"We could get to know each other better. We could have talked about this five years ago. . . ."

"I don't want to talk to you, because you're black and I'm white!"

"If we had gone to school together, maybe it wouldn't bother you so much."

Afterward, the marchers talk among themselves and to the reporters trailing them. "Talk like that back there has its effect. Not now, but maybe tonight, or tomorrow night, or three weeks from now."

They continue, slowly, hour by hour, looking for conversations that will open up communication with the people in the countryside.

Knots of men gather in front of gas stations to stare, not to talk. "Howdy," says a black marcher. From somewhere in back of the crowd comes a weak "Howdy." Maybe there is hope. Suddenly, a crack like a rifle. The marchers jump. The crowd laughs—it was only a backfire.

They sing a tune based on a gospel song that has traveled around the world.

By midafternoon, they cross the border into Georgia. The police who had protected them in Tennessee disappear. There are no Georgia troopers in sight. Nervously, some of the reporters break off from the group.

Into poor country now—rocky pastures, hard clay, bitter men and women who

Come by Here

Come by Here, composed in the 1930s by Rev. Marvin Frey of Ossining, New York, is another example of a gospel song written by a white man in the North, and then passed from hand to hand (no, ear to ear) among black people, who added words, changed rhythms, changed notes. Missionaries took it to Angola; the song returned to the U.S.A. as *Kum Ba Yah.* The greatest compliment that people can pay a songwriter is to think his or her composition is an old folk song. The fact that the second half of the melody resembles a widespread European melody (used also by *Hatikvah* and *Twinkle Twinkle Little Star* among others) does not detract from the miraculous achievement of this great song. Thank you and bless you, Marvin Frey!

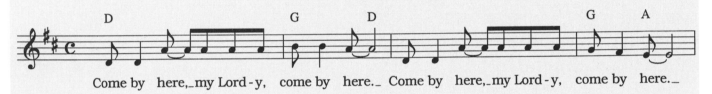

Come by here, my Lord-y, come by here. Come by here, my Lord-y, come by here.

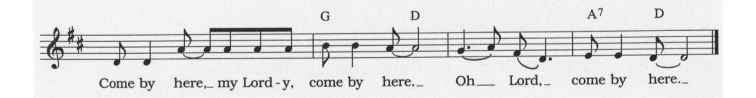

Come by here, my Lord-y, come by here. Oh Lord, come by here.

VERSES ADDED BY THE CIVIL RIGHTS MOVEMENT

Churches burning here, come by here . . .

Someone's starving, Lord, come by here . . .

Someone's shooting, Lord, come by here . . .

We want justice, Lord, come by here . . .

We want freedom here, come by here . . .

Alabama, 1964.
© 1983 Dan Budnik / Woodfin
Camp & Associates

scratch a miserable life from poor, ugly ground. A teen-ager stands in front of a diner, a can of beer clutched in one hand, his other hand a fist, clenching and unclenching.

With each passing hour the number of hecklers grows. A waitress watches from a cafe doorway: "The sons of bitches should be in a mental institution!"

A man drives by slowly, passes the group, then drives by the other way. As he passes, he leans out of his car: "Those look like pretty good niggers. Why do they march with the damned Jews?" His car roars off.

Cars full of teen-agers come by, Confederate flags waving from their aerials; their riders gawk, heckle, then drive on.

By late afternoon, the marchers reach their first night's stop, at Hooker, Georgia. It is a black Baptist church of white clapboard, set by the edge of the woods, with a mountain stream running right through its yard. The elders were supposed to give them the key, but no one is there when they arrive, so the group sits outside, chatting and singing. At about five o'clock a group of teen-agers comes with the key. The teens set up a baseball game in the yard, boys and girls running around, catching and dropping balls, squealing at one another, while the marchers cook their supper and start to quiet down for the night. A young black boy rides down the hill on his bicycle, giggling and shouting, "No brakes! No brakes!" Little by little, the marchers realize that the teen-agers aren't there just by accident. They are around to see if the marchers will need any help.

Nothing serious happens. Cars drive by and slow down; a porky-faced white man with only a few strands of hair on his head growls, "We won't do it at night. We'll do it in broad daylight."

But a white teen-ager from Chattanooga hops out of his car and slinks nervously toward the church. Looking around for a white face, he fixes on Bob Zellner, a soft-spoken but quick-tempered SNCC worker from Alabama. "Could . . . could . . . could I use the bathroom?" squeaks the boy. Jesse Harris, a young black marcher from SNCC, laughs and puts his hand over the boy's head: "Lord, protect this one. He is an innocent!" The boy uses the facilities so quickly he stains his pants, and runs back to his car.

Marcher Dick Haley, a quiet ex-professor and assistant director of CORE, looks across at the parked cars. "I'm hopeful," he remarks. "They were totally hostile at first. I think we've caught their imagination. Now some of them just like to watch. . . . In one way, they've become part of what we're doing."

Bill Hansen, a white member of SNCC, with a lower jaw that sticks out at a funny angle as a result of a beating in an Albany, Georgia, jail, begins a diary:

"8:30 PM   Cars have been gathering in front of the church for almost an hour now. There seems to be about 35 whites, most of them young. Eric Weinberger is out there talking to them. . . . Zellner and Chico are asleep. Eric just came in. He said they don't seem hostile out there. . . . It's getting chilly. . . .

"10:00   We have only one bucket of coal. We turned out the lights and prepared to go to sleep. About a half hour later cars with headlights pulled into the yard. They stayed for quite a while, but I went to sleep. I don't know what time they left."

May 2

The next day, the walkers get up from the cold church floor where they spent the night, and go outside to wash in the stream. It is beautiful, but ice-cold. Hopping around, they dress as fast as they can to keep from freezing. A truck arrives with coffee and doughnuts, courtesy of the NAACP. It carries a telegram for Bob Zellner, from his mother. He tears it open. It says, "Bob, I've never asked you to do anything for me before, but in the unlikely event that you are allowed into Alabama, please drop out of the march till it gets past Birmingham, or your grandfather and your uncles are going to kill you." Everyone laughs. But Zellner knows it's not that funny: "Grandpa is a real hard-core Klansman. Probably loading up the shotgun for me right now."

Refreshed now, with the hope that the power of their belief and their openness will change the angry landscape within people, the marchers continue.

"Yellow-bellied sons of bitches," yells a man from a Georgia Ford.

"Moore died not in vain, Moore died not in vain, Moore died not in vain, I know. Deep in my heart I know that I do believe, Moore died not in vain I know. . . ."

They pass through the Georgia town of Trenton, the county seat—just a white courthouse and four shopping streets surrounding it. The buildings are in disrepair, the stores shuttered, closed. Cars parked, watching them from a distance. The red dust swirling at their feet. Georgia clay country.

"Wait till you get to Alabama!" shouts someone from one of the cars. "Wait till you get to Alabama! We'll get you in Alabama!" Tomorrow, they will cross into Alabama.

From Bill Hansen's diary: "9:00 AM   The terrain is one hill after another. Winston Lockett of CORE is carrying Bill Moore's sign and leading the line this morning. Alabama cars are becoming very numerous. There definitely is trouble ahead—it seems there is a mob waiting for us at the Alabama border. . . .

"9:35 AM   A Cadillac with Georgia plates came across to our side of the road and tried to run us down. It missed Eric, Jesse, Sam, Chico and myself by about three inches. . . .

"10:45 AM   My feet are hurting terrifically and legs are aching from my hips to the end of my big toes. I've taken off my boots and changed into my sneakers because of the big blister on my heel."

The marchers stop to rest by a roadside gully. The cars stop, watch; the passengers, mostly young, climb out and slowly walk toward the gully. As the crowds grow larger, state-trooper cars appear. One marcher, Bob Zellner, wearing a green Alpine hat, stands for a minute and sings a song, just to raise his spirits. When he sits down again, with the hat beside him, a man comes forward and steps on the hat. He stands there, daring Zellner to push him off. The crowd draws closer. This is what they were waiting for. Zellner quietly speaks to the man for a moment. The police step in and the man turns away. The marchers decide to move on.

It is growing hot now. There is no breeze.

From Bill Hansen's diary: "2:30 PM   Eric has been limping for the last hour now. No one is really paying attention to anything anymore except the feet of the person in front. My legs ache everywhere, and from indications, so do everyone else's. Up and down. Up and down these mountains.

"4:00 PM   We have finally stopped for the day. Everyone is completely shot. We are 6.8 miles from the Alabama line. Newsmen who have driven to the border tell us a couple of hundred people await our arrival, along with Al Lingo and the Alabama State Police."

That night they are to stay at Rising Fawn, Georgia. But no one has arranged housing for them there. Some black teen-agers from Rome, Georgia, pick them up in a 1947 Chevrolet and a green 1952 Ford and take them to their homes for the night. They will continue the march early the next morning.

May 3

By the next morning, two hundred cars, including patrol cars and what seem to be FBI cars, accompany them. An airplane flies back and forth overhead.

Today they will cross into Alabama. They begin to march in single file, the crowd following on foot and in cars. The thin voices of the marchers: "Moore died not in vain, Moore died not in vain . . . I know. Deep in my heart, I do believe, we shall overcome. . . ."

A little blonde girl watching them from the roadside reaches down into the strewn garbage and wrappers and finds a tiny blue flower. She smells it and then rubs it slowly along her cheek.

Today the march is led by Sam Shirah, the white son of an Alabama preacher. He has sent a telegram to his old Sunday-school teacher, now governor of Alabama, George Wallace, asking that they be allowed to pass through Alabama safely. Wallace had once been a parishioner in Sam's father's church. Wallace ignores the telegram.

The highway is clogged with gawkers; the mob continues to walk behind and alongside the marchers, lobbing dirt bombs and soda bottles and beer cans at them. The hecklers grow louder, more daring: "Head it up, coon! Troopers ain't gonna help you in Alabama!"

"You'll never make it through Fort Payne, Alabama!"

At a filling station, two teen-agers spray soda from a bottle onto the legs of the marchers. At a rest stop, a white man with a crew cut breaks from the crowd, hits Winston Lockett in the neck with a bottle, and then disappears.

A rock smashes one of the marchers in the head. Bob Zellner can hear the terrible *bong* it makes on his co-marcher's skull. "Blood began to trickle down," he recalled later, "and as I watched I could see the lump just swell up like an egg. But he wouldn't touch it. You could see he wanted to touch it, but he didn't want to give them the satisfaction of seeing him in pain."

They are lonelier now than ever. The local black people and the newsmen, who have kept them company all through the march, have had to leave because of the escalating violence. People are afraid of being identified with the group, afraid of the smell of death and martyrdom that accompanies them.

As they continue marching, the crowd closes in behind, smelling blood now, pelting them with pebbles and eggs. The Georgia troopers make no effort to stop them. In a few minutes, the marchers will be in Alabama.

"Ain't gonna let George Wallace turn me 'round, turn me 'round, turn me 'round."

At the state line a row of Confederate flags strung across the highway. Cars parked all along the road, fifteen hundred people, by press estimates. Standing on the Alabama side, a line of state troopers with riot helmets.

"The opposition lined the road as far as you could see—with their CBs and their trucks and their gun racks. . . . TV cameras trained on the state line," recalled Zellner. "Everyone was waiting for us to cross."

Woman on Alabama roadside.
© 1981 Bill Strode / Black Star

© Henry Wilhelm / Black Star

The line of marchers, dusty, their clothes smeared with dried egg, moves forward. "The silence of the kill fell over the crowd," said one journalist. The marchers walk faster; suddenly, they are over the line. The crowd swarms behind them, shouting, running. A line of troopers runs in to protect the marchers from behind. Another row of troopers stands in front, blocking their way.

"You are welcome as individuals," shouts Col. Al Lingo, "but not as a group. I order you to turn back and disperse."

They stand silent. "Arrest them!" shouts Lingo.

The marchers drop to the ground, curled up in the fetal position of nonviolent resistance. An officer jabs them with an electric cattle prod. The marchers jerk and writhe on the pavement, but refuse to get up. Finally, the troopers carry them to the waiting patrol cars, jabbing them again and again with cattle prods.

"Stick him! Stick him!" "Kill him! Kill him!" come the shrieks from the crowd.

Bob Zellner later recalled, "They grab Sam, who is first in line, and I hear the crowd screaming, "Kill him! Hang him! Kill him right here!" I start to worry—if that crowd tried to lynch us, how could the cops stop them? Then I realize—if the crowd is going to lynch us, the cops wouldn't want to stop them, so there is no sense worrying."

"We're going to have law and order regardless of what it takes," explains Lingo.

Five weeks later, the marchers are finally released from jail. At Huntington College, George Wallace is speaking at a Methodist conference. From the audience, Sam Shirah's mother asks her son's old Sunday-school teacher, "George, how come you put my son in jail?"

"I had to," explains Wallace. "The people were trying to kill him."

"Well," she asks, "why didn't you put the people who were trying to kill him into jail?"

Wallace thinks a moment: "There were just too many of them."

The march that had begun with such ideals ran into a wall of such bitterness and hatred as to make its goals almost impossible. The nonviolent movement seemed to bring out the best in people, their selflessness, generosity, courage, and the worst— jealousy, fear, pettiness.

The miracle did not happen.

Profile: BOB ZELLNER

Bob sits in the living room of his Manhattan apartment. Paintings and masks from Cuba and Central America decorate the wall. A contractor and master carpenter, he does special custom woodwork and furniture. Now he is doing an office for Harry

Belafonte. It is the kind of work his family has done for several generations, and something he has wanted to do since he was a child.

Basically I got into the movement to defend my own rights. In 1961 I was studying sociology in Huntington College in Montgomery, a conservative Methodist school. In a course in race relations we had to do a paper presenting ideas for solutions to the "racial problem," as they called it. This was a routine assignment. We were supposed to go the library. But a group of us had a better idea—we told the professor that we wanted to go to the Montgomery Improvement Association. Since nearly everybody in class, myself included, had been to the White Citizens Council, and had been bringing in pamphlets and such, it seemed right to speak to the other side.

"Well," he said, "you can't do that. It's breaking the segregation law and it's too dangerous."

Well, I felt really confined. I was no rabble-rouser and no revolutionary, but my mother and father had taught me a sense of fairness, and this just wasn't fair. We were pretty curious too. This was 1961—the sit-ins were going on, and there was something really exciting in the air. The greatest thing, though, was that these kids doing the sit-ins were our age. They were college kids, all dressed with white shirts and ties and notebooks, just like us. And somewhere inside, I've got to confess, I felt that they were having a hell of an adventure and it was for a real cause. We didn't actually want to get involved in the sit-ins, but we did want to get closer, see what was going on.

Well, it just so happened that the Montgomery Improvement Association was being sued by the city of Montgomery, and all the luminaries—Dr. King and Reverend Abernathy—were right in town, in the courthouse every day. So the five of us figured that we would speak to them in court. Even if we couldn't go to the Improvement Association, anybody can go to a public trial. So, during the recess in the trial, we eventually got up the nerve to introduce ourselves and shook their hands—which in the South was a verboten thing—and told them that we were students at Huntington College. We gave them a letter signed by some classmates saying that there were some white people who didn't subscribe to the segregationist line.

They were very friendly and open. I got up the nerve to tell Reverend Abernathy about our paper on race relations and ask him if we could meet with some black students from Alabama State and some of the Montgomery Improvement Association people. "Sure," he said. "I'd be happy to set it up, but you may get arrested for violating the segregation laws."

We explained that we had thought about that, and we weren't ready to demonstrate and we weren't courting arrest, but if they wanted to arrest us for something so ridiculous, so be it.

So he set up this clandestine meeting with students and a couple of members of the Montgomery Improvement Association. He snuck us onto the campus of Alabama

State. It was very secret, very exciting. We had to sort of infiltrate their meetings.

Then we found out about these mass meetings going on every night. Well, we asked Reverend Abernathy if we could go to a mass meeting, and he said, "Sure, but if you do that, you'll probably be arrested." Well, we weren't dying to go to jail, but if they wanted to arrest us it was their problem. "OK," he said, "as long as you understand that."

The next night he had a deacon from the church meet us outside of the mass meeting and sneak us inside. When we got in there, we saw the reason for all this precaution. All around the church, up on the balcony, sitting in back, down near the pulpit, state investigators were writing down people's names, taking pictures, taping the whole proceedings. If they saw us breaking the segregation law we'd be dead ducks in minutes. So the deacons kept us way in the back out of sight, incognito. Well, they must have seen us, because one of the deacons came over and told us, "The police are coming down the stairs and they say they are coming to get you guys." We tried to sneak out the back. But they must have gotten a good look at us.

The end of that week—Saturday—there was a workshop at the church. Reverend Abernathy said, "OK, you can come to the church, but they'll definitely get you." After the workshop, Reverend Abernathy came and said to us, "Well, you know they've got the church surrounded and they're waiting to arrest you guys."

We said, "OK. But at least we should go through the motions of trying to escape so we could tell our parents that we weren't courting arrest." That was still very important, then. He sort of chuckled and said, "Well, OK, you can try, but they're on all the doors and they're going to get you."

So he took us to the back so we could sneak out, and then he and Dr. King went out the front door. And I sort of peeped out the door and saw everybody move en masse around to the front of the church to see Dr. King. So we just ducked out quick, walked up the steps to the sidewalk, and just sort of drifted towards the exit of the campus. We figured they would get us any minute, but pretty soon we realized we were going to make it.

We got back to campus, and about an hour later, we were all down to dinner. Then the president and the dean started coming down, and I saw them picking us all out. Then they came over to us and said, "Meet us in the office in twenty minutes! You're in big trouble!" Turned out the police were still surrounding the church, waiting for us to come out.

The upshot of that was they asked us to leave school and the Klan burned crosses around the dormitory. The next day it was in the papers: our pictures, the story— FIVE WHITE BOYS SUSPENDED FROM HUNTINGTON COLLEGE. The dean called us hoodlums. The editorials called us ingrates and radicals.

The attorney general of the state of Alabama called us into his office. This was really big time—the state seal and everything. He bawled us out and he told our parents that we had fallen under Communist influence and he told us that they had

our eye on us! I said, "Goodness, you mean there's Communists here in Alabama?"
He said, "They don't live here, but they come through here."

I started to feel ashamed, like I was a real criminal. Then I would ask myself, What had I done wrong? I attended some meetings—I tried to inquire. Luckily my parents understood what I was doing. The other four boys were yanked away from there so fast!

After that, I couldn't go back. I didn't mean to get into the movement, but the state didn't give me a choice. You couldn't make a little inquiry unless you were willing to go all the way! That summer I joined SNCC.

It wasn't very long till I actually got arrested. In fact, the very next time I went back to Huntington to visit friends, I got arrested by William B. Painter, a state investigator I'd met at those mass meetings, and Al Lingo, head of the highway patrol, whom I would get to know very well. I was just having coffee with John Hill, who was one of the five, and Sam Shirah, who hadn't yet gotten into the movement. As we stepped out of the coffee shop, I saw Willie B. sitting in a car with this strange guy in a highway-patrol outfit. I said to the others, "I'm probably about to be arrested." My friends said, "Oh, Bob, don't be so paranoid. They can't arrest you, you haven't done anything."

Meantime, Willie B. is motioning me to come over to his car. So I try to slip my wallet out and give it to Sam or John. I don't want the police looking through my wallet for names and appointments. But my friends don't see what I am doing.

Willie B. and this strange big guy in the highway-patrol outfit step out of the car. "We'd like to speak to you, son—"

"Am I under arrest?" I say, and I keep trying to slip my wallet to Sam or John, only they still don't see anything. They are dumb struck.

Then the big strange guy looks at me and says, "You're under arrest."

"What's the charge?" I say.

He stops and thinks for a minute, then he says, "Conspiracy." Obviously, he hadn't even thought about what he was going to charge me with. That guy turned out to be Al Lingo.

So they put me in the car in the back seat, and I roll down the window to get my friends' attention and give them my wallet. But by now they are completely paralyzed. So as the car pulled away, I threw my wallet out to them. They didn't see a thing. They just walked away. Later a dean found it and sent it to me in jail. The police got it anyhow.

I don't think I would have gotten into the movement if it hadn't been for my father. He was an exceptional man. He had started out as an organizer for the KKK— a good one, too. When he came back from Europe, he had changed. He quit the Klan, took up the ministry, and became an outspoken integrationist—a real radical as far as the South was concerned.

Most of the original people in SNCC came from southern church backgrounds.

What we had in common was much more than what we had as differences; at least for a while we were really unracial—we were so black and white we weren't even black and white. I'll give you an example: Sometime much later, a couple of old SNCC members were organizing for the antiwar movement—one was black and one was white—and they were talking to some GIs. The black guy kept saying "honky" this and "honky" that, till his partner started getting uncomfortable. "But I'm a honky," he said. The black guy just turned around to his partner and said, "Shut up, nigger!"

Bob's hair has gone to gray now. It is shorter than it used to be. He is sitting on the stoop talking to a war veteran, a janitor, a doorman. The conversation is easy. You can see the friendly laugh, the comfortable open way with people, that made him one of the movement's best organizers.

Been Down into the South

Bob Zellner wrote this song in December 1962 while spending thirty-five days in the East Baton Rouge Parish prison in Louisiana. With Chuck McDew, an early SNCC chairman, he had gone to visit a fellow civil rights worker, Dion Diamond, in jail. They ended up getting arrested too. The first charge was vagrancy; then, when they pointed out that they had money and bus tickets, the charge was changed to "criminal anarchy."

He and Chuck were put in adjoining cells. They couldn't see each other, but they could talk and sing. They went through all the freedom songs they knew and then started making up new verses to other songs. Bob remembered a song he'd learned at a Methodist church camp in Alabama. The song was *Been Down into the Sea*, with verses like:

> I want to go to heaven, I want to go right.
> I want to go to heaven, all dressed in white.

As you can see, some of the verses they sing are almost identical to verses known in old spirituals, and others are verses from the 1960s, which went from song to song. The tune is a cousin to the better-known *Them Bones Gonna Rise Again*.

This transcription is by Ethel Raim.

I want to go to heaven but I want to go right,
Been down into the South.
I don't want to go without my civil rights,
Been down into the South.

Segregation is chilly and cold,
Chills my body but not my soul.

Freedom sounds so mighty sweet,
Soon one day we're gonna meet.

I been knockin' on doors and spreadin' the news,
And gettin' big holes in the bottom of my shoes.

Yes I've got big holes in the bottom of my shoes,
But this is one battle we can't lose.

If you don't think I've been through Hell,
Just follow me down to the Parchman jail.

You can talk about me just as much as you please,
Well the more you talk I'm gonna bend my knees.

The only thing that we did wrong,
Stayed in the wilderness a day too long.

The only thing that we did right
Was the day we started to fight.

We are fighting both black and white,
Fighting for our civil rights.

VII

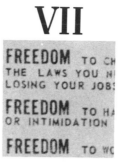

1963
The Jackson Movement
"Mississippi Goddam"

When my sons are grown, they're going to find Jackson even better than New York City.
—*MEDGAR EVERS, 1963*

Plans for this year's Dixie Week at the University of Mississippi include the Rebel Flag Raising Ceremony . . . , assassination of Lincoln . . . , salute to the Confederate dead . . . , the appearance of the Ku Klux Klan . . . , and a Dixieland Band. . . . A slave auction will be one of Wednesday's attractions.
—M BOOK, *UNIVERSITY OF MISSISSIPPI, 1954*

Segregation had many limbs and faces. But the heart of the beast was Mississippi. Deepest of the Deep South states, more rural, poorer, less educated, and far more dangerous than any of the others, it straddled the nineteenth and twentieth centuries: on one hand, desperately poor, divided like a third-world dictatorship between the majority in unheated tar-paper shacks and a few very wealthy citizens, all whites; on the other hand, a comfortable homey state, like a huge small town, where everyone knew everyone else and few native sons and daughters, black or white, willingly left.

Movement people spoke of Mississippi in the hushed voice reserved for a fearful enemy. Segregation might be bent and bruised, but it would never die until the stake went through its heart in the Magnolia State.

Edwin King, white minister at black Tougaloo College, in Mississippi, and candidate for the Freedom Democratic party: *Things became infinitely worse* [after the 1954 Supreme Court decision banning public-school segregation]. *First there was a sweep of violence through the state—lynchings, one after the other, like the murder of Emmett Till. Any black who attempted to integrate his school, or register*

FREEDOM CANDIDATES

AARON HENRY

FOR

GOVERNOR

REV. ED KING

FOR

LIEUTENANT
GOVERNOR

WHAT IS THE FREEDOM VOTE? ▮▮▮▮ IT IS A PROTEST VOTE TO ACHIEVE ....

▪ **VOTES**

▪ **JUSTICE**

▪ **JOBS**

▪ **EDUCATION**

FREEDOM TO CHOOSE THE MEN YOU WANT TO GOVERN YOU AND THE LAWS YOU NEED FOR A GOOD SOCIETY WITHOUT FEAR OF LOSING YOUR JOBS OR ENDANGERING YOUR FAMILY...

FREEDOM TO HAVE A JUST TRIAL WITHOUT FEAR OF BRUTALITY OR INTIMIDATION BY POLICE....

FREEDOM TO WORK AT ANY JOB FOR WHICH YOU ARE QUALIFIED, TO EARN A GUARANTEED WAGE WITHOUT FEAR OF HUNGER AND WANT....

FREEDOM TO LEARN, TO ATTEND GOOD SCHOOLS, TO BE ABLE TO FINISH SCHOOL WITHOUT FEAR OF HAVING TO DROP-OUT AND GO TO WORK. THIS MEANS ONE GOOD SCHOOL SYSTEM, NOT TWO IN-FERIOR ONES.

WHAT TO DO ON ...

NOVEMBER 2, 3 and 4

ALL REGISTERED AND UN-REGISTERED VOTERS 21 OR OVER:

GO TO THE FREEDOM VOTING CENTER IN YOUR AREA. YOUR PASTOR AND LOCAL LEADERS CAN DIRECT YOU TO IT. IF THERE IS NO VOTING CENTER IN YOUR AREA, MAIL YOUR BALLOT TO:

WHAT TO DO NOV. 5

ALL REGISTERED VOTERS:

ON YOUR OFFICIAL BALLOT, WRITE IN THE NAMES OF AARON HENRY FOR GOVERNOR AND REV. KING FOR LIEUTENANT GOVERNOR. DO NOT VOTE FOR THE DEMOCRATS OR THE REPUBLICANS....VOTE FOR FREEDOM.

NOW

EVERYBODY WANTS FREEDOM

...GAINING FREEDOM COSTS MONEY...VOTE ON NOVEMBER 2, 3 OR 4, BUT GIVE NOW FOR FREEDOM.

SEND ALL CONTRIBUTIONS TO:

Aaron Henry Headquarters
1072 Lynch Street Room 10
Jackson, Mississippi

to vote, would get shot or beaten, and would certainly lose his job. By 1956, '57, they had silenced the black community.

Then they turned on the white community—the Citizens Councils soon became a quasi-official arm of the state. Anyone who spoke out for integration, who did not give unquestioning support to segregation, would find himself unemployed, black-listed. By 1959, they had silenced every "disloyal" newspaper, or teacher or clergy-man or businessman. I saw the "decent" middle-class people clam up, as this home-grown fascism took over the state. . . . People wanted this terror to go away, they wanted segregation to end, but they said nothing, and it grew worse and worse.

But little by little the civil rights movement reached Mississippi. In the delta and the small agricultural cities, civil rights workers helped local people build grass-roots organizations. In Jackson, the capital, with just over 150,000 people, local black leaders tried to create a movement like the ones in Birmingham and Montgomery. Robert Smith, the first African American from Mississippi to run for Congress since Reconstruction, Aaron Henry, Medgar Evers of the Mississippi NAACP, and a group of black clergymen organized a "Jackson movement" to ask Mayor Allen Thompson to form a biracial commission to look into the problems of segregation in Jackson. Thompson "graciously" admitted them to his chambers, and in front of newsreel cameras took their requests "under advisement." After that he refused to see them.

Symbol used by movement ministers in Mississippi. Courtesy Ed King Collection, Tougaloo College

OPPOSITE. *Courtesy Ed King Collection, Tougaloo College*

To dramatize their demands, movement leaders staged a three-person sit-in at a Woolworth's lunch counter and a ten-person picket line at J. C. Penney's. The city's response—over a hundred police lined the five-block Capitol Street shopping district, with rifles and riot gear.

At 11:15 A.M., on May 28, 1963, Anne Moody, a senior at Tougaloo College, sat down at the Woolworth's lunch counter with several other students and teachers. For three hours, while the police watched, the crowd kicked, punched, and threw Anne and her friends on to the floor again and again.

Anne Moody: *The mob started smearing us with ketchup, mustard, sugar, pies. John Salter [a teacher] joined us, and was hit on the jaw with what appeared to be brass knuckles. Blood gushed from his face and someone threw salt in the open wound. . . . A Negro High School boy sat down. . . . The mob took spray paint and sprayed the word "nigger" on his white shirt. . . .*

Finally, Anne and the others escaped with the help of the Tougaloo College president and several faculty members.

Afterwards, I sat in the NAACP office, thinking that the whites had a disease, an incurable disease in its final stage. I thought of the young Negroes who had just begun to protest as young interns. When these young interns grew up, they would be the best doctors in the world for social problems.

"We can cage a hundred thousand agitators," boasted the mayor.

Five days later, four hundred students from the city's four all-black high schools gathered at Farrish Street Baptist Church for prayer and a workshop in nonviolent resistance. Then, carrying small American flags, two by two, they began to march toward Capitol Street. They had not even reached the tracks which separate the black section of Jackson from the all-white downtown when eighty-seven policemen charged the march with rifle butts and clubs, bashing and pushing.

Edwin King: *There was no resistance. Each pair simply walked up to the police to replace those who were arrested and beaten in front of them.* Soon, with the street littered with crumpled American flags, and signs saying "We Want Freedom," all four hundred were under arrest. They were heaped into a closed garbage truck, ripe with the flies and stench of summer garbage. When the youngsters sang to keep up their spirits, the police beat on the side of the truck to silence them.

Mayor Thompson set up temporary jail facilities at the fairgrounds just behind the capitol; Governor Ross Barnett told him he could use the facilities at the Parchman

state penitentiary as well. The press called the temporary jail in the converted animal pens the "Fairgrounds Motel." Arrested boys were loaded into the cattle stockade, and girls into the hog pens. Into each area came a barrel of baloney, a barrel of milk, and a barrel of water. The police threw slices of bread onto the dirt: "Eat it, you dogs!"

Edwin King: *That evening a guard announced, "We're gonna finish this in Jackson, tonight. We got gas for you niggers!"*

"What does he mean!" whispered a college co-ed.

"He's just trying to scare us," muttered a Tougaloo student. . . .

"What's that?" cried another girl, pointing to the far end of the building.

Ugly, whirling clouds of gray-white smoke poured through the heavy mesh of screened windows. The cloud came closer. . . . The ceiling began to disappear in the horrible fog, the lights casting a pale beam through the terror. . . . One white

LEFT AND OPPOSITE. On the steps of the state capitol, Jackson, Mississippi. © Matt Herron / Black Star

policeman laughed and shouted, "God, it stinks in here. Let's get out of here."

The police left. Outside, one shouted to the men, "Block that door! Shoot any black bitch that tries to get out!"

A girl screamed, "It is poison! They are going to kill us!" . . . Other girls screamed and crouched down, huddled near the concrete floor, as the smoke poured over their heads. . . . As the stench hit they began to gag.

Outside, a white policeman laughed, "That'll kill their crabs . . . and their fleas and their bedbugs! Hah hah!" Choking, the girls begin to get up. This was not poison gas but insecticide—the same gas that got sprayed on the streets every summer night to kill the mosquitoes. They were not going to die, not tonight. . . . But the terror had left a mark on every youngster, like a knife wound in the guts. . . .

The next morning the Jackson Daily News' favorite cartoon character, "Leftie Wing," a bearded beatnik with dark glasses, spouted tears and cried, "Police Brutality (they've hurt my feelings) Boo Hoo!"

Medgar Evers, a field director for the Mississippi NAACP, had spent his whole adult life trying to organize for civil rights in the Magnolia State, a job that has been likened to "trying to pick a plantation's entire cotton crop singlehandedly—one boll at a time, in the middle of the night, with a gun pointed at your head." On June 12, 1963, the thirty-seven-year-old Evers stepped from a car in front of his three-room Jackson home. From inside the house came the fuzzy roar of a TV set tuned to a station that had gone off the air. Myrlie, his wife, had fallen asleep waiting up for him again. Quietly, he reached into his pocket for his keys. Three rifle shots tore the darkness. Evers lay on his front stoop, bleeding to death.

Four days later, six thousand black people from all over Mississippi walked behind his casket for the two miles from the church to the funeral home.

Edwin King: *This time, they gave a "parade permit," that's what they called permission to walk behind a coffin. Martin Luther King came, Wilkins from the NAACP, James Farmer from CORE, and thousands and thousands of people. It was a quiet procession—the police had ordered "no singing." I guess they did know the power of the songs. Way at the tail end the SNCC kids were marching—some of the other organizations considered them too rowdy. The last thousand or so marchers never got near the funeral home. So they stood out in the street, waiting quietly. After a while, one of the SNCC kids started to sing—it was Oh Freedom. It was very quiet, very soft, very sad. Then someone else picked up the song, and someone else. Soon the verses started getting closer and closer to the situation here in Jackson—"No more killing, no more killing, no more killing over me. And before I'll be slave, I'll be buried in my grave. . . ." Then it got to "No more Thompson," he was the mayor. "No more Thompson, no more Thompson . . ." and "No Ross Barnett, no Ross Barnett . . ."*

By now, the police were getting very twitchy, and the whole crowd outside the funeral home was singing.

Myrlie Evers, Jackson, Mississippi, 1963. © 1975 Flip Schulke

Mississippi Goddam

Words and music are by Nina Simone.

a-bout Mis-sis-sip-pi god - dam.

Hound dogs on my trail, School chil-dren sit-ting in jail,

Black cat cross my path, I think ev-'ry day's gon-na

be my last. Lord have mer-cy on this

land of mine. We all gon-na get it in due time,

Don't be-long here I don't be-long there, I ev-en stopped be-liev-

- ing in prayer. Don't tell me, I'll

Picket lines, school boycott,
Try to say it's a Communist plot.
All I want is equality,
For my sister and brother, my people and me.
You lied to me all these years,
You told me to wash and clean my ears.
Talk real fine, just dress like a lady,
And you'd stop calling me Sister Sadie.
But this whole country is corrupted with lies,
You all should die and die like flies.
I don't trust you anymore,
You keep on saying, "Go slow."
That's just the trouble—too slow,

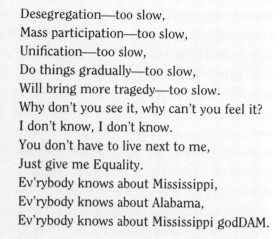

Desegregation—too slow,
Mass participation—too slow,
Unification—too slow,
Do things gradually—too slow,
Will bring more tragedy—too slow.
Why don't you see it, why can't you feel it?
I don't know, I don't know.
You don't have to live next to me,
Just give me Equality.
Ev'rybody knows about Mississippi,
Ev'rybody knows about Alabama,
Ev'rybody knows about Mississippi godDAM.

Then someone else started a song—"This little light of mine, I'm gonna see it shine. . . ." Now, the words got even closer to the situation here in Jackson." All over Jackson, I'm gonna let it shine. . . ." The police were really getting nervous. Finally everyone was singing "All over Capitol Street, I'm gonna let it shine. . . ." The police heard that one word, and they broke ranks, retreating like crazy toward downtown. That's what started it. Someone just picked up their finger and pointed it straight toward the capitol—"All over Capitol Street, I'm gonna let it shine."

The march started—orderly, solemn, but singing, through the black section, straight toward Capitol Street, a mile away. It was as if all the frustration of the last month suddenly let loose. People poured out of the houses and the restaurants and the shops. The march passed a seedy section with a lot of bars, and people poured out of those too—it was as if the whole black population of Jackson was joining in.

The march reached Capitol Street. They were singing "No more killing, no more killing, no more killing over me. . . ."

That's when the police attacked. No arrests this time—this time they were beating with their sticks. They ran up to TV cameras and threw them on the ground. They didn't want any witnesses!

This crowd got furious. A lot of them never had any nonviolent training. Someone threw a bottle—a rock. Suddenly there was a shot—the police were shooting at the crowd.

The march leaders realized that they had to break this up quickly. People like John Lewis from SNCC started running through the crowd: "Please go home. Someone is going to get killed!" People began leaving, but the crowd didn't break up fast enough to suit the police. They started to charge. That's when John Doar [from the Justice Department] jumped between the police and the marchers. He turned his back to

Oh Freedom

This 145-year-old song, like most great works of art, contains contradictions. After a triumphant opening line, the verse ends implying an acceptance of death. In 1935 black sharecropper John Handcox changed the last line to "Take my place with those who loved and fought before," and this is how it spread through the CIO unions of the thirties. The young 1960s freedom fighters changed it to "I'll fight for the right to be free." And there have been other last lines. But the old last line keeps coming back. Perhaps it's partly the beauty of the *o* sounds contrasting with the *ee* sounds. Even "Lord" becomes, in the Deep South accents, more like "Lo'd." Whatever the reason, the old line keeps getting sung by black and white, and that's how we print it here.

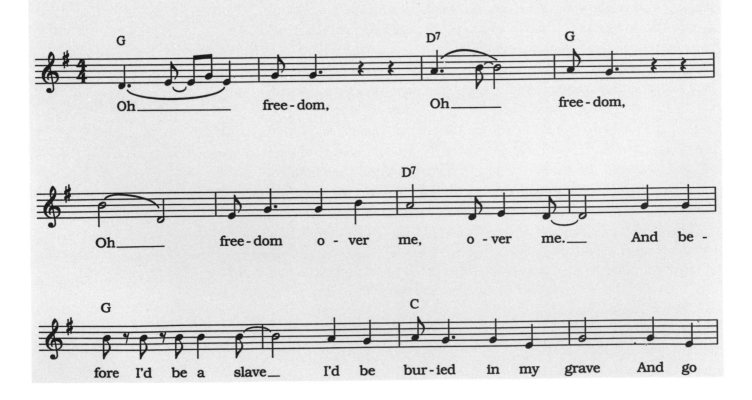

the police and said to the crowd, "Please go home." The police stopped rather than run over him. The people did go home. It was a brave thing to do, but a lot of us wondered why he didn't turn and face the police and say to them, "Please go home." That was the last big street demonstration of the Jackson movement.

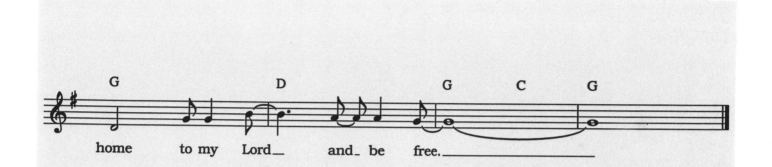

No more mo'nin',
No more mo'nin',
No more mo'nin over me.
And before I'd be a slave
I'd be buried in my grave
And go home to my Lord and be free.

No more slavery . . .

No more weeping . . .

There'll be singing . . .

In the 1960s, new verses were added:

No segregation . . .

No more shooting . . .

No burning churches . . .

No more Jim Crow . . .

No more Pritchett . . .

In actual practice, old and new verses were mixed together.

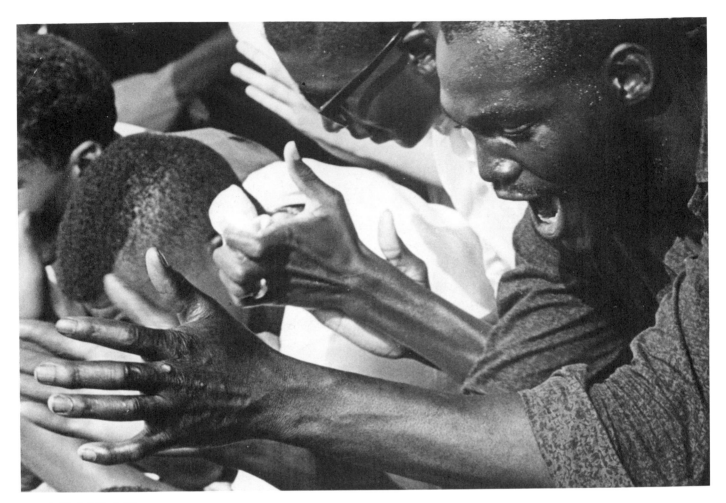

© Bob Fitch / Black Star

Profile: JUNE JOHNSON

June's soft-spoken manner and gentle Mississippi voice give little clue of the powerful and strong-willed individual beneath the surface. June was fourteen years old when the movement came to her town of Greenwood, Mississippi. She was in the eighth grade.

I was curious at first. In the mornings, on the way to school, I would meet Bob Moses at the corner of Broad Street and Avenue H. He was my favorite. He would take my books and walk me to school and I would ask him all the questions: "What are you doing here? The white people say you're troublemakers." He would laugh and say, "That's not true. We're here to teach people to be first-class citizens and to become registered voters."

I got really interested when he told me that the movement needed people like me to help canvass the community and recruit people to go down to the courthouse to register. So I got trained, and kept going to the freedom office. My mother got so angry—she gave me a spanking every time I went there. But I kept going and I kept getting more whippings.

That spring there was to be a SNCC training session in Atlanta and I wanted to go so bad. But my mother said, "You've never been out of Mississippi!" and "Who are those people?" and "You may get into trouble," and blah blah blah blah blah. So I convinced Bob Moses to come to my house and talk to my mom. She finally said, "Yes, but you have to stay at Annell Ponder's house in Atlanta." Annell had been in Greenwood as part of Dr. King's group, teaching people to read and interpret the Constitution so they could pass the literacy tests. So Mom knew her. The trip came and it was so wonderful. Lawrence Guyot and Hollis Watkins and all those people were singing, and I had never seen so much joy and so much spirit and so much honesty.

The next trip came up a few months later—to Charleston, South Carolina. This was the later part of '63. Myself, Annell Ponder, Evester Silver, and Mrs. Fannie Lou Hamer went together.

During this trip, June and the others went to see the citizenship school on John's Island which had been started by Septima Clark of Highlander and a group of local citizens. They attended workshops in nonviolent techniques, and they got some practical experience by helping out at a local demonstration. After four days, they started back to Greenwood.

At Columbus, Mississippi, at the Trailways bus terminal, we had a two-hour layover. When we got in line to get on the bus, the driver threw us all to the ground. There was a little white girl in back, Pearl. He took her to the front of the bus and said "nigras" must get in last and we must sit in the back of the bus. Mrs. Hamer stepped forward and told him that this was an interstate bus and he was in violation of our civil rights. She wanted his badge number so she could file a report with the bus company. . . .

Finally we got on the bus. As we were proceeding to our next stop—Winona, Mississippi—we noticed the bus driver stop at every little town and make a telephone call. We all feared that we were going to run into some problems. When we got to Winona, the highway patrol, police officers, white people, were all over. We went into the terminal, sat at the lunch counter. The waitress said, "We don't serve niggers," and she told us to leave. That highway patrol and police officers came in with billy sticks and pushed us out of the place. So we were very disturbed. We decided that whatever would happen, would happen to every one of us—we would stick together.

I walked behind the highway patrol car so I could get their tag number. There was a big white fat guy standing outside the car, with a tee shirt on and overalls and pulling on a knife. He went back inside and told the highway patrol something and they came out and arrested us all.

At the jailhouse, they put us into a cell. But three police officers stood in front of me and said, "Not you, bitch." Next thing I knew they had stripped me of everything I had on and they just started beating me. They said we had made the worst mistake in the world to come to Winona, Mississippi, with that integration "shit," and they weren't going to have it in their town, and they were going to make sure we never came back.

After they took me back to the cell, they came and got Fannie Lou Hamer and took her in the back area of the jail. We could hear the echo of the beating she was getting. It is my understanding that they took off her clothes, sat on her legs and made the jail inmates beat her. She never overcame that whipping. To the day that she died, she suffered. Then they beat Annell Ponder. They beat all of us, and then they told us to get rid of the evidence.

Then, three o'clock that morning, we were handcuffed, taken out of the cell, and tried on the street in front of a mob, right there in Winona. I was found guilty, immediately. But I refused to tell them I was twenty-one—they wouldn't believe I was only fifteen and I was big for my age. So the judge said they would send me to a detention center.

They wouldn't let us make phone calls. But, the deal was there were two people left on the bus and they didn't know it. Those two people went to Greenwood and told Bob Moses and everybody what had happened to us. But when they called, the police denied that we were in the jail. Lawrence Guyot came down personally to see us. They beat him brutally. You couldn't even recognize him.

But word got to Attorney General Robert Kennedy, and phone calls started coming in. But still they wouldn't release us. I remember going in to take a shower. This black guy who worked around the jail, they put him up to turning the hot water on me, and I was scalded. I still have a scar on my leg.

Then, on the night of June 11, they took us from our cells at gunpoint and made us sign statements that nothing had happened to us, that none of the officials had done any beatings, that we had done it to ourselves, and that we had gotten kind treatment while there. The next day my mother, Hollis Watkins, James Bevel, Andy Young, and Bernard Lee came to get us out. That's when they released us. . . . That day we found out Medgar Evers was killed.

June and the others sued the police for violating their constitutional rights. The trial took place later that year in Oxford, Mississippi.

The trial began . . . the day John Kennedy got killed. . . . When the court in Oxford found out what kind of case this was, they dismissed all blacks from the jury. There was only one black restaurant in that town and they were afraid to serve us. So the Justice Department people who were pleading our case brought us hamburgers and Cokes, which we ate up in their office. We couldn't sleep in that town—the Holiday Inn was segregated, and nobody would put us up. So we slept in Holly Springs, sixty miles away, on the Rust College campus. Sometimes we stayed at the Reverend Boonfield's home.

While the trial was going on, the students from Ole Miss* would come with rebel flags in their hands and sit in the courtroom and wave the flags and laugh at the testimony which we gave. The three prisoners who beat Mrs. Hamer testified that they had been told that if they didn't beat Mrs. Hamer, they would be killed. And at the end, their court found against us—they said we had not proved our case.

But I'll tell you, all these experiences made me a fighter. I was fifteen years old, and I was a fighter.

I stayed in Greenwood for almost another twenty years. I ran for a seat on the county board of supervisors, and the power structure put together a sixty-thousand-dollar campaign to stop me. I ran for the justice-court judge seat. I sued the Republican party for gerrymandering, and we won, and we got a good congressman in. In 1979 we sued the city when they tried to tie up revenue-sharing money and spend it on a computer instead of dividing it between the white and the black communities for community-development work. In 1983 I helped a good friend, the mayor of Tchula, Mississippi. He was a bright articulate person. The white establishment tried to put a murder on him. We had to put together a national and an international campaign to save him. But we got him acquitted.

Then my Doberman pinscher turned up dead, my house got broken into in broad daylight and the police ignored it, and I found myself getting arrested every day. A good friend of mine advised me to leave town while I was still alive.

But I've got a mother and eleven sisters and brothers there, and I go back all the time. If I move back, I'll run for public office again. I'm not finished.

*The University of Mississippi. The nickname Ole Miss has a double meaning. On Mississippi plantations, slaves used to refer to the plantation owner's wife as "Ole Miss." The plantation owner's daughter was "Young Miss."

Field hand, Mississippi delta.
© *1966 Bob Fletcher*

VIII

1961–1964

The Mississippi Delta—"A Tremor in the Middle of the Iceberg"

I met a very wise old man sitting on a stump. He said to me: "If you want to be smart and live a long life like me, when a white man tells you to do something, do the opposite.
—*SAMMORAH MUHAMMAD, FROM JACKSON*

*R*ural Mississippi was even more isolated than the towns of the state. Without the trappings of city sophistication to connect it to the rest of the country, it was, as historian James Silver described it, a tight "closed society." It was Klan country. The night riders had swapped their horses for pickup trucks, but they still indulged in beatings and lynchings to keep the social order in place. As recently as 1955, they had beaten Emmett Till to death, tied him to a piece of cotton-gin machinery, and dumped him into the Tallahatchie River for, allegedly, whistling at a white woman. A whole generation of white and black Mississippians grew up with the news photo of Till's water-bloated corpse tattooed into their minds.

Into this world in the summer of 1960 came a single black man from the Bronx, Bob Moses. This quiet, bespectacled math teacher from the Horace Mann School in New York was traveling through the state to find some local black activists to come to a SNCC conference in Atlanta that fall.

One choking hot afternoon, he got off the bus in the dusty town of Cleveland, in the delta area.. He was tracking down Amzie Moore, vice president of the state's six-hundred-member NAACP.

Moore was at the post office, where he worked as a janitor. Because of his activism, it was the best job he could get. "Let's walk outside," he said to the northerner.

They stepped out the back of the post office and walked through the streets of Cleveland. As Moses explained his reason for being there, Moore just looked at him. Finally, Moore shook his head: "Mississippi isn't the rest of the South. I don't know what I would have to say to those sit-inners. You sit in over in Nashville, you go to jail. Sit in here, they'll bash your brains in, murder your family, and then put you in jail." Moses' heart sank. Here was one of the state's most aggressive civil rights leaders. If he had no hope, who would? Amzie explained that in Mississippi, everything was run by the Citizens Councils—from the police to the judges to the state politicians straight up to the governor. They worked as a united front to squash any attempt at integration: if the police didn't stop you, the sheriff would, or the courts would, or the governor, or the state's unofficial militia—the Klan.

Moore looked carefully at the northerner. There was something open about him. "As soon as you met Bob, you felt like you had known him for your whole life," says Hollis Watkins. Moore wondered if he could trust him with some ideas that had been running around in his head. "Why don't you come to the house for supper and we'll talk."

For the next several days they continued to meet. Amzie drove Bob around the state, introducing him to other civil rights workers. By summer's end, they had worked up a plan.

Seventy-five years earlier, Mississippi's white legislators, the state's so-called "redeemers," had undermined Reconstruction and stolen the vote from the Negroes. They used a voter-registration test that could be rigged so that no black person could pass. They used terror, so any black foolish enough to try to register would find himself out of work, or lying in a ditch with all his bones broken. By 1960, less than 5 percent of Mississippi's voting-age black people were registered. Moses and Moore agreed that the only way to win equal education and economic opportunity, the only way to stop the Klan and the Citizens Councils, was to strike "at the soft spot of segregation—the state machine—the political structure." To get the politicians where they lived—to get back that vote.

Bob Moses: *Till then I hadn't really seen a place for myself to fit into the movement. Atlanta was sort of crowded—there were organizers and a student movement and SCLC. But in rural Mississippi there wasn't anything going on—nothing focused. Here was a project that I could work on, where I could make a difference. Also, with Amzie I wouldn't be coming in cold. He was what I like to think an organizer should be—working behind the scenes, helping set up things.*

Amzie was special. He didn't have a formal education; he still had his common roots, which didn't have that sort of institutional stamp a university can put on you. On the other hand, he had a very special analytical and well-read mind. So he could talk to the people and he could talk to the powerful. He knew people all around the state. They listened to him and respected him.

Other people were afraid of the student movement or were already committed to

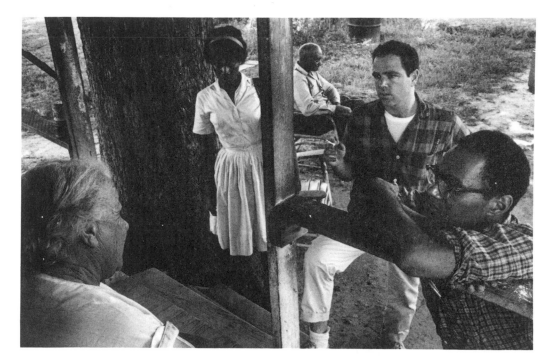

Bob Moses organizing door to door, 1962. © Danny Lyon / Magnum

their own organization. He was the only one I met who was really ready for the students, who saw their potential for helping the black people in Mississippi.

Bob and Amzie charted a state-wide registration drive, run by local Mississippians who knew and understood the people, aided by northerners and students who would be safe from economic reprisals. From this seemingly non-confrontational plan, the Mississippi freedom movement was to grow. Before the next six years were up, nearly thirty people would die, hundreds would be shot and beaten, and thousands would go to jail. But segregation's back would be broken.

In 1961, Moses and a small group of SNCC and NAACP workers began their Magnolia State registration drive in the city of McComb, in the southern part of Mississippi. All summer, the workers made the rounds of the black homes. Little by little, fear and suspicion turned to interest, and finally to enthusiasm. The people asked for classes to help them pass the difficult voter-registration exam. E. W. Steptoe, the local NAACP leader, turned his home into a registration school. His neighbor Herbert Lee, the father of nine, volunteered to drive civil rights workers in his car to speak to blacks who lived way out in the country. Every day, another small group went to the courthouse to register.

Before the summer was over, white violence lashed out. It began with beatings, such as the attack on Travis McGill, a SNCC worker from New York who was leading a group to register in Liberty. Fifteen local whites surrounded him as he tried to enter the courthouse and beat him nearly unconscious. That same week, Moses was beaten over the head and face with the butt of a knife; John Hardy, from Tennessee, got smashed over the head with a pistol and thrown in jail. Finally, on September 25, Herbert Lee was shot to death with a bullet to the head fired by a white state legislator, E. H. Hurst. The murderer was acquitted on the grounds of self-defense.

In the ensuing protest, hundreds went to jail. From his cell, Moses sent a message to those on the outside: "We are smuggling this note from the drunk tank. . . . Twelve of us are here, sprawled out along the concrete bunker; Curtis Hayes, Hollis Watkins, Ike Lewis and Robert Taylor are sitting up and talking—mostly about girls; Charles McDew ('tell the story') is curled into the concrete and the wall. . . . This is Mississippi, the middle of the iceberg. Hollis is leading off with his tenor, 'Michael row the boat ashore, Alleluia; Christian brothers don't be slow, Alleluia; Mississippi's next to go, Alleluia.' This is a tremor in the middle of the iceberg—from a stone that the builders rejected."

Teen-ager at county fair.
© Robert S. Reiser

The next summer, SNCC moved its attentions northward into the delta, to Leflore County, where Emmett Till was murdered. Here, in the city of Greenwood, the Mississippi "iceberg" began to split.

It began with a single twenty-one-year-old youngster.

Sam Block: *They dropped me off in Greenwood in June of '62. I had no car, no money, no clothes, no food, just me. . . . The first thing I had to do was find a place to stay. Some students I knew found me a place with Mrs. McNease, the elementary-school principal. She didn't know why I was there. As soon as she went to school, I went to work—talking to people, hanging out in pool halls, wherever people were—the laundromat, the grocery stores.*

I found a lot of angry people. A lot of blacks had been murdered in Leflore County. Emmett Till was one of the few that got publicity. The people who were most receptive were the older people. The young people crossed the street when they saw me coming.

Finally, we got our first meeting of about 15 or 20 people . . . at the Elks Hall. . . . At our first mass meeting we sang freedom songs and Mr. Cleveland Jordan told the people, "We've been wanting somebody help us do something. Well, here he is. Don't be scared of him. Treat him just like he is one of us because he is."

Soon, 21 people, ages forty up to eighty years old, were ready to go down and register. At the courthouse

Michael Row the Boat Ashore

In 1867, an ex-officer of the Union army published in the North a book entitled *Slave Songs*. In 1954, Tony Saletan found a copy in a library in Boston and went through it page by page. He selected this song and these verses to teach me. I taught it to the Weavers, who sang it at their '55 reunion concert. In '59 some pop singers made it a hit record. Then (not before) it spread through the South again and got many new verses.

—*Pete Seeger*

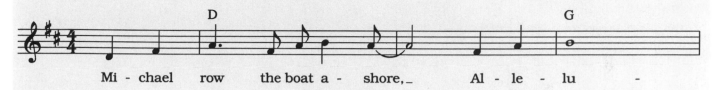

Michael's boat is a freedom boat, Alleluja.
If you stop singing then it can't float, Alleluja.

Jordan's river is deep and wide, Alleluja.
Get my freedom on the other side, Alleluja.

Jordan's river is chilly and cold, Alleluja.
Chills the body but not the soul, Alleluja.

Christian brothers, don't you know, Alleluja,
Mississippi is the next to go, Alleluja.

we met Mrs. Martha Lamb, county registrar. Mr. Ledbetter, 70 years old, was first in line.

Mrs. Lamb shook her head, "Now Ledbetter, you know you can't read and write."

"I know I can't but I can answer questions. Whatever questions you want to ask me, just ask me, and I will answer it. . . ." he said.

She got so mad she told him, "I don't know many questions that I could ask you that you could answer, but how many bubbles are there in a bar of soap?"

Old man Ledbetter stood back and looked at her and said, "If I don't answer this question I'm gonna flunk this test, ain't I?"

She said, "Yes, that is your question."

"Well, I don't want to be an ignorant man all the rest of my life. Mrs. Lamb, tell me how many bubbles there are in a bar of soap, so when somebody asks me again I can let them know."

Mrs. Lamb got so furious she called Sheriff Smith . . . who spit in my face and told me to leave Greenwood. . . . I said, "Sheriff, if you don't want to see me around here . . . the best thing for you to do is pack your bags and leave, because I am staying."

Two more field secretaries joined Block—Lawrence Guyot, a man of almost 280 pounds, and Luvaughn Brown. The night they arrived, the police raided the SNCC office, and the three men escaped by squeezing out of the bathroom window and sliding down the TV antenna, no easy feat for Guyot. The next day the Greenwood project got Willie Peacock, its fourth member.

Food for displaced share-croppers, Mississippi.
© 1966 Bob Fletcher

Willie Peacock: *For a long time we just visited people in Leflore and neighboring counties—knocked on doors and talked to people about the vote. We had to let the people know that we weren't going away, we were there for the long haul.*

Hollis Watkins, next to join the project: *But the state found new ways to keep local people in line. These were tenant farmers and cotton pickers who had recently lost their jobs to machinery and were kicked off the land; they were squatting somewhere and eating courtesy of the government. They were vulnerable targets for retaliation.*

When people continued to listen and to attempt to register, the county just cut off their food. By winter, people were literally starving.

Sam Block: *The Vassels, the first family we visited, their house was cold. You could look through the holes in the floor and see the ground. What hurt me most was this newborn baby, lying in the bed—there were some springs but no mattress. There was a coat on top of the springs and this baby was covered with raggedy clothes.*

SNCC sent an appeal to the North for food. In Ann Arbor, Michigan, in Cambridge, Massachusetts, students and faculty responded with a fury. Between Christmas and Easter, Ivanhoe Donaldson, a "one-man transport operation," drove twelve truck-loads of food and medicine the thousand miles from Michigan to Mississippi.

Their constant presence and their help turned things around.

Bob Moses: *We stymied . . . the anxious fear in the Negro community, seeded across town and blown from . . . white sunken sink to windy kitchen floors and rusty old stoves, that maybe you did come only to boil and bubble and then burst out of sight.*

Hollis Watkins: *When Willie and Sam and I talked to people, we knew what their lives were, because we had grown up in the same place. So, talking to people was like talking to our next-door neighbors.*

Willie Peacock: *One night in February, we held a mass meeting. It was the largest one yet—we had to hold it in the First Christian Church. It was powerful. We couldn't stop singing freedom songs. Those songs had a real message that night: Freedom doesn't come as a gift. It comes through knowledge and power—political power. It comes from the vote. That night I went to bed at the office. That next morning, people started knocking on the door first thing in the morning. They were ready to go down and attempt to register. They kept coming and coming—they knew they probably wouldn't be allowed to register, but it was their right to try.*

We hadn't but one car to get people to the courthouse, and people were afraid that if they used their own cars, they'd be tagged and arrested later, on the way out of town, so they decided to walk to the courthouse—two by two, in a line, so they could be sure to arrive safely. It was the first movement march—marching didn't begin in Birmingham. It started in Greenwood.

After that, the segregationists began a reign of terror. Sam Block was thrown in jail. Bob Moses' car was sprayed with machine-gun fire. Moses escaped, but Jimmy Travis, who was traveling with him, was badly wounded. The voter-registration office was set on fire, all of the equipment and records burned. Six white men with a shotgun blasted Sam Block's car, nearly killing Block and Willie Peacock. Bullets tore through the wall of the home of George Greene, a Greenwood civil rights worker, narrowly missing the bed where his three children slept. All across Mississippi, violence accelerated. Aaron Henry, local head of the NAACP, had his home bombed, his drugstore burned. Hartman Turnbow, the first black voter applicant in Holmes County, watched his fire-bombed home explode. The Jackson police clubbed students, and the Klan killed Medgar Evers.

But, as Willie Peacock says, while "their activities increased, . . . ours increased even faster. More and more black people were beginning to demand their rights." Courageous Mississippians began to emerge. Fannie Lou Hamer, the middle-aged sharecropper from Ruleville, Mississippi, tried to register to vote, lost her job, fled for her life, and survived jailings and beatings to become one of the most powerful organizers from Mississippi. Hartman Turnbow led more neighbors to register to vote, and then survived bombings, fires, and arrests to challenge Mississippi's white delegates to the Democratic convention. Annie Devine, from Canton, Mississippi, gave up the safety of a small business to try to integrate one of the most rabidly segregationist cities in the state.

Sam Block: *People began to come out of the woodwork. Like Mrs. Laura McGee. Her land was almost taken away because her brother, Gus Coats, had attempted to register to vote and was shot in the head. Gus had to be hidden in a casket and* shipped to Chicago. . . . Now the Federal Land Grant Bank was trying to take her farm from her. We raised the money to stop them. Her sons became the first two students to go down to desegregate the local theater. After Jimmy was shot, Mrs. McGee donated the farm to us for a fund raiser—Pete Seeger, Theodore Bikel, Bob Dylan, Jackie Washington and others came. From there, I think, Bob Dylan was inspired to go back and write "Blowin' in the Wind."

We had entered a new phase. People had taken over the movement themselves. Local leaders were directing it themselves.

Hollis Watkins: The movement in Mississippi was under way and nobody could stop it. It was a wildfire.

The dangers that these people faced made them different from other civil rights workers. In other states the movement consisted of a loose coalition of African Americans and liberal European Americans. But in Mississippi, there were few liberal whites with whom to unite. The price for liberalism was too high. Those who entered the movement were joining a small, united, and almost entirely black community.

In 1964, Amzie Moore of the NAACP and Bob Moses and several other SNCC members proposed that it was time to enlarge this little band—it was time to focus the attention of the nation on Mississippi—it was time to bring in the volunteers from the North.

With the help of volunteers from northern universities, an umbrella group called the Council of Federated Organizations, or COFO, would register voters in a "Freedom Democratic party," which would elect a slate of delegates for the 1964 Democratic convention. The new slate could publicly challenge the legitimacy of the official segregated delegates at the convention. It would "open up the political process to Mississippi's black people and nurture a new generation of local black leaders." To this end, COFO would also set up Freedom Schools and community centers to educate the black citizens, many of whom had never learned to read and write. The project would be called Freedom Summer.

Veteran Mississippi organizers objected, afraid that all of the careful gains which they had made in building up local active communities would be undone by this flood of northerners—that the local people would lose control of their own movement.

Moses and Moore argued that the bright light of national attention which the volunteers would focus on Mississippi would "confront, break open and finally put an end to the violence."

Bob Moses: We had progressed through a series of murders—Herbert Lee in 1961, the attempted assassination of Sam Block and Jimmy Travis and myself, and then the assassination of Medgar Evers in '63. The violence was escalating into higher and higher levels.

SDS pamphlet, 1962.
Courtesy Avon Rollins

Freedom Is a Constant Struggle

This transcription is by Ethel Raim, from the singing of the Freedom Singers.

By Roberta Slavitt. Copyright © 1965, 1989 by Stormking Music Inc.
All rights reserved.

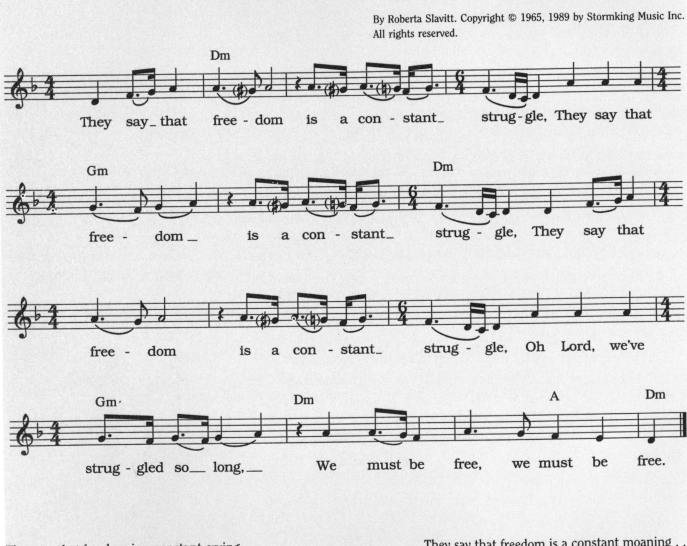

They say that free-dom is a con-stant_ strug-gle, They say that
free-dom _ is a con-stant_ strug-gle, They say that
free-dom is a con-stant_ strug-gle, Oh Lord, we've
strug-gled so_ long,_ We must be free, we must be free.

They say that freedom is a constant crying . . .
Oh Lord, we've cried so long . . .

They say that freedom is a constant sorrow . . .
Oh Lord, we've sorrowed so long . . .

They say that freedom is a constant moaning . . .
Oh Lord, we've moaned so long . . .

They say that freedom is a constant dying . . .
Oh Lord, we've died so long . . .

Mississippi was being used as a sounding board for rallying the nation to the problems of the South. The nation was beginning to respond. Every time the nation would respond with a civil rights law or a court ruling, the state would increase its violence against blacks. And nothing was coming back to help. The black people who lived in the state, the people we were trying to organize, wanted help from the North.

Then they murdered Lewis Allen—the man who witnessed the murder of Herbert Lee two and a half years earlier and testified against the murderer. I felt like we had gone full circle. When Herbert Lee was murdered, there was nothing for us to do but just dig in. But now we had come back to the same point, and we didn't have to take it. That's when I spoke out for the Summer project—something to bring national focus on Mississippi.

"The rest of the country has never felt much responsibility for what goes on in Mississippi," said Ella Baker. "These young people will make the rest of the country wake up!" The argument for inviting white volunteers finally won. Veteran Mississippi civil rights workers prepared for the volunteers.

Hollis Watkins: *By the time '64 came around, we'd mobilized maybe 750 people in the Greenwood area, people who would give homes and food and protection and support to that whole army of students coming from the North. With news that northerners were on their way, hysteria spread through the segregated white community. An invasion was coming—a foreign army of "bearded Yankee liberals and Communists!" Mayor Thompson of Jackson deployed a baby-blue tank to repel the invaders; the state passed five separate bills prohibiting "assembly for effecting political change." Governor Paul Johnson cried, "These kids aren't any good. Some of them are even idealists!"*

On June 20, as the first wave of volunteers drove toward Mississippi, Ella Baker voiced her hope: "Even if segregation is gone, we will still need to be free; we will still have to see that everyone has a job. Even if we all vote, if some people are still hungry, we will not be free. . . . Singing alone is not enough. We need schools. . . . We are fighting for the freedom of the human spirit, a freedom that encompasses all mankind."

The next night the opposition answered. Three civil rights workers, Michael Schwerner of CORE, Andrew Goodman, a volunteer from New York, and James Chaney, a Mississippi high-school student working full-time for the movement, disappeared on a road just a mile outside of Philadelphia, Mississippi. The police claimed that the three had been arrested for speeding, had paid their bail, and then were released in the middle of the night. Movement people knew they could not have voluntarily left jail at night. That was a cardinal rule: stay in jail till morning. Their co-workers knew that they were probably dead.

The episode might have passed as another unexplained lynching, but for the press attention focused on the Mississippi Freedom Summer, and the alert communica-

© 1980 Charles Moore / Black Star

tions network of COFO. Within a day, everyone in the country knew about the disappearance. The county and state police, the FBI, and the Justice Department all joined in the search for the three missing men.

Even experienced organizers found the first half of that summer the most terrifying that they ever lived through.

Matt Jones: *We all learned to drive in a very special way. We tried to teach everyone certain rules. At night never let a car pass you. You know why—when they are alongside of you, they might pull a shotgun. Go across a cornfield, anything.*

Don't travel at night is another rule. If you do travel, be prepared to circle around and get out of there. When you're in jail, and they come to you at eleven and they say, "You can go now, you're released," don't believe them. Stay put till the next morning, when somebody can come and get you. But, a lot of the kids from the North didn't listen—that's how those tragedies happened. They thought they knew. Believe me, we who came from down there, we knew the South.

Willie Peacock: *I remember talking to Schwerner again and again, warning him, "These are bad people. They'll hurt you." But he seemed to want to prove us wrong, to show that there was goodness in people. . . . People from the North just didn't understand what pure evil can be.*

Two days later, the blue Ford the three had been driving turned up on a county road, ten miles outside of Philadelphia, Mississippi. It had been doused with naphtha and set afire. All that remained was a burned-out wreck. There was no sign of the three missing men.

Bob Zellner: *We were in Oxford, Ohio, for the orientation session, training volunteers, when we heard about the missing boys. Someone had to go down with Rita [Schwerner] to look for her husband. We were convinced that they were dead from the beginning and that the Kluxers were anxious to kill more.*

We went into Neshoba County to ask the black people if they had any information that would help us. We knew that they wouldn't give information to anyone except someone from CORE or SNCC. If they told the police or the FBI it was just like telling the Klan.

One night we followed a tip and went to the burned-out church which the boys had been investigating right before they disappeared. When we got there I realized something was wrong. It was just starting to pale into daylight. When we pulled into the yard of the church, we were suddenly struck in the eye with this blinding light. The whole place was surrounded by pickup trucks. We were pinned there, in a tiny

Corvair car—me and Rita Schwerner and this white lawyer from the North.

I didn't even stop. I just turned around and slowly started to drive away. They fell into line behind me. I really turned on the gas then. We were speeding along this dirt road. After about two or three miles it was getting light enough to see. They had pulled this flatbed truck across the road so that our way out was completely blocked— we had driven into a trap. We were about to be ambushed.

Well, on the side of the road were these piney woods with tall trees and some underbrush. They figured we couldn't get through it, but I had a feeling that we had an outside chance. The pickup trucks were coming up to us, and the lawyer was shouting that we should get out and talk to them. I said oh no—they didn't go to all this trouble to have a discussion!

So I just kept the car going as fast as I could, and we jumped the ditch, and plowed through the underbrush and drove into the tall woods. I had to keep moving fast so I didn't get bogged down—they would have killed us for sure. I had to keep dodging between the trees. Your mind is working much faster—you do everything by reflex. So you zip through one opening, and you're watching for your next opening between the trees, and you're calculating your third one. Like a video game. We ripped that whole car apart on both sides, that's how tight it was, and squirted out on the road on the other side of the truck.

All the pickup trucks were stuck on the other side of the flatbed, and they were too big and heavy to go zipping through the woods after me. Then I saw they were starting to move the flatbed out of the way, so I kept going as fast as I could. I drove into Philadelphia and went straight to the motel where the FBI was staying. I rushed in and pounded on the door. It turned out to be the room of Claude Sitton and Carl Flemming, a couple of reporters I knew from the Freedom March. Flemming said, "Zellner, what are you doing here? Are you trying to get us killed?!" Then they saw Rita, and said, "Oh my God!"

I told him I was looking for the FBI. Carl said, "Zellner, the FBI is down there!" and he pointed to another room. Then Sitton yelled out, "Carl, where's your manners, boy? Bring those people in here and give them a drink of whiskey."

By now, the Klan was all around the building, leaning against their pickup trucks and smoking cigarettes. Gun racks on their cars. There wasn't a tag, there wasn't a license plate to be seen. So we all walked down to the FBI room together. The Bureau boys opened up, looked at me, looked out at the cars, and hollered, "What's the matter, Zellner, you trying to get us killed!"

We said, "We will not leave this county till we have a look at the burned-out car!" Well, the FBI looked at us, and looked at the mob, and said, "No, we can't do that— only the sheriff can."

Of course, we knew the sheriff was in the Klan, together with his deputies and those guys out there in their pickups and the guys who had killed the civil rights

workers. But we figured we'd make all the stink we could. So they called the sheriff down and we chewed him out right there in front of the press and his deputies and the FBI. We hollered at him for his feeble investigation. He was sputtering! So he said, "Yeah, I'll take you to the car. You can have five minutes, and then I'm taking you to the county line, and then God rest your souls—"

We figured we probably would be all right. Maybe we'd be battered to hell, but they probably wouldn't kill us. Too many people had seen us together; they'd never get away with killing us—that time.

On August 4, after paying $25,000 to an informer, the FBI found the bodies of the three missing civil rights workers buried under a newly constructed dam on a farm near Philadelphia, Mississippi. Goodman and Schwerner had been shot in the chest. James Chaney, the black man, had been savagely beaten and chain whipped before being shot three times. Eighteen men were arrested, among them the Neshoba County sheriff and deputy sheriff. The Ku Klux Klan Imperial Wizard, who reportedly had masterminded the murders, declared that "this was the first time Christians had planned and carried out the execution of Jews"—Schwerner and Goodman were Jewish.

Remarkably, despite the Klan's violence, it turned out to be a summer of joy for many people.

Sammorah Muhammad: *I remember, we decided the community would feed all these kids coming down south. So we got our baskets and our brown bags and went door to door asking if people had a can of soup or beans or corn or rice or whatever you have to donate to help us feed the kids who have come down to help us. Then we'd go and have a feast. We had it between my mother's house and Miss Viola's house; we'd cook the meat and feed them—a community feast.*

Out of the fear and the violence, out of a thousand arrests, thirty-five bombings and thirty church burnings by white extremists, out of the deaths of six freedom workers, but most of all, out of the growing confidence of the long-repressed black Mississippians, came a summer of extraordinary achievements—forty-seven Freedom Schools, models for the Vista and Head Start programs of the next decade. Hundreds of new local community leaders and the first generation of Mississippi children ever to go to school in an atmosphere that gave dignity to everyone regardless of color. The registration in the Freedom Democratic party grew to sixty thousand. Hazel Palmer, co-chairperson of the Hinds County Freedom Democratic party, said, "We want the world to know that we can do things for ourselves in Mississippi. . . . Scare us and scatter us was their way. . . . But now they've done all they can do, and we will not be scattered. They'll have to kill more than one at a time."

But there was another price, often forgotten—the bitterness of the civil rights workers who had been organizing in Mississippi since 1961.

Hollis Watkins: *There were a lot of gains from that summer, but there was a lot of pain and a lot of loss also—I don't know if it had to be that way. The community was close, pulling together, directing itself, and along came this organized "army" with its own goals and its own program. And for three months they took over— people started depending on them. They were educated and spoke well, so people listened to them and respected them, and then—in three months, they were gone, and the community was scattered. In '65, it was just the original group of us again, and we had to pick up the pieces.*

Willie Peacock: *We went through a phase of real regret. Until summer of '64 we were in charge of our part of the movement. We understood it. In '64 it was cut from under us, and we were left hanging with nothing to do. The people came down here, to our state, to our movement, to our people, and they wouldn't listen to us. They were from the Ivy League; they knew more than us bumpkins. That was painful.*

But in the end, the established segregationist attitudes began to break apart. One Saturday night, a local man, an avowed segregationist, dropped by the Ruleville community center to talk to movement people, to find out what they were up to. The police came by, and seeing him there, told him to leave before there was trouble. "No trouble here," he told them. "You don't understand," they said. "You leave or you'll go to jail." He stayed, and he was arrested, and he came again.

Mississippi segregation would thrash and lash out for years with diminishing strength. But the stake had been driven into the beast's heart. It was dying.

Bob Moses: *The other civil rights organizations wanted to surround Mississippi and then move in to desegregate. As it turned out, that strategy would have been disastrous. Because during the next couple of years, with the continued assassinations—Malcolm and King and Kennedy—the whole political leadership was wiped out and the movement collapsed and the country shifted to the right and this new wave of racism started coming out. But, luckily, there was no place in the whole country where the state itself could propagate segregation. If Mississippi's segregationist state apparatus had been left intact, saved for last, there would have been no last. It would be like having South Africa right in the middle of our country.*

Edwin King: *If it hadn't been for nonviolence, if we had fought them as they fought us, the hate would have never died. Mississippi would have been Northern Ireland.*

COFO office, Biloxi, Mississippi, 1964. Thorsten Horton / courtesy Highlander Center

Woke Up This Morning

Reverend Osby, of Aurora, Illinois, made up this revamp of an old gospel song ("I woke up this morning with my mind stayed on Jesus") in the Hinds County jail during the freedom rides. It later spread to Albany and all the surrounding communities. In Mississippi it went from the jails to McComb, where one of the earliest voter campaigns began; 120 students had marched out of Burgland High School in protest over the murder of Herbert Lee, a voter-registration worker, and the expulsion of their classmate Brenda Travis, who had participated in a sit-in at the local bus station. Early that Wednesday morning, October 4, 1961, I had arrived at the Negro Masonic lodge in McComb for a SNCC staff meeting. To my inquiry, "How are you this morning?" Charles Sherrod, Bernard LaFayette, Chuck McDew, and the other SNCC people answered in chorus, "We woke up this morning with our minds stayed on freedom!"

—*Bob Zellner*

It takes two or more people to sing this song right. For convenience we've put it in a high enough key so tenors (or altos) can lead, and everyone else can come in on the wonderful answering phrase. The interlude is sung only occasionally, not after every verse. When you get to know the song well, you'll be adding still more parts.

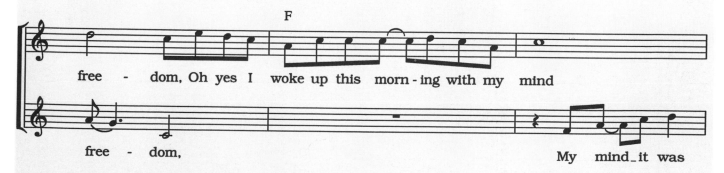

walk   with your mind   on   free - dom, Got to   talk   talk,_ you got to

talk   talk,_ you got to   talk   with your mind   on   free - dom,

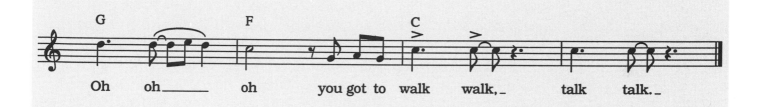

Oh   oh_____   oh   you got to walk   walk,_   talk   talk._

Ain't no harm in keep'n' your mind—
—In keeping it stayed on freedom.
Ain't no harm in keep'n' your mind—
—In keeping it stayed on freedom.
Ain't no harm in keep'n' your mind—
—In keeping it stayed on freedom,
Hallelu, hallelu, hallelujah.

Walking and talking with my mind—
—My mind it was stayed on freedom . . .

Singing and praying with my mind—
—My mind it was stayed on freedom . . .

When the song gets going well, innumerable "frivolous" verses can be added:

Doing the twist with my mind—
—My mind it was stayed on freedom . . .

Whatever verses you choose, you should end with:

Ain't no harm in keep'n' your mind—
—In keeping it stayed on freedom . . .

Woke up this morning with my mind—
—My mind it was stayed on freedom . . .

Profile: SAM BLOCK, WILLIE PEACOCK, AND HOLLIS WATKINS

Willie Peacock, a solid-looking man in his forties sits alongside a desk in the office of a realty company in Jackson, Mississippi. Hollis Watkins, slighter and shorter, sits behind the desk, deep in thought. Both speak slowly, quietly. The remarks of Sam Block come from an interview by Joe Sinsheimer in *Southern Exposure*, Summer 1987.

Block: *It's very interesting how I got into the movement. My mother worked for a federal district judge. She cooked, she did everything for their family. I used to mow his lawn. One Saturday it rained and I was unable to mow. But there was a basketball tournament that night, and I needed the money. So I walked the four–five miles to his house, and knocked on the front door. "Judge," I said, "I wanted to know"—He said, "Wait a second. First thing you know is you don't come to my front door for any goddamned thing. Now you get your snotty-assed black ass away from here and go around to the back door."*

My mother had always taught me that this man loved me. But he really hurt me. I went around to the back and asked him if I could borrow the $2 I would have made mowing so I could go to the basketball tournament. . . . He said he would talk to me in a couple of hours.

I waited all morning across the street at a seed company warehouse, and called him from one of the company phones. The judge couldn't speak to me then, but he promised to call me back. When he called back, the phone got picked up by someone in the office, a white man. Not knowing I was on the phone, the two men talked.

The judge said, "I was calling for this snotty-nosed black nigger boy. His goddamn old mammy has been working for me all her goddamn life. And you know how niggers are. They want to know if you can give them something or they can borrow something". . . .

By that time tears had begun to come into my eyes. It hurt so much because my mother still believed this man loved us. I got behind the seed sacks and I cried like a baby. . . . That's when I started to make up my mind that if I ever got a chance to help people, especially black people, I would do it. I was about ten years old.

Peacock: *I grew up in Tallahatchie County. That's near where Emmett Till went to visit his grandparents and got killed for supposedly whistling at a white woman. Near where I lived was a town called Mount Bayou. Black leaders from around the state would come and meet there—mostly NAACP people. I remember their first campaign was a state-wide appeal—"Don't buy gas where you can't use the rest room." There was T. R. McGraw, who was a doctor in a black hospital in Mount Bayou. They always gave me hope that we could do something to make things better. When this thing happened to Till in '55 something stirred in me—how could one human being treat another human being like that? I vowed to work to eradicate that.*

Watkins: *I was in Los Angeles visiting with my sister and her husband. I was deciding whether to live out there or come back to Mississippi, and I started reading about the freedom rides. I got curious about what was going on. When I got home— I lived in southern Mississippi, near McComb—I heard that Martin Luther King was in the area. I went looking for him, but never found him. He had just left. But I met Bob Moses and then Marion Barry. Barry spoke to us about using direct action—sit-ins and such. So myself and Curtis Hayes, both of us eighteen years old, sat in at Woolworth's. First open act of defiance they'd seen since Reconstruction. They jailed us for thirty days for breaching the peace. Three days later, another group of young people tried to sit in at the bus station. Six of them this time. They jailed them for eight months! But one of them, Brenda Travis, was thrown out of the high school. When they heard about it, 80 percent of the students walked out. They accused us of "contributing to the delinquency of minors."*

Block: *My uncle and Amzie Moore owned the only two black service stations in that little town. . . . Amzie lived a block or so from our house. I respected him. He was one of the few people in the Delta who was willing to take a stand in the 50s when they murdered Emmett Till.*

In the Spring of '62 Amzie asked me to come over to his house to meet Reverend James Bevel of SCLC and Bob Moses of SNCC. They asked where I would like to work in that movement. I told them "Greenwood, Mississippi." Because that was in Leflore County where Emmett Till had been killed. So, Bob, Hollis Watkins, Curtis Hayes and myself packed into Amzie's old '49 Packard car and headed up to the Highlander School in Tennessee. We spent a week in discussions and non-violent training. . . . It seemed like the happiest part of my life. That's where I learned my first freedom songs. One that stuck with me the most was one Bob taught us on the long ride back—Woody Guthrie's "This Land Is Your Land, This Land Is My Land."

When they dropped me off in Greenwood, Bob told me, "Sam, you know that you could be killed. . . . You really want to go into Greenwood?" There were tears coming out of my eyes, but I said Yes.

After our first meetings, I realized how much those songs I had learned, those freedom songs, could help pull us together. It was an organizational glue. I asked people to think about a song they might want to sing that night and then change that song. Think about freedom, interject your own feelings, your own words. . . . Out of that came freedom songs we'd be singing all across Mississippi.

Watkins: *If you are black and from the South, especially Mississippi, there is a special spiritual element that is part of you. When you organize here, you are working and organizing among religious and spiritual people. Willie and I understood that—we're from Mississippi. Singing and music is an integral part of all that. You sing to throw off weight, your burden. When you are weighted down and your spirit is low, your mental capacity is also low. But when you sing, and you let go of that weight, you rise up, you feel good about the decisions you've made or the ones you are about to make. You feel good about the jobs you are going to do, and you feel good to be part of the group that's going to do them.*

Peacock: *When you sing, you can reach deep into yourself and communicate some of what you've got to other people, and you get them to reach inside of themselves. You release your soul force, and they release theirs, until you can all feel like you are part of one great soul. Sometimes when Hollis and I were leading a song, we could feel it. We were together with the people, and they would not let us go, you knew you could not cut the singing short until it reached a conclusion. The singing could go on for hours.*

When you have that kind of unity and that kind of communication, there is nothing the police can do to stop you. They can put you in jail, but you can sing in jail and organize the inmates and the other prisoners.

We always ended our meetings with We Shall Overcome. *That's a song around the world wherever there is struggle, but it started here in the United States. It is a song says whatever we have been through and whatever we have to go through, and whatever conflicts we've had in the heat of the day, now we are refocusing and rededicating ourselves to our main object. . . .*

Watkins: *That song was like the end result of all of the hard fighting. We are going to overcome, no matter what, no matter how; no matter how hard or how difficult or how long, we SHALL overcome! We sang it with our arms crossed with the right over the left, showing that the right will finally be victorious, and by holding each other's hand, the common bond pulled together all of the people.*

Block: *Then one night we got a call. It was Bob Moses. "Get to Leflore County Hospital immediately. Jimmy [Travis] has been shot. Somebody passed us with a submachine gun and sprayed bullets into the car. We don't know whether he is going to live or die." By the time Willie and I got to the hospital, Jimmy was lying on the table and I understand they refused to treat him. . . . We took him to Jackson where he was operated on. He was shot in the neck—paralyzed, stayed in the hospital for months, but he eventually recovered.*

Watkins: *You never knew when something would suddenly happen. One day I was in the office sitting in a chair and some white men burst in the door, holding a noose—"Get ready, nigger, we're going to hang you tonight." Or one day we went to use the rest rooms in a service station, and the attendant came swinging a rifle at us because we used a white man's toilet. Sometimes you'd do things that would amaze you, later, anyhow—like the time we visited someone's shack to talk to them about registering, and the plantation owner came after us with a shotgun, and chased us, shooting and barely missing, and then, the next week, we were right back at the same person's house; or the time they were tailing us in an unmarked car that we knew was Klan and probably full of guns, so we decided to tail them in our own marked and unarmed car. We weren't being brave, we were trying to stay alive.*

Peacock: *In one day we'd drive out to help some organizers in Clarksdale, then go over to Sunflower County and go over to Ruleville, where Mrs. Hamer lived, and take some people down to vote, then we'd go on to Greenwood to get ready for a mass meeting at night. There were no more than twelve of us working the whole state, but if you asked Governor Barnett how many there were, he would have said there was an army! We were so busy, some days we didn't even eat!*

Everything I've heard about soldiers in combat describes us—the never-ending tension, the exhaustion, the constant danger. We were guerrillas. The difference was we weren't going in to fight and win, we were teaching people who were already there how they could win. You don't liberate people—you teach them how to liberate themselves.

The rare times we would get a few hours to get away from everything, we'd just go crazy.

Watkins: *Somebody, just a local person, would pull down the shades, put up a pot of food, and we'd sing and talk and joke till maybe two in the morning.*

Peacock: *Probably saved us from burn-out.*

Watkins: *Course, by 7 A.M. the next day, we'd be back at work.*

Peacock: *My greatest relaxing was fishing. I'd go in the woods near my grand-mother's place near Greenwood. Sometimes I'd just sit in the woods and think.*

Watkins: *My relaxation was my family. Just spend the day with family and friends, just be loose, or maybe spend all day singing with the choir, let those songs lift me, lighten me.*

Peacock: *One time when Bob Moses took us up to New York to show us off to all the Friends of SNCC, we did go a little crazy!*

Watkins: *We were hicks, and Moses tried to introduce us to New York culture, and we didn't really know what to do!*

Peacock: *But that trip might have saved our sanity. A lot of our friends were beginning to burn out. We didn't realize it, but we were on the verge of burning out ourselves. It was so easy to not take the time off, to work day after day after day, because there was so much to do, and so many loose ends you had to be there for, and so few of us to pick up the pieces.*

We trained people to fill in, to take over for us, training and training, especially young people. But the more people you trained, the more you wanted to do and the bigger your job got.

Block: *In the end, I think that many of the problems we had were within ourselves. Being under all that pressure in a hostile environment gets to you. Twenty-four hours a day, seven days a week. You should work for three months and then go into retreat for two–three weeks, and then come back. You can't expect the same person to go on and on without getting battle fatigued. There was no organizational glue that we could use to sustain ourselves. There was nothing, and when there is nothing, a lot of people get hurt. It takes its toll. It destroys you. I am still paying the price.*

The movement continues.

Watkins: *I've stayed South for the last twenty-five years, still fighting it out. That which we thought we would overcome still has not been overcome. There is still a fight. To register people, to educate people, to change not only national politics but local politics—school boards and county officials and town officials. Those are the people who can really change things.*

Peacock: *Today, with all the politics and the voter registration going on, it is like the days of the movement. It is not on the same level of intensity, but it's got a lot of the ingredients. While we're sitting here, communities are getting organized, schools are getting reorganized, people are registering and voting; people all around the state are fighting to get rid of the good-old-boy politics of Mississippi. A lot of old firebrands like Hollis are out there changing the state.*

There is a lot to be done down here. You can't do it without money. People come in and do interviews and books and films about Mississippi. It would be good if they put something back into the state so we could continue our work.

Watkins: *This is the first place people come for information, and the last place they think of to give anything to. It would be great to have an information and money network, a freedom network, to inform and to fund community projects through the Deep South, beginning right here in Mississippi.*

Block: *I often think about going back to Mississippi and working, because I think the problems are still just as alive now as they were in the sixties. In the last five years we have lost much more than we have gained. A lot of black leaders have been picked off and thrown into prison for one reason or another, all across the country. Black politicians, black organizers, men and women, civil rights activists of all races. People have sort of gone underground. But I think there is going to be a volcanic eruption sometime in the near future. People are just going to put themselves out there and you will find them at the Rainbow Coalition. . . . because it is already there and people identify with it. But people themselves will explode and take leadership. They are tired of being underground, of being ignored and taken for granted.*

Interlude
July 4, 1964, Klan Rally

*I*n July 1964, George Wallace went to Atlanta to stand with other southern leaders and pledge his undying support of segregation. SNCC sent a delegation to protest.

Matt Jones: *Jim Forman thought it was important that a group of us go to make our presence felt. So thirteen of us got together and went down to the stadium there. Only, when we get inside we realize something is wrong—everyone gets really quiet. Up on the stage is George Wallace and Ross Barnett from Mississippi. As we walk in, I notice people closing in behind us. Suddenly I noticed that we'd gotten cut off from most of our group. Most of the thirteen were still outside. Now it was just me, one other black guy, and a white girl, Carol Ableman. This was not any political rally—this was a meeting of the Grand Wizards of the Ku Klux Klan.*

This woman took a glass with Coke and ice in it and threw it down on us, and then this man stood up on a chair and did this Tarzan yell. And suddenly they came running down towards us—there must have been ten thousand of them, holding up these metal chairs and swinging them at us. And then this lady who threw the Coke started this chant, "Kill the nigger! Kill the nigger!" and they all started chanting. This policeman nearby saw what was happening and turned away. This Japanese photographer was standing nearby, and started taking pictures of me and the crowd, and before he knew it, they were hitting him with chairs too.

My friend Chuck [Charles Neblett, one of the Freedom Singers] was trying to climb out, over this wire fence, but the crowd was on him too—hitting him with chairs. By now I was flat on the ground, covering my head, trying to protect myself, and this old man lay down next to me. At first I thought he was trying to be friendly, trying to help, but he just got down there so he could hit me. Eighty years old and he kept punching at me. Some lady was hitting at me, and I said, "If you get me out of this, I swear I'll never come back." I thought I was going to die. No doubt about it.

KKK member.
UPI / Schulke Archives

Suddenly the policeman grabbed me, and backed me up to the fence, then stood between me and the crowd and somehow worked me around onto the other side of the fence. Then he put me into the police van. Carol was out there too. She seemed OK. It seems she had been lying there, and the crowd was getting ready to go after her when this Citizens Council man yelled out, "Don't touch her, she looks like my daughter." That's how she survived. Except she never forgave herself for getting away while we two got so badly beaten. To this day she has always faulted herself for what happened.

In the police van, my friend looked half dead, and I was spilling blood from my face and my head, and we kept saying to each other, "Don't worry. . . ." We didn't know what we were saying, we were in shock. Well, they didn't take us to jail—they took us to the hospital and dropped us at the emergency room.

The nurse shaves my head and says, "Oh, you've got a little cut there. . . ." I look in the mirror, and there is a huge gash on my skull. Through my fog I realize that if I stay there, some racist doctor is going to sew up my skull. Probably without any anesthetic. What am I going to do? Lie. I told the doctor, "I just had a fight with my wife and she hit me on the head with a frying pan." The doctor looked at me—he looked mean as any cracker I'd seen. "You can't fool me. I know why you're here." My heart sank. He was probably in the Klan himself. "By God, son, I am with you." I was amazed. You can't make assumptions. You never know what's inside of people. I saw the policeman being bandaged, and I said to him, "I don't know why you did it—but thank you for saving me."

Afterwards, Forman asked me to write a song about it. I couldn't do it. I was so mad at him—he wanted to use this incident for the movement. Man was all business. I was so mad, I wouldn't write a note about it.

For the first time, I was really scared. I kept thinking, I'm going to get a gun. I'm going to practice. I'm going to protect myself against these crackers. It wore off, though. I can't live like that.

IX

1963–1965
Selma, Alabama

*S*elma is the seat of Dallas County, Alabama. In 1963, when Bernard and Colia LaFayette began a SNCC registration drive in Selma, fifteen thousand black adults were working and raising families there, but only 153 could vote.

Bernard LaFayette: *They had told us that we might as well scratch Selma off the list because people there weren't ready for a movement. We didn't get any different impression when we went there. We couldn't find a place to live—people were afraid to put us up. In fact, the only organization we could find was something called the Twelve High Club. They called themselves that because there were twelve people in the group and by twelve they were all high. . . . But we worked on the assumption that no matter how bad a place is, some people have courage. Mrs. Amelia Boynton befriended us and let us use her office. We set up classes. We went into the country—people there are close to the earth, they are religious, warm and very friendly. Mostly, they're unafraid; they own most of their own property and stores so they're more independent. When the country people went down to register, the city folks realized that they were getting left behind. So they went to register. By September, two thousand people went to the courthouse, six hundred actually got registered.*

In October of that year, Sheriff Jim Clark tried to put a stop to this. As 250 people lined up to register at the courthouse, the sheriff, a troop of armed, helmeted deputies, and a group of photographers greeted them. "Does your employer know you are here?" Clark asked the registrants. "Would he like to get a picture of you with these Communists?" The registrants stayed in line. After an hour, the first person was allowed in to try to register.

Clark arrested every person in line who was carrying a sign. "No demonstrating," he said.

Another hour passed—the next person in line was permitted to enter. Anyone who left the line, to go to the bathroom, to drink from the water fountain, got a jab in the side or a smack on the head from a

billy club. They were not allowed to get back in line. More time passed—another person was permitted to enter the building.

James Forman of SNCC, the author James Baldwin, Charles Neblett, the Freedom Singer, and Amelia Boynton, one of Selma's few registered black voters, stepped over to Clark. "Can we bring some drinks and sandwiches to the people in line?" Clark dared them to try.

Two tried. Deputies surrounded them, threw them to the ground, and beat and stamped on them. Their arrest warrant read, "inciting to riot." By three-thirty the registrar had allowed another person into the courthouse.

Albert Turner had been trying to register for years. "I was a college graduate. I thought I had enough intelligence to pass at least a voter-registration test. . . . But they had tests! They had tests asking how many words in the Constitution! They had tests asking what side the moon was on! They had a book with about three–four hundred tests in it. They had it fixed, so if you were black, you could never pass."

Selma, like the rest of Dallas County and nearby Lowndes County, was Klan country, Citizens Council country. This was the birthplace of Bull Connor. Pure Wallace country.

Said Sheriff Jim Clark, "You are an agitator. You are the lowest form of life."

SNCC, the Dallas County Voters League, and local ministers kept up the registration drive through 1964. But Clark and his "posse" continued to fight, with arrests and beatings. By court order any meeting of more than three blacks could be broken up by the police. But the mood of the city was changing.

Bernard LaFayette: *I saw some great changes. Many people had gone to jail, people you never would have expected to stand up. Some of the kids I had worked with, whose parents and grandparents and teachers had argued with them and threatened and disciplined them, ran up to me to say, "My grandmother went to jail! Man, I can't believe it. My grandmother's in jail!" The principal of one high school, who once threatened to arrest me for coming on the school grounds and talking to the students about the movement, actually led a march of teachers asking for the right to vote.*

Selma's blatant disregard of African American voting rights became a national scandal. In January 1965, Hosea Williams, Martin Luther King, and members of SCLC joined the drive. Twice a month, on registration day, Williams, King, and groups of blacks would line up in front of voter-registration headquarters, only to be attacked and driven away by police. These attacks went unrecorded by local TV cameras. But on January 19, the national press was there. Amelia Boynton stood with several hundred black citizens waiting to register at the courthouse: "Clark had a big club in his hand and he yelled to me, 'Where you going? . . . You all got to line up in the alley!' Before I could gather my wits, he jumped behind me, grabbed me by my coat, propelled me around, and started shoving me down the street. I was stunned. I

Do What the Spirit Say Do

This transcription is by Ethel Raim, from the singing of the young people in Selma.

Do what the spir - it says do, __ We're gon - na

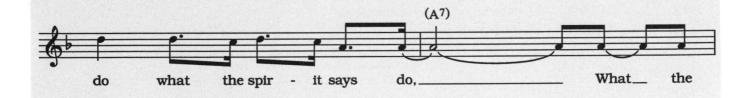

do what the spir - it says do, _____ What __ the

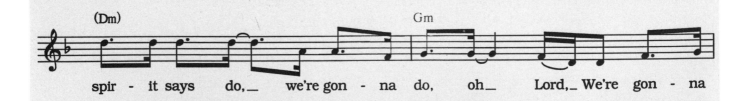

spir - it says do, _ we're gon - na do, oh _ Lord, _ We're gon - na

do what the spir - it says do. _

You gotta do what the spirit say do,
You gotta do what the spirit say do,
And what the spirit say do, I'm gonna do, oh Lord,
You gotta do what the spirit say do.

You gotta march when the spirit say march,
You gotta march when the spirit say march,
And when the spirit say march, you better march, oh Lord,
You gotta march when the spirit say march.

You gotta sing . . .

You gotta moan . . .

You gotta picket . . .

You gotta vote . . .

You gotta move . . .

You gotta pray . . .

You gotta preach . . .

You gotta shout . . .

You gotta rock . . .

You gotta cool it . . .

You gotta love . . .

You gotta die . . .

Governor George Wallace,
Alabama state house.
© 1963 Flip Schulke

saw newspapermen and cameramen all around me, and I said, 'I hope the newspapers see this! Damn it, I hope they do!' "

The nation saw, and the respected black teachers from Selma saw and risked their jobs by publicly marching to the courthouse and joining the movement. After that, everybody marched. "The beauticians got a group and they marched; the undertakers got a group, they marched. Selma had the marchingist movement since Birming- ham!" said one citizen.

When King got arrested, five hundred children marched. They went to jail! The next day three hundred more youngsters marched. The police chased them for six miles with cattle prods and clubs. TV cameras followed the brutality, and millions of Americans watched it on the evening news.

One fourteen-year-old said, "We was singing 'I love everybody,' and one of them stuck me with a cattle prod and said, 'You don't love everybody,' and I said, 'Yes, I do.' "

Malcolm X came to show support: "If white people realize what the alternative is, perhaps they would be more willing to listen to Dr. King." It was to be one of his final speeches.

On February 18, in the nearby city of Marion, Alabama, the violence exploded. Willie Bolden, who had been a street hustler in Savannah, Georgia, before joining SCLC, later recalled the night.

Willie Bolden: *After the speeches we decided to have a short march to the court- house to protest the arrest of our co-worker, James Orange. We filed out, and turned toward the courthouse. The cameras were shooting. All of a sudden we heard cameras being broken and newsmen being hit. I saw people running out of the church. . . . The troopers were in there beating folks while local police were outside beating any- one who came out the door.*

A big white fella came up to me and stuck a double-barreled shotgun in my stom- ach. "Somebody wants to see you," he said, and he took me across the street to this guy with a badge and red suspenders and chewing tobacco. "See what you caused," he said, and he spun me around, "I want you to watch this."

There were people running over each other and trying to protect themselves. I began to cry. . . . One guy was running toward us. When he saw the cops he tried to make a U turn and he ran into a local cop. They just hit him in the head and it bust his head wide open. Blood spewed all over and he fell. When I tried to go to him, the sheriff pulled me back and stuck a .38 snubnose in my mouth. . . . I was scared to death! He said, "Take this nigger to jail." So they took me, and they hit me all over the arms and legs and thighs and chin. There were others there got beaten the same. . . . There were literally puddles of blood leading all the way up the stairs to the jail cell. . . .

Shortly after I was in there we heard the shots. That's when Jimmy Lee Jackson got killed. The cops were beating on his mama, and he was headed toward his mother and that's when they shot him.

With the lights shot out by the police, and news cameras broken, this massacre was never filmed.

The next night the Klan and state troopers poured into Marion and Selma looking for more excitement. Night marches had become downright deadly. But a couple of days later, James Bevel, one of SCLC's most important strategists had an idea, and on Sunday, February 28, he announced it to the congregation at Brown Chapel. "Esther, chapter 4, verse 8: '. . . charge her that she should go in unto the king, to make supplication unto him, and to make request before him for her people.' . . . There is a decree of destruction against black people in Alabama, but we cannot stand by any longer and see it implemented. . . . I must go to the king!" And when the congregation shouted approval, Bevel shouted it again and again: "We must go to Montgomery and see the king!"

Albert Turner: *We were going to get killed or we were going to get free.*

Martin Luther King and civil rights workers at burned-out church, Alabama. Courtesy Highlander Center

This May Be the Last Time

I first learned this song first from Woody Guthrie. It's an old one, sung widely in white churches as well as black. If you don't have a tenor or alto to lead this, try shifting keys.

—*Pete Seeger*

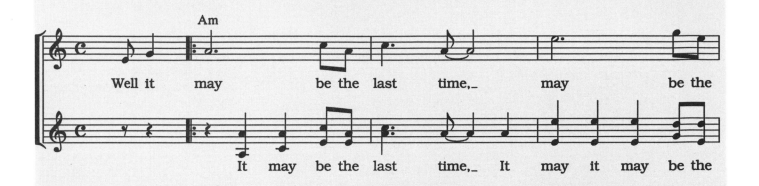

E   Am

may be   the last   time,   I don't   know_   This   may be   the last   time We

may be   the last   time,   I don't   know_____

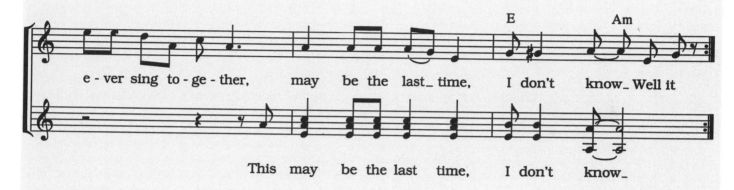

E   Am

e - ver sing to - ge - ther,   may   be the last_ time,   I don't   know_ Well it

This may   be the last   time,   I don't   know_

It may be the last time
We'll ever pray together . . .

It may be the last time
We can walk together . . .

It may be the last time
We can dance together . . .

It may be the last time
We'll hold hands
    together . . .

On March 7, a Sunday, 525 began the fifty-mile march from Selma to Montgomery.

Rev. Henry Hampton: *Moving on a serpentine path from the low hills of the north, the Alabama River runs crooked beneath the Edmund Pettus bridge. . . . There is little beautiful in this river. "Alabama" is its white name, but to the Negroes of Selma and the Black Belt it is the "river of tears." Too many black bodies have stained its muddy water, too many fathers, brothers, distant relations. . . .*

It is here on this dry dusty 1920s bridge that the marchers came on Sunday, "Bloody Sunday." They came marching across, black and four abreast, pulled together by their fear. . . . It was here just past the bridge that they were stopped. . . .

They knew. They must have known, for to be black in Alabama leaves few secrets. They knew as they paused forty seconds and as the rasp "troopers advance" rang out. . . .

The women fell first. With the thud of billy clubs, they fell, legs askew. . . . The children began to run in circles and the troopers would stand in wait and club them as they passed. . . .

The men lay across the bodies of the women and screeching children. The troopers flailed at the living hulks beneath them. . . .

It was a quiet spring day. Sheriff James Clark lifted his head toward the wind, and methodically fired. The bright canister lofted gently over the heads of the streaming troopers and landed amidst the retreating demonstrators. With a hollow sound more canisters clanked on the soft asphalt, spouting clouds. . . .

And now, those who were unable to run, too dazed, too unconscious, to run. . . . were inched back to Selma. Back from the light of the distant goal of Montgomery, back into the world a hundred years ago, back into Selma, this black crowd was inched, pushed, shoved, beaten, horse-prodded, back across the bridge, down Broad Street, back to the church where it had begun.

Sheyann Webb, eight years old in 1965: *I saw those horsemen coming toward me and they had those awful masks on. They rode right through the cloud of teargas. Some of them had clubs, others had ropes, or whips, which they swung about them like they were driving cattle.*

This time the confrontation happened in full view of the TV news cameras. It was seen in living rooms across the country.

King sent hundreds of telegrams to ministers, to friends of the movement: "No American is without responsibility. . . . Join me in Selma for a . . . march to Montgomery on Tuesday morning March 9." With two days' notice, 1,500 people stood at Brown Chapel ready to march to Montgomery. Nuns and priests and rabbis and ministers and hundreds of others. But the state would not grant permission for the march. King asked them all to stay in town for a few days. They agreed.

The city panicked. Helped by segregationist government officials, rumors swept

the state that "Communists masquerading as ministers," were invading Alabama.

Orloff Miller, Unitarian Universalist minister: *Most of us went to Selma without even a toothbrush because we thought it was a one-day event. . . . But when Dr. King asked us to stay, many of us agreed. . . .*

That night Jim Reeb [a Unitarian minister from Boston], *Clark Olsen* [a Unitarian minister from Berkeley], *and myself went to Walker's Cafe for dinner. A lot of our colleagues were there. . . . After dinner we started across the street. There was a group of four or five white men. They yelled, "Hey, you niggers!" We did not look at them, but we quickened our pace. . . . They ran to our side of the street, right behind us. Suddenly one of them swing a club. It caught Jim Reeb full on the side of the head. . . . We took Jim by ambulance to University Hospital at Birmingham, sixty-five miles away.* [Reeb died a day later from a fractured skull.]

. . . It's a terrible thing to say, but for some reason it took the death of a white clergyman to turn things around. Tuesday was the "turnaround day" not only for the March but also of how America saw the civil rights struggle . . . When Jim Reeb was killed, people came from all over the country. Selma became a flood of demonstra-

Ad from Albany, New York, paper, March 1965.

tors. People went to Washington and Johnson said, "Where have you been all these years?" Where had we been?

Thousands came to Selma, neighborhoods sent entire delegations.

Jimmy Collier, SCLC: *We were watching this film on television, Judgment at Nuremberg. It's a powerful film and it ends with the question, "Will there be another war?" Right after that they bring on this newsreel showing the people in Selma being beaten down by the possemen. . . . I had to go to Selma and do something. I didn't know what.*

Sheyann Webb: *Our house was full of people. They'd sleep in sleeping bags on the living room floor, anywhere there was space. . . . There'd be so many people out at the church singing freedom songs. They'd go on all night. I'd fall asleep listening to them.*

Oh Wallace

In 1964, shortly before the Selma–Montgomery march, James Orange was driving a van along Highway 90 from New Iberia to Atlanta. Others in the van were asleep. He heard a rock tune on the car radio, and before the end of the trip had made up these new verses. The response ("dat da da da dat") is of course done by the chorus, after every verse line of the soloist.

Copyright © 1968 by James Orange.

Chorus — Am

Oh Wal-lace, you ne-ver can jail us all,

Oh Wal-lace, you know se-gre-ga-tion's bound to fall,

da dat— da da da dat   da da da da da da dat   da dat— da da da

Verse

dat.   I said   I read   in   the   pa - pers   (dat —   da   da   da

dat)   just the o - ther   day   (da dat— da da da dat)   That the free - dom

fight - ers   (dat— da da da dat)   Are   on their   way.—   (da dat— da da da

dat) They're com - ing by   bus   (da dat— da da da dat)   and   air - plane

too.   (da dat— da da da dat)   They'll   e - ven   walk   (da dat— da da da

dat)   If you ask   them   to.   (da dat— da da da dat)   Oh——

Don't you worry about
Going to jail,
'Cause Martin Luther King
Will go your bail.
He'll get you out
Right on time,
Put you back
On the picket line.

I don't want no mess,
I don't want no jive,
And I want my freedom
In sixty-five.
Listen Jim Clark,
You can hear this plea,
You can lock us in the house,
You can throw away the key.

Now I'm no preacher
But I can tell,
You've got to straighten up
Or you're bound for hell.
You can tell Wilson Baker
And Al Lingo
That the people in Selma
Won't take no mo'.

Well this is the message
I want you to hear,
You know I want my freedom
And I want it this year.
So you can tell Jim Clark
And all those state guys too
I'm gonna have my freedom
And there's nothing they can do.

You can push me around,
You can throw me away,
But I still want freedom
And I want it every day.
You can tell Jim Clark
And Al Lingo
It's time for them
To end Jim Crow.

Route Eighty
Is the way we'll come,
I know them boys will have
A lot of fun.
You might see black
And a few whites too,
They're looking for freedom
Like me and you.

I saw James Orange
Just the other day,
He was getting ready
To be on his way.
He had a white shirt on
And some blue jeans,
Just come on to Eighty
You'll see what we mean.

You know Jack and Jill
Went up the hill
And Jill came down
With the Civil Rights Bill.
Don't want no shuckin',
Don't want no jive,
Gonna get my freedom
In sixty-five.

At noon on Sunday, March 21, three thousand marchers again set out across the Pettus Bridge to walk the fifty miles to Montgomery.

Sheyann Webb: *I remember watching those people marching along. I would never forget the sight. And I said to Rachel (my friend), "It seems like we're marching to heaven today."*

And she says, "Ain't we?"

Fifty miles—five days, in heat, in cool, in rain.

Bruce Hartford, SLCC worker: *Only three hundred people were allowed to walk most of the way because of the injunction—the rule was we could have an unlimited number of marchers on the four-lane road leaving Selma, and the four-lane road leading into Montgomery. But on the two-lane road which ran most of the way we were limited to three hundred marchers.*

My job was to help set up the campsites for the marchers, and then to guard the campsite at night while the marchers slept. It was raining. You slept in mud up over your ankles, sloughing through it to get to the can. The food was terrible. By the time the food was driven from Selma to the campsite it was cold. People were exhausted all the time—people weren't used to marching ten, fifteen miles a day.

Despite the hardships, or maybe because of them, the marchers grew closer and closer to one another.

Question (along the march): "What is freedom?"

John Shuttels, sixteen years old: "Someday, everyone will be together, able to associate with each other, eat at the same places. . . . Negroes would have a chance to be sheriff, mayor, governor even."

Ten-year-old child: "Freedom means for your mother to get a better job."

Cliff Moton, thirteen years old: "I have to do it. . . . People should have done it before now. . . . Freedom is to be what you want. . . . When I grow up, I want to be a carpenter, and to vote, so my children won't have to be in this mess like we are now."

Selma–Montgomery march.
© Steve Schapiro / Black Star

Right! Right!

The songwriters and the young singers of Selma were creating one great song after another right before our eyes. One woman saw me trying to notate a melody and said, smiling, "Don't you know you can't write down a freedom song?" All I can do is repeat what my father once told me: "A folk song in a book is like a photograph of a bird in flight."

I saw a woman of sixty or so with a sign, tied across a small cheap suitcase, that read, "If you don't vote, don't squawk—register!"

—*Pete Seeger*

We were marching along and some old army guys were calling cadence: "Hup hip, to your left, to your left, right left." I started thinking it wasn't quite right. The word "right" is affirmative. We want to get to Montgomery, right? So I said, "Why don't we accent on the right foot?" And so "a-right, right," and then we could put together verses, and the answers from the group would be "right, right." And so I started singing.

—*Len Chandler,* singer / songwriter / organizer

Pick 'em up and lay 'em down, (Right! Right!) Pick 'em

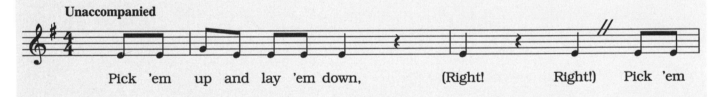

up and lay 'em down, (Right! Right!) Pick em up and lay 'em down,—

(Right! Right!) All the way from Sel - ma town. (Right! Right!)

Oh the mud was deep,
 Right! Right!
The hills were steep.
 Right! Right!
Now we've made some level ground
 Right! Right!
Let Wallace hear the sound.
 Right! Right!

I've been walking so long
I've put blisters on the street.
Well I caught the Freedom fever
And it settled in my feet.

Did the rain come down,
Well I thought I would drown.
Then I thought of Sheriff Jim,
Something said you'd better swim.

There was a guy named Jim Letherer who had one leg. He went all the way. There was a picture of us in the *N.Y. Times* and it said something about the last leg of the march. Jim said, "Hey Len, make me a verse."

—*Len Chandler*

Jim Letherer's leg got left
But he's still in the fight.
Been walking day and night,
Jim's left leg is all right.

I been walking so long
My feet done turn to wheels.
I don't think no more of riding,
I disremember how it feels.
Is freedom all . . . .
 Right! Right!

Bruce Hartford: *The day we reached the outskirts of Montgomery, a thunder-shower hit. If you've never marched in a thundershower, let me tell you—people had ponchos, forget it. It was like swimming. There wasn't a dry spot on anybody.*

But now we hit the four-lane road and people could join. We started to sing and a complete change came over us. The sun came out. A shuttle started going, carrying in new marchers from Montgomery, letting them out and going back for more. The numbers kept growing and growing. Soon we had two thousand, three thousand, people.

On the right side of the road, all lined up, were these tourist motels. In the lobbies were the black maids, janitors, in their uniforms, and they were just looking. You could see, you could just know, what was going on in their minds—they wanted to come out and join the march, and they were afraid of losing their jobs. Wanted to join, afraid to come out. Suddenly, in one swoop, one rush, they just ran out and joined us. They were liberated. We were all liberated. To me that was the high point. I'll never forget that—it symbolized everything that was happening.

Price Cobbs, psychiatrist: *I was glad I had my dark glasses on, because for ten* miles tears were streaming down my cheeks. I wasn't prepared for the overwhelming feeling of love. I didn't realize that people of every color, every background, could really feel together. I was surrounded by Negro teen-agers from Montgomery, wonderful kids with a kind of pride and freedom I'd never seen before. They kept calling to the whites on the sidewalk, "Come on and join us. We want you too!" They really meant it.

Thursday morning, the marchers dug out of the mud at their final campsite, in the shadow of St. Jude's Church. They had reached the outskirts of Montgomery.

Theresa Fulton, from California: *The streets were lined with people. Many were crying silently. Everyone wanted to join, but didn't dare. We were singing and victory shouting as hard as we could, so loud that sometimes I lost breath. Sometimes we joined hands.*

I was excited. I felt I was floating. . . . The sky was clear gray. I looked back many times, but I could not see the end of the march, or its beginning for that matter. We reached the state house and waited for the end of the marchers to catch up. It took an hour and a half. . . . It did not occur to me that it was extraordinary to sing "Black and white together" in front of the Alabama state house. . . .

When I came home from the march, I scraped some of the thick clayey mud from my shoes and saved it. It was as if I wanted to keep some tangible proof to testify for me that the march had really happened and that I was really there.

That night volunteers drove the marchers back to Selma. Scattered and alone, they made easy targets for Klan revenge. Viola Liuzzo, an Italian American housewife, and Leroy Moton, the black teen-ager who had carried an American flag the length of the march, were heading back to Montgomery to pick up more marchers. On Route 80 they spotted a car without plates following them. As the car overtook them, a rifle barrel poked from its open window; the gun blast hit Mrs. Liuzzo in the face—her car rolled into a ditch.

Leroy lay on the seat with his eyes closed. He heard the Klansmen's car stop and their door open. He held his breath as they peered into the Oldsmobile: "They're dead."

Selma had cost another life, but as a result of these events, the Voting Rights Act was passed by Congress with an enormous margin. Nearly half a million black people now registered to vote. "Don't lose it," said one examiner to a woman registrant. "Don't worry," she said. "I'm too proud to lose it."

In the midst of the battle of Selma, one of the nation's most important African American leaders was shot down while addressing a Sunday gathering in New York City. Malcolm X had lived much of his life in the angry northern inner cities; he matured from a wild young man to become the major organizer in the Black Muslim movement and ultimately an internationally respected leader. Some were frightened by his fiery rhetoric, but when he died, this "master teacher," as he was called, was

Newly registered voter at courthouse. © 1964 Bob Fletcher

beginning to build his Organization of Afro-American Unity into an interracial coalition of all people who had been left out of the American dream.

"I'm not a politician, not even a student of politics. . . . I'm not a Democrat, I'm not a Republican, and I don't even consider myself an American. . . . I am one who doesn't believe in deluding myself. I'm not going to sit at your table and watch you eat, with nothing on my plate, and call myself a diner. . . . I'm not an American. I am one of the 22 million black people who are the victims of Americanism. . . . I see America through the eyes of the victim. I don't see any American dream; I see an American nightmare."

That summer, the northern cities exploded.

Four days after the Voting Rights Act became law in August 1965, a traffic incident in Los Angeles touched off a four-day urban riot far larger than anything that had happened in the South. There was no underlying social or political program, but a tremendous outpouring of anger. Terror of black revolution flamed up, although, despite all the burning and looting, it was police attempts to stop the riot that killed most of the people. For the next five years, riots would continue to explode across the country, and the attention of the press would shift away from the southern movement.

Profile: BRUCE HARTFORD

Bruce is sitting in a hotel room in New York City. He is in town as a member of the executive board of the National Writers Union. His home is in San Francisco. As he speaks, Bruce's voice quickens and lightens and takes on a swinging southern lilt, as if the twenty years have disappeared and he is back south again.

My mother was a union negotiator. She told me that once they wrapped up negotiations in a day because she was so pregnant with me that the management was afraid she'd give birth right at the bargaining table. So I was an activist even before I was born.

Bruce joined the movement while a college student in Los Angeles, where he worked with CORE. After graduating in 1965, he went south to work full-time with the SCLC. After a year in Alabama, he was sent by SCLC to Grenada, Mississippi.

Grenada is in the delta about thirty miles east of Greenwood. What you would call hard-core Mississippi. In that year I was there, we reached about three or four peaks of activity. It was a regular cycle the town went through. We would start a major campaign—school desegregation or something. We would start our daily marches. After a few weeks of demonstrating, we'd have three or four hundred people marching every day. They would bring in mobs of Citizens Council and Klan people from around the state—two or three thousand people. They'd attack us, and throw rocks

Burn, Baby, Burn

I made up this song while the riot in Watts was going on. I was searching for ways to try and express what I thought these fellows in Watts were trying to say by burning the town down.

—*Jimmy Collier*

Mid-dle of the___ sum-mer___ bit-ten by flies and fleas, Sit-ting in a crowd-ed a-part - ment,___ A-bout a hun-dred and ten___ de-grees___ I went out-side___ ___ The mid-dle of the night___ All I had___ a was a match in my hand___ But I___ I want-ed to fight___ So I said a

burn, __ ba - by burn, __   Burn, __ ba - by, burn __ __   No-where to be, __   No one to see __ (I said a) No - where to turn, __   Burn, __ ba - by,   burn. __

I called President Johnson on the phone,
The secretary said he wasn't there.
I tried to get in touch with Mr. Humphrey,
They couldn't find him anywhere.
I went into the courtroom, with my poor sad face,
Didn't have no money, didn't have no lawyer,
They wouldn't plead my case,
So I said, Burn, baby, burn . . .

I really wanted a decent job, I really needed some
    scratch
(I heard people talking about a dream, now, a dream
    that I couldn't catch),
I really wanted to be somebody and all I had was a
    match,
Couldn't get oil from Rockefeller's wells,
Couldn't get diamonds from the mine,
If I can't enjoy the American dream, won't be water
    but fire next time,
So I said, Burn, baby, burn . . .

Walkin' around on the west side now, lookin' mean
    and mad,
Deep down inside my heart, I'm feeling sorry and sad,
Got a knife and a razor blade, everybody that I know is
    tough,
But when I tried to burn my way out of the ghetto,
I burned my own self up,
When I said, Burn, baby, burn . . .

        Learn, baby, learn,
        Learn, baby, learn,
        You need a concern, you've got money to earn,
        You've got midnight oil to burn,
        Burn, baby, burn.

I really want a decent education, I really want a decent
    place to stay,
I really want some decent clothes, now,
I really want a decent family,
I really want a decent life like everybody else,
So I say, Learn, baby, learn . . .

and firecrackers at us. The press would hear about it. After a few days we'd march; they'd beat us up, but it would be on television. After a few more days the governor would send in state troopers to defend us. Finally the mob would leave and the TV cameras would leave. And we'd be back where we were, until we started a new initiative.

Some of those night marches were unbelievable. They had this central square. And we'd march around the square. I remember this one night. The white mob was around the entire square. But it was clustered most strongly on this one side of the square, where the real Klan leaders were. Since we were going around the square, we would routinely go past this one part of the mob. They became like a wedge sticking out from the mob, pushing into us.

We were singing. Somehow, I can't explain it, through the singing and the sense of our solidarity we made a kind of psychological barrier between us and the mob. Somehow we made such a wall of strength that they couldn't physically push through it to hit us with their sticks. It wasn't visual, but you could almost see our singing and our unity pushing them back. You could see it most clearly when we passed this wedge they made. You could see those Klan leaders trying to push into us. They got within a few feet of us, but they couldn't get closer. By our singing, we actually pressed them back from us, pressed them away from us. Eventually the only way they could get through was to bombard us with rocks.

When we started to retreat, and we stopped singing, it was like they had broken our bubble. They moved in on the back of the march and started to beat us up.

People think of nonviolence as this esoteric philosophical moral thing, without understanding the actual strengths of it. You can feel this psychological shield. It is very powerful. I don't think you can build this shield on a nationalistic or hate basis, and I think that when SNCC lost the idealism based on love, it lost the ability and the interest in creating that kind of glorious nonviolent shield.

Bruce stayed in Grenada for nine months, while the campaign there dragged on and on against almost militarily organized Klan and Citizens Council opposition.

The stress is what gets to you. Day in and day out. My friend was talking to a federal mediator on the street one day, when a car pulls up and sprays them with machine-gun bullets. They had to duck under a car to stay alive. Another day a pickup trucks pulls up to me while I'm walking along and the guy jumps out and starts kicking me. I curl up in a ball and he kicks and kicks and my glasses fall off. So his son jumps out of the truck and starts jumping up and down on the glasses— but I had the foresight to have glasses made of safety glass. The kid kept yelling, "Daddy, Daddy, they won't break!" Another time, two of us were walking along the street. This guy suddenly appeared with a shotgun. He stuck it right at our heads: "I'm gonna kill you motherfuckers!" "Go ahead, motherfucker," said my friend. He went away. But how many times can you take it? You never know when it's going to *happen. The tension, the terror, wears you down. It eats a hole in your stomach. You live on Gelusil.*

I wasn't into alcohol; I was afraid to try drugs in Mississippi—I'd get twenty-five years. And my love life was nothing great. But singing! Singing was the fun! The relaxation! I remember once we were driving through Lowndes County in a VFW microbus. I noticed in the rear mirror there was a truck coming up on us with the Confederate flags and the rifles in the back—these dudes looked bad. I don't know what the hell's gonna happen. We were scared. Suddenly, right in front of us, the sky turned black. It was only eleven in the morning. Then the sky turned green. Tornado sky. We're driving straight into this thing. Behind us, the truck is coming up closer, so we couldn't stop. Suddenly, wind started to shake us. We pulled up close to a Trailways bus, but the gusts kept threatening to turn us over. And the rain is howling. So we sang. We sang Wade in the Water. And we rocked that car for forty–fifty miles. Singing was my release. I can't sing a lick. I was voted twice the worst singer on the SCLC staff. But I loved it and I led songs. You don't need to be a good singer to sing, you just should love it.

It was a real movement of people. People feel good about it, about themselves; people give each other rides, give each other dinner. A real sense of community. It was expressed in the singing and the courage. It was expressed in the way people could rise out of themselves and, like someone said, become Gideons.

The exhilaration, the way we grew so close to one another, was a drug that was instant addiction. It was so compelling, so emotionally satisfying, so profound, that I will probably search for it for the rest of my life. It is like a transcendental love. The people who experience the kind of communities we had in Birmingham or Albany or Jackson or Montgomery or Selma or St. Augustine or Danville, or wherever the movement really took hold, will never get that out of their blood. I've searched ever since for something as potent. I tried to find it in the antiwar movement, and the student movement. I guess the only other time I really saw it was around Delano, California, in the early days of Cesar Chavez and the grape strikes.

It doesn't last long—there are too many pressures pulling it apart. But for a brief instant you have a flash of what a society of the future could be, of what mankind is capable of. A flower blossoming just for a moment. I don't even think we have words to describe it.

Interlude
Annie Devine and the Congressional Challenge

Annie Devine was one of the three representatives elected by the Freedom Democratic party in 1964. At the beginning of the congressional session in 1965, Victoria Gray, Fannie Lou Hamer, and Annie Devine entered a challenge for the three Democratic Mississippi seats. At the opening session they sat with Congress. Representatives walking through the tunnel from the House office building to the Capitol that day met an incredible sight. As Mary King, of SNCC described it, the tunnel was lined with poor rural Mississippians, standing about twenty feet apart. "With their work-worn overalls, faded dresses, and their posture bowed from physical work, they held themselves solemnly. They stood with such dignity and such presence, saying nothing, but looking each member of Congress straight in the eye as he or she passed."

That day 149 congressmen voted to challenge the seating of Mississippi's representatives and to recognize the three women.

For four months the challenge was debated in committee. For the first time in history, white Mississippi congressmen were subpoenaed and questioned by black Mississippi farmers. In the end the farmers lost. But the attention they brought helped pave the way for the Voting Rights Act of 1965.

Profile: ANNIE DEVINE

She sits in the living room of a small ranch-style house in the town where she has lived most of her life—Canton, Mississippi. She talks slowly, thoughtfully. One hand wears a woolen glove to help reduce the ache of arthritis.

The hurt we had back then was always with us. But people were conditioned to deal with the hurt. You see I have arthritis in this hand. I wear this glove for comfort and warmth to protect it. But I've had the ache so long, sometimes I forget about it and I don't wear my glove, and then, oh gracious, I get most miserable. That's how it was with us—you forget about the hurt sometimes, but it never goes away.

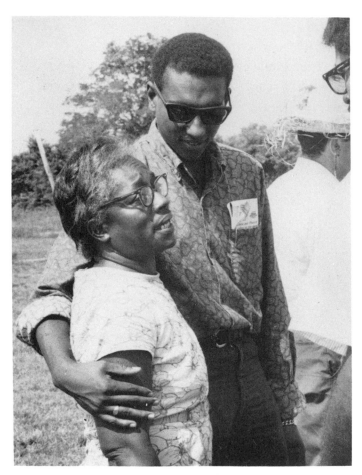

Annie Devine and Stokely Carmichael, Mississippi, 1966. © Charmian Reading

When I got involved I wasn't hurting as much as some people. But I always knew, from the time I was a little child, that something was seriously wrong. We were conditioned to hurt—we were used to it. But that didn't make it less.

Dave Dennis and some others came up from Louisiana to do voter education. It started such hatred. But it woke us up—just like Fannie Lou Hamer from Ruleville, a woman who thought she had it made because she was timekeeper on the plantation, a couple of steps higher than the people who just pulled the cotton sacks. But sometimes it just takes a word or a question: Are you free? And you realize how much you hurt. Then you try to stand up, and they beat you and they jail you like they did with Fannie Lou Hamer, and you decide, Well, I'm here. Whatever it takes I'm going to go through with it.

Fannie Lou was one of the strongest people I have ever known—a strong mind! But she was also humble and lovely too. She and Victoria Gray and myself lived in Washington for six months. I'll never forget her. She used to sing this song—"I've been 'buked and I've been scorned. . . . But we'll never turn back, no we'll never turn back, till we all are free."

I got up one morning and said to myself, "I've been here since I was two years old and I got to be afraid of these folks. I'm not scared of them anymore." I went in to register to vote. The registrar had a gun on the wall. I didn't even think. I just filled out the form and left and came home.

We had a meeting at a church here called Pleasant Green. Outside were about six police cars and they were taking pictures of everybody and getting the names of people who had jobs, which were very few of us, and people who had cars, which were very few of us. The policeman asked me where I lived. I was safe because it was the federal projects, where he had no control, and then he asked me where I worked. Again I was safe because I worked for a black insurance company—something he didn't even know existed.

The governor got on television and was talking all that stuff about how black folks were happy and this was all caused by outside agitators. By the time outside agitators reached Canton, we were already organized. We knew what was going on. When the volunteers started coming in '64, we were ready and we found places for them to stay. When the city of Canton realized that there were volunteers right here in the city, they went crazy.

Before I knew it I was involved in teaching people about citizenship and federal projects which could help them. What hatred that provoked! I had doors shut on me. We had food cut off, and clothing—we had to have it sent in. They threw people out of their homes. I remember a meeting up in Mount Beulah with seven hundred farmers who had been displaced off of their land. "I've lost my dwelling place," they'd say—not "my home," because that was the man's house, "Mr. Charlie's house" to say it the way it should be said. So we tried to go up and occupy the barracks.

Only once did I experience the violence that was within people. I was with Dr. King when he went from Canton to Philadelphia. We were marching toward the courthouse and these people came toward us on horses; they rode through the crowd. First they found the media people—anyone with a camera or anyone writing notes, whether they were FBI or they were newsmen. They lashed out and smacked the cameras and the papers from them. Then they rode through the crowd and scattered the people as they rode. You know what? I was looking at one of the men as they rode through the crowd. He fell off his horse and the folks were on him quick as a jack rabbit, beating him for life.

But the march kept going on. The heart was lost and the mind was lost and all you could do was look. There was no thought or feeling. The mind was just dulled. We did recover, and we got to the courthouse and King and Abernathy knelt in prayer. People were saying, "This is no time to pray." But they did, and we got out of there without getting killed.

In 1967 I got involved in CGM—the Head Start program in Mississippi. It helped mothers who could not keep their children in school and could not even feed their children. Since then the people have gotten homes, the children have grown up with respectable jobs, some have been very successful. That's more than happened in the fifty years before that. If there is any benefit for black people that came from the movement, that was the most outstanding one as far as I'm concerned.

We accomplished so much in the sixties—for a while, we thought we'd won the power over our own lives. Now it seems to have faded away. We're not the ones who are running this society anymore.

I miss the unity we had then. It was so easy to get us all together. You made yourself available. You wanted to be there. Today, maybe you'll get a few people together for fifteen minutes, but that's not how you change anything. Why did we let it die out? Why did we allow "we" and "us" to change into "me, me, me"? Now everyone has to race just to stay alive, just to keep a roof over their head. Something has gone very wrong.

I don't have what it takes in me to hit the street again. I don't have the know-how to stand up and make speeches. Even talking about it now, I don't know where to start. But others are doing it—others still have hope and energy. That's good. That's good. I pray that they keep their hope and their strength.

Alabama, 1965.
© *Flip Schulke / Black Star*

PART THREE

BEYOND
THE WALL

Many people grew bitter and impatient, not simply against the wall itself, but against the millions of Americans who, by their apathy, allowed it to stand. . . . [Thus, as the segregation wall crumbled, it revealed another prison of mistrust, fear, and hatred. But even that wall showed cracks.] What was remarkable was how many people had broken free and were determined to act out their freedom in every aspect of their lives; they were even free from the need to hate, which is one of the greatest freedoms of all.

VINCENT HARDING

Lowndes County,
Alabama, 1965.
© 1976 Flip
Schulke

X

1966
The Meredith March

*B*y mid-1966, the Voting Rights Act had been law for almost a year. Since the Selma march, the civil rights movement had slipped to the back pages of the newspapers, supplanted by an expanding undeclared war in Vietnam. But to those in the South, where little girls were chain-whipped for trying to attend integrated nursery schools, where ministers got killed for trying to register voters, segregation was still very much alive.

In June 1966, James Meredith, the first African American to gain admission to the University of Mississippi, set out on a "march against fear" across his home state, from the Tennessee border to Jackson. On the second day out he was shot and wounded by a sniper in a passing car.

Civil rights workers around the country vowed to continue his march to Jackson, Mississippi. Only two years before, when postman Moore had been killed, a dozen lone SNCC and CORE workers were willing to go on such a march. Now, with the civil rights movement "legitimized" by the press and public opinion, thousands of people were willing to take part.

But this march was different from the ones before it. You could sense it almost as soon as the march began. "I'm not for that nonviolence stuff anymore," said one young SNCC staff member. "If a white cracker touches me, I'll knock the hell out of him." "What we need on this march are more blacks, not more northern white phonies!" said another. At one point, Martin Luther King tried to unite the crowd with *We Shall Overcome* and some singers fell silent on the verse "Black and white together." Most startling, walking alongside the column of marchers was a small group from Louisiana carrying snubnosed machine guns—the Black Deacons.

King threatened to leave the march unless it was interracial and nonviolent. The other groups agreed. The next day 350 marchers set out to walk the two hundred miles to Jackson. To the whites lining the road it was the last chance to save their "southern way of life." They threw bottles and

The Movement's Moving On

Len Chandler made up this song when students at Hunter College arranged for a special commemoration of John Brown's raid on Harpers Ferry. He set his words to the music of *John Brown's Body*. That extraordinary tune has been used for dozens of songs, most notably *The Battle Hymn of the Republic* and *Solidarity Forever*.

Mine eyes have seen injustice in each city, town and state
Your jails are filled with black men and your courts are white with hate
And with every bid for freedom someone whispers to us, "Wait."
That's why we keep marching on.

CHORUS

Move on over or we'll move on over you
Move on over or we'll move on over you
Move on over or we'll move on over you
And the movement's moving on.

You conspire to keep us silent in the field and in the slum
You promise us the vote and sing us, "We Shall Overcome,"
But John Brown knew what freedom was and died to win us some
That's why we keep marching on.

Your dove of peace with bloody beak sinks talons in a child
You bend the olive branch to make a bow, then with a smile
You string it with the lynch rope you've been hiding all the while
That's why we keep marching on.

It is you who are subversive, you're the killers of the dream
In a savage world of bandits it is you who are extreme
You never take your earmuffs off nor listen when we scream
That's why we keep marching on.

I declare my independence from the fool and from the knave
I declare my independence from the coward and the slave
I declare that I will fight for right and fear no jail nor grave
That's why we keep marching on.

Many noble dreams are dreamed by small and voiceless men
Many noble deeds are done the righteous to defend
We're here today, John Brown, to say we'll triumph in the end
That's why we keep marching on.

screamed at the marchers. To King it was the last chance to hold together a movement that was threatening to fly apart into a dozen factions. To the marchers it was terrifying.

Bruce Hartford: *I had been south for almost a year. But I had never been to Mississippi. I was so frightened I didn't go to the bathroom for three days.*

Bill Pearlman, SNCC worker and Freedom Singer: *My job was to run up ahead and make arrangements for water and food for the marchers. It was brutally hot. I'd drive by myself to local farms. . . . It felt like being all alone in a strange and dangerous country.*

But the press was bored. "Mile after uneventful mile," said one observer, "they sat in their press truck looking out at the shacks where the essence of the march was made flesh in the lives of Negroes whose median income was 600 dollars a year . . . overlooking Negro cotton choppers heading for their $3 day in the sun."

As they headed south, tension grew. "Why are we marching, anyway?" asked Charles Evers, the brother of Medgar Evers. "I don't see how walking up and down a lot of highways helps. I'm for walking house to house, fence to fence, to register more Negro voters." The marchers agreed to register voters in their path. In Grenada five hundred blacks registered, and Bob Greene of SCLC stood by the town's statue of Jefferson Davis and said, "We want this joker, Jeff Davis, to know that the South he knew will never rise again!"

White resistance grew more blatant—bottle throwing, screaming, charging at the line of marchers. Police protection grew weaker and weaker. But in spite of everything, the marchers continued. Their number grew to four hundred, five hundred, six hundred. At night, King went to the local churches to preach—hundreds, sometimes thousands, of local blacks would come to listen and to sing.

Cleveland Sellers, SNCC worker: *By being there and showing that he really cared [King] helped destroy fear that was hundreds of years in the making. . . . The people trusted him. . . . He made it possible for them to believe they would overcome.*

In Greenwood, Mississippi, where Sam Block, Willie Peacock, Hollis Watkins, and a handful of other workers first cracked the Mississippi "iceberg," the coalition began to break apart. On June 17 the group prepared to set up tents on the grounds of the all-black high school. "No camping here," announced the police. Stokely Carmichael, the new chairman of SNCC, continued to erect his tent. With that, two policemen hoisted him into an open-backed truck and took him to jail.

Carmichael had been one of the most devoted SNCC workers in Mississippi. He had been a fervent supporter of nonviolence. But the disappointment of Freedom Summer and the murder by southern bigots of his best friend, Jonathan Daniels, a white minister, poisoned any hope that the whites in power would give up anything voluntarily.

That night there was a huge rally to protest the arrest. Carmichael arrived before the rally's end. His clothes were rumpled and torn, his face swollen. The crowd grew quiet.

Cleveland Sellers: *"This is the twenty-seventh time I have been arrested—and I ain't going to jail no more!"* [Carmichael said]. *The crowd exploded into cheers. ". . . We been saying freedom for six years—and we ain't got nothing. What we're gonna start saying now is BLACK POWER."*

. . . Willie Ricks, who was as good at orchestrating the emotions of the crowd as anyone I have ever seen, sprang into action. Jumping to the platform with Stokely, he yelled to the crowd, "What do you want?"

"BLACK POWER!"

"What do you want?"

"BLACK POWER!"

"What do you want?"

"BLACK POWER! BLACK POWER! BLACK POWER!"

The phrase electrified the crowd. They applauded and stomped and screamed. It seemed to encompass all the ideas of black pride, voting power, and political power in two simple words. The press went mad. Since the beginning of the movement the press had taken every sign of black aggression as the beginning of the apocalypse, the black people's revenge against white America. Now, right there on the stage with Martin Luther King, someone had uttered what sounded like a war cry. All night the wire services buzzed with the new phrase, along with warnings about the impending race war.

That night, Carmichael explained his intent to journalist Paul Good: "Whites get nervous when we don't keep talking about brotherly love. They need reassurance. But we're not going to divert our energies to give it to them. . . . Whites never give anything. You can only talk to them on the basis of political power."

The next day, the march resumed. On the walk, King tried to temper the impression made by Carmichael's speech. In Yazoo City, when a group of Black Power advocates began chanting, "Hey, hey, whatdaya know! White people must go!" King shouted to the crowd, "Some people are telling us to be like our oppressor, who has a history of using Molotov cocktails, who has a history of using atomic bombs, who has a history of lynching Negroes. . . . I'm sick and tired of violence! I am tired of the war in Vietnam! I'm not going to use violence, no matter who says so!"

Far from the march, the effect of the phrase "Black Power" was even more devastating. Movement leaders had always taught that you can't win when you're mad. In a nation whose history was so often ruled by violence and revenge, the movement was determined that for once violence would not hold sway. The phrase "Black Power" implied to many that SNCC and CORE would take a violent tack. The floodgates of hate would open. The nation would drown in racial warfare. Unsympathetic public officials and media people who wanted to attack the movement found the perfect excuse to do so.

Greenwood, Mississippi, June 17, 1966. © Bob Fitch / Black Star

    Fearing a public-relations disaster, King begged Carmichael to stop using the phrase. Carmichael said, "The crying need is for black people to organize themselves and to consolidate economic and political resources to gain power. The Irish have done it. The Italians have done it. The Jews have done it. Why can't we?" And King: "It's not the program, it's the slogan. This one isolates us, confuses our allies, and gives whites who might be ashamed of their bigotry an excuse to justify it."

    Soon enough, violence came. It had nothing to do with slogans.

    The march had arrived in a driving rainstorm at Canton, Mississippi, a city of about ten thousand people, thirty miles north of Jackson. On the grounds of the all-

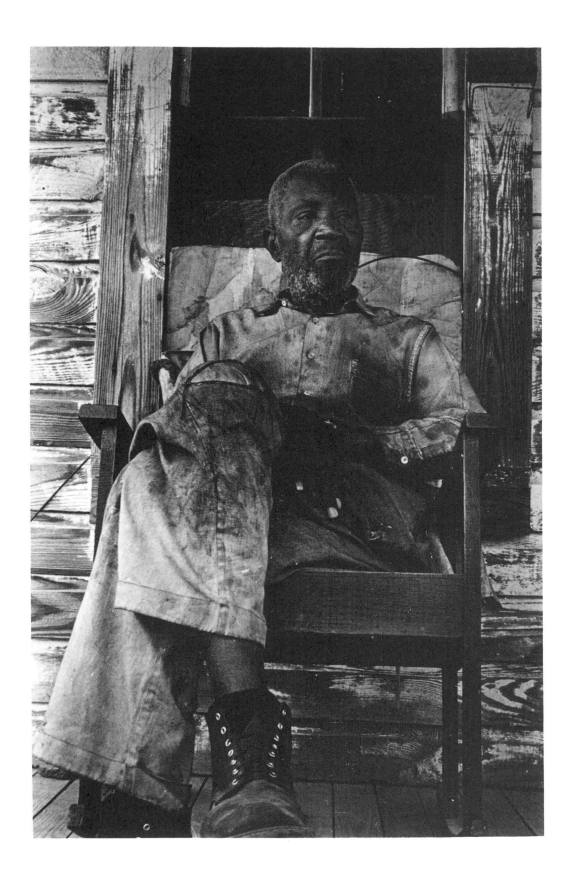

Uncle Tom's Prayer

In the fall of 1963, Matt Jones was a field organizer in the bloody Danville campaign. Despite the support of masses of young and old people in the city, several influential ministers and teachers were reluctant to speak out and support the campaign. Matt thought, These people are not bad; they are just afraid. He tried to put himself in their place, and came up with this song.

I am an Un-cle Tom, Lord,__ That's what the peo-ple say.__ But I ain't no Un-cle Tom, Lord,__ I'm just a lit-tle a-fraid.. Oh, help me, Lord,__ to stand up_____ and be__ a man, and fight se-gre-ga-tion__ as long as I can.

Well, what about my house, Lord,
You know those notes are high.
Well, you know I need my house, Lord,
That ain't no lie.

Oh, what about my job, Lord,
What shall I do?
You know if I join that line, Lord,
You know my job is through.

black elementary school, the marchers began setting up a big circus tent for people to sleep in. A small fist fight had broken out somewhere in the crowd, and the press jumped from the truck to cover it.

Paul Good: *A damp El Greco twilight sopped up sound, the grass in the field moistened to a vivid green, while vast purple clouds hung overhead. Work stopped when state troopers formed file on file, as if drawn up for parade, at the end of the field. They were goggled, clunky at the hips with their shotgun shells and tear gas canisters girdled around them.*

Bruce Hartford: *The cops were lining up, saying we couldn't set up. I wasn't particularly paying much attention—the cops were always lining up and threatening. Suddenly, up went their shotguns, and tear gas is going off all over. They were shooting tear gas out of those guns. I remember one shell arced over and hit the truck with the tent, and the people standing on the truck went flying in every direction. . . . I try to find my way through there, and I'm yelling at people, "Don't rub your eyes!"*

The police moved in behind the gas, gun-butting and kicking anyone—any child—in their way.

Edwin King: *I was standing next to Ms. Annie Devine when it happened. I remember throwing myself on top of her to protect her while they moved in, kicking and beating while they went.*

Mrs. Warwick, a heavy-set black woman, tried to rise after being stunned by the gas. A trooper kicked her back down: "You want your freedom, nigger. Here it is!" Within minutes the gas was so bad all two thousand marchers fled the schoolyard, running into the surrounding community. The police pursued, beating, and shooting gas as they went.

As the smell of gas began drifting into nearby homes, people came boiling out into the open. They were furious at the police. Some began throwing things and shouting. Most opened their doors to shelter the escaping marchers. The police began lobbing gas into the homes. The attack went on and on, spreading wider and wider, for another two hours before the police captain finally called off his men—they were out of gas shells.

Bruce Hartford: *I don't know what they were trying to do. You take two thousand people, you throw tear gas at them, where are they going to go? I guess subconsciously the police thought we would vanish into thin air. They didn't figure that if you chase people from point A they will have to run to point B. And they will not be in a good mood. . . .*

The next day you couldn't walk through the community without your eyes burning. And you would get repeats. When you get so much tear gas it gets into your skin. Then, even days later, when it got hot and you sweat, the moisture would reactivate the dried tear gas and it was like getting a tear-gas attack again.

The next day half of the marchers walked through the white area of Canton. Martin Luther King took a group that had pledged themselves to nonviolence to Philadelphia, Mississippi, where three civil rights workers had been killed two summers before. On Main Street, he led a small memorial service. A crowd of local whites surrounded them. Right behind King stood Deputy Cecil Price, caressing a blackjack.

"Today, we have seen men with hatred in their eyes," said King, "men who want to carry America back instead of forward. . . . I believe in my heart the murderers of those three boys are around you at this moment."

"They're right behind you," shouted a white farm boy in the crowd. The sheriff smiled and nodded. Another from the crowd rolled a cherry bomb under King's feet. It exploded like pistol shot. The small group of marchers flinched.

King looked out at the thickening crowd of onlookers, and he was sure he was going to die here. He continued: "I'm glad to have our white brothers out here. They don't understand the movement because their minds are closed. The hate in their hearts hasn't allowed God to speak to them or to let them see we love them."

He knelt on the courthouse steps. A huge white man in coveralls shouted, "Let me get my hands on that son of a bitch, and I'll love *him!*" But somehow, miraculously, they didn't attack that time. After a few moments of silent prayer, King, Abernathy, and the three hundred mourners rose and walked out of the square.

That night King again called his contacts in Washington to get some help from the government. Attorney General Katzenbach and President Johnson ignored the request. "I don't know what I'm going to do—I know I'm going to stay nonviolent

Grenada, Mississippi, 1966.
© *Charmian Reading*

no matter what happens. But a lot of people are getting hurt and bitter, and they can't see it that way anymore." As long as he lived, King never heard another word from the president.

The next day, fifteen thousand people stood before the state house in Jackson. The band played *When the Saints Go Marching In.* King, Carmichael, Floyd McKissick (Farmer's successor as head of CORE), all spoke. But the coalition that had made the movement possible was flying apart at a faster and faster rate.

Bruce Hartford: *There was some tension on the march. Some of the black SNCC workers didn't want us whites on the march. But we respected one another. We all had the same blisters. We all dodged the same tear gas. But later, when people who had never participated in the movement rose to the top, there weren't the ties to hold us all together.*

The issue of "blackness" grew within the ranks of SNCC, until at the 1967 general meeting it split the organization in half. After a long, bitter, unhappy debate, the few remaining white members of SNCC were asked to resign. The wounds created by this battle eventually killed the organization.

Bob Zellner: *Our organization couldn't have lasted. We lived and worked in a fever. We were the shock troops of the movement. . . . We were irreverent. We were bodacious. We were kids and we changed this country. It was not the great "leaders." It was us. We dragged the leaders. We were kids and we changed America.*

Ev'rybody's Got a Right to Live

Words and music are by Rev. Frederick D. Kirkpatrick. I met "Kirk" on the Poor People's Campaign in '68. Tall (he'd been a Grambling College football player), he had a voice that could fill a hall with no need of a mike—could sing high or low. Tragically, he died, aged only fifty-one, in New York City in 1986. May his songs carry on.

—*Pete Seeger*

Ev' - ry - bo - dy's got a right to _ live _____

Ev' - ry - bo - dy's got a right to live _____ And be -

fore this cam - paign fails we'll all go down in jail. _ Ev' - ry - bo - dy's got a

right to _ live. _____ On my way to Wash - ing - ton _

feel - ing aw - ful sad think - in' 'bout an in - come that I ne - ver had.

Black man picked the cotton
A long time ago
He has been a victim
Since they bought him to this shore. *(No Chorus)*

Black man dug the pipeline
Hewed down the pines
Gave his troubles to Jesus
Kept on toeing the line. *(Chorus)*

Black man dug the ditches
Both night and day
Black man did the work
While the white man got the pay. *(No Chorus)*

Now look a-here, Congress
This is a brand new day
No more full-time work
And part-time pay. *(Chorus)*

I want my share of silver
I want my share of gold
I want my share of justice
To save my dying soul. *(Chorus)*

Martin Luther King, 1967.
© *1983 Dan Budnik / Woodfin*
Camp & Associates

Interlude
Martin Luther King, Jr.—The Power of Nonviolence

*D*iane Nash: *People think of nonviolence as something very strange and abstract and kind of wishy-washy. Nothing could be less true. Our goal was not just to gain power; it was really to heal the torn-up community around us—to rehabilitate our community. Nonviolence was a way to fight and to heal at the same time. You can't kill somebody to make a beautiful community. We never believed that ends justify means. Instead we believed that, as Mahatma Gandhi of India said, everything is really a series of means. . . . The way we fought was, not by hitting and hating the person who oppressed you, but by withdrawing your support from the system—in order to be oppressed you had to cooperate with the oppressor; if you stopped cooperating, the system couldn't work. Nonviolence took as much courage as hitting someone with a pipe—but the results were much deeper.*

Jim Keck, in 1966 a young seminarian working with SCLC in Chicago: *At first a lot of us took the attitude that Dr. King was some sort of a wind-up doll. I mean, we'd drive him around the city and hear him give the same speech over and over. . . .*

This changed one muggy night in June.

King sat in front as, one by one, the tenants of a building walked to a microphone to tell about the rats, roaches, lead paint—you name it—they lived with it. . . .

Then, all of a sudden, five blacks we didn't know came to the microphone. They said that this building's landlord was good for the community and that these people were lying. The last one, a woman, said she's the rent collector, and she launches into this speech about these tenants being filthy and dirty and a disgrace to Negroes. Well, a lot of people in the audience started to murmur and say things like "She's right, it is our fault. We are no good."

King expected to give, you know, sermon number 68. But now it was completely on him to pull this out.

He walked calmly to the pulpit and, without any notes, . . . talked about how, after 400 years of slavery, we do have cultural problems, that a lot of testimony we have just heard is true. But we are not a people who have to be preoccupied with our problems. . . . We have a country to save, America, and we have to press on. We have to learn not to be down on one another. Then he looked at the five people who gave the testimony and said, "I understand you are trying to raise families, and we all forgive you. We've all had to do what you did today for the sake of our families."

Well, lo and behold, the five each got up and admitted they'd been lying, and the last woman, in tears, asked Dr. King for forgiveness. And the whole audience was screaming, "We forgive you!" People were out of their seats, yelling "Amen!"

I have never before or since heard a person deliver a speech like that. After that, the smart-alecking about King came to an end.

Martin Luther King and his wife, Coretta, at airport, 1967. © Dan Budnik / Woodfin Camp & Associates

XI

1968

Memphis, Tennessee

As the movement changed, the ideals of the first days gradually gave way to a division about goals and tactics, an impatience with the whole theory of nonviolent protest. SNCC and CORE worked on trying to build black awareness, but as the splits in the organization grew worse, they became more and more occupied with factional fights. SCLC worked on registering voters in 1966 and 1967. It tried, unsuccessfully to bring the nonviolent spirit to the cauldron cities of the North.

By 1967 Martin Luther King realized that another enemy, deeper than segregation, an enemy of both white and black, lay at the root of much of the violence—poverty. King felt that the movement had to go beyond matters of race, to a campaign against poverty, a campaign that would embrace poor people regardless of color. The old idealism, the old conviction, sparked to life. A poor people's march on Washington was planned for the following spring. At the end of April 1968, thousands of poor people would converge on Washington and erect a shanty town in view of the Capitol. There would be a long mule train from Mississippi, the poorest state in the nation. King hoped that this, together with sustained demonstrations and rallies and selected boycotts, would arouse a "moribund, insensitive Congress to life."

The strain of trying to put together a national campaign, far larger and more ambitious than anything he had done before, began to show on King. He had moments of terrible dread and depression, but somehow always managed to shake them off. April 22, the kickoff day for the Poor People's Campaign, drew closer and closer.

Then, in mid-March, he received a call from his friend Jim Lawson. In Memphis the garbage collectors had struck for a living wage and the blatantly racist city government had tried to break up the strike with Mace and night sticks. The black community and the liberal whites had come together to support the garbage collectors. Lawson told him that the people there were desperate for the movement to remain nonviolent. King came to address the people and saw a spirit akin to what he had seen in Selma and Birmingham.

On April 3, he spoke to two thousand people at the Clayborne Temple in Memphis. "Only when it is dark can we see the stars," King said. The stars were the masses of people in Memphis, New York, Africa, Latin America, Asia, everywhere, saying, "We want to be free."

On the afternoon of April 4, King stood on the balcony of his room at the Lorraine Motel. He saw one of his young co-workers, Jesse Jackson, down in the parking lot. "Jesse, I want you to go to dinner with us this evening. And be sure to dress up a little tonight, OK?" he joked. "No blue jeans, all right?" Jackson laughed and nodded. There was a pop like a firecracker. A bullet fired from a high-powered rifle across the street struck King in the throat and knocked him backward. His friends and staff ran to him and tried to staunch the bleeding with towels. In less than an hour he died.

Avon Rollins: *I was hurt as if my daddy and my mommy both had been killed. White folks turned on their TVs and saw the fires and they thought the world was coming to an end. It was like The Christ was coming back. They were frightened for the first time. It's the strangest thing how frightened white people get of black people. They made all kinds of concessions that they wouldn't have made before. . . . Why did it have to take a death and fires and destruction to wake people up?*

In five years a generation of young leaders, black and white, had been murdered—Medgar Evers, John Kennedy, Malcolm X, Martin Luther King, and later that spring, Robert Kennedy. That summer, a nation numb from too much pain watched thousands of protesting young people being bludgeoned into unconsciousness outside of the Chicago Democratic convention. Millions asked, Is there any hope for America? Or for the human race, for that matter?

Coretta Scott King at her husband's funeral.
© *1968 Flip Schulke*

OPPOSITE. *Selma, Alabama, 1965.*
© *Dan Budnik / Woodfin Camp & Associates*

The Torn Flag

Pete Seeger: I had a poet uncle once who wrote,

I have a rendezvous with Death . . .
At midnight in some flaming town.

In 1968 I swiped his line and used it for a new verse.

At midnight in a flaming angry town
I saw my country's flag lying torn upon the ground.
I ran in and dodged among the crowd
And scooped it up and scampered out to safety.

And then I took this striped old piece of cloth
And tried my best to wash the garbage off,
But I found it had been used for wrapping lies.
It smelled and stank, and attracted all the flies.

While I was feverishly at my task
I heard a husky voice that seemed to ask,
"Do you think you could change me just a bit?
Betsy Ross did her best, but she made a few mistakes.

"My blue is good, the color of the sky.
The stars are good, for ideals oh so high.
Seven stripes of red are strong to meet all danger,
But those white stripes, they, they need some changing.

"I need some stripes of deep rich brown;
And some of tan and black; and all around
A border of God's gracious green would look good there.
Maybe you could slant the stripes; then I'd not be so square."

I woke and said, "What a ridiculous story.
Don't let anyone say I suggested tampering with Old Glory."
But tonight it's near midnight, and in another flaming town
Once again I hear my country's flag lies torn upon the ground.

Who really owns America? The chief of a northwestern Indian tribe fighting for its fishing rights said, "We are the stewards of this land. Notice that we did not say 'the owners.' The Great Spirit owns all this earth. We are but his stewards."

And so I'd say also, take it from an old blacklisted singer who has had to fight most of his life against people who wanted to make him an outcast in his own home: this land belongs to the hard-working people who love freedom. Woody Guthrie had a great verse which should be sung now:

> Was a great high wall there
> That tried to stop me.
> Was a great big sign there said Private Property;
> But on the other side
> It didn't say nothin'—
> This land was made for you and me.

John's Island,
South Carolina, 1968.
© Robert Yellin

Epilogue
"This Little Light of Mine"

Movements come and go with the temper of the time, but does the spirit that created the civil rights movement, and that was hardened in its fires, continue to shine?

At Highlander, Myles Horton, Guy and Candie Carawan, Hubert and Jane Sapp, and dozens of others maintain the school that helped give birth to the civil rights movement, bringing people together to celebrate their common humanity and build their own grass-roots movements.

The community organizing that Hollis Watkins and Willie Peacock have done in southern Mississippi has helped to change the lives of tens of thousands of black people and poor people throughout the state. Hollis works for the Center for Constitutional Rights, training people around the state to help voters to register and develop their own political voice.

Bob Moses' program to teach advanced math to inner-city children is now moving into the Boston school system. To Bob, it is a new kind of freedom school. In the sixties the fight was for political freedom; now it is for economic freedom. His wife, Janet, also a civil rights worker, is finishing her medical residency in pediatrics.

Bernard LaFayette has returned to the school he left twenty-seven years ago, the American Baptist College, in Nashville, Tennessee. He is now the school's vice president. He spends available free time traveling around the country and working for the New York State Martin Luther King Commission, teaching people the philosophy and methods of nonviolent social change.

Marion Barry has become the mayor of Washington, D.C. Julian Bond served on the Georgia state legislature for twenty years, and has become a distinguished radio and TV commentator and political adviser. John Lewis was elected to Congress from Georgia's Sixth District in 1986. James Forman is actively working in Washington to make the District of Columbia the fifty-first state. Andrew Young served in the Carter administration before becoming mayor of Atlanta.

Dr. Bernice Johnson Reagon became head of black American studies at the Smithsonian Institution in Washington. With her group, Sweet Honey in the Rock, she travels around the U.S. and the world showing black and white audiences the rich musical and cultural traditions of African America. She has become one of the nation's most inspiring song leaders.

Bob Zellner: *I've got a lifelong commitment to political struggles. Each of us does it in our own way. There are still many things that we can march people off to—and we're all marching people off to things in our own way.*

Dottie Zellner: *To me the movement didn't end. Since then, I've organized a union, worked with emotionally disturbed children, and worked in the women's movement; the place where I work now, the Center for Constitutional Rights, is a movement place too. One way or another, I've always been in the movement.*

Danny Lyon: *Why do I go to Haiti? Why do I take pictures of the Tontons Macoutes* [Haiti's death squad] *throwing this guy down the stairs? Why do I believe that the ordinary Haitian people threw out Duvalier and could have really made their government work if the U.S. wasn't so anxious to pull the plug on them? It comes out of my movement experience twenty years ago. It changed me—I grew to love ordinary people; I saw that they could really have power and overcome the rich and the pow-*

LEFT TO RIGHT: *Bob Zellner, Praithia Hall, Cleveland Sellers, Charles Sherrod, Bob Mantz, Hollis Watkins, Silas Norman, Charles McDew, Casey Hayden, Dorie Ladner, Lucy Montgomery, and Joyce Ladner at Trinity College, Hartford, Connecticut, 1988.*
© *Charmian Reading*

erful, if only they can get together and act. I saw people become aware of their own power. I know it works.

With skill and persistence Jesse Jackson has worked since 1980 to reform the Democratic party. His Rainbow Coalition has added to the voter rolls millions of African Americans, native Americans, Latinos, and other previously disenfranchised people. In a speech to the Democratic convention in July 1988, Jackson said: "America's not a blanket woven from one thread, one color, one cloth. . . . Farmers, you seek fair prices, and you are right, but you cannot stand alone. Your patch is not big enough. . . . Workers, you fight for fair wages. You are right, but your patch is not big enough. . . . Women, you seek pay equity. You are right, but your patch is not big enough. . . . Blacks, Hispanics, when we fight for civil rights we are right, but our patch is not big enough. . . . Conservatives and progressives, when you fight for what you believe, right wing, left wing, hawk, dove, you are right from your point of view, but your point of view is not enough. . . .

"Pool the patches and pieces together, bound by a common thread. When we form a great quilt of unity and common ground, . . . the people can win."

In April 1988, Jack Chatfield, a former SNCC field secretary, currently a professor of history, brought together dozens of civil rights workers for a three-day symposium at Trinity College in Hartford, Connecticut. Youngsters traveled from Michigan, from Maine, from campuses and neighborhoods torn by racism and despair, to see if the experience of the last generation could speak to theirs.

Chuck McDew, former chairman of SNCC: *There is a part in the Torah that says, "If I am not for myself, who will be for me? If I am only for myself, what am I? If not now, when?" I decided that I cannot only be for myself, I cannot only fight for my own dignity. I'm having to deal with racism now because my father didn't deal with it then, and if I don't deal with it now, my children would face the same evil twenty years from now—"If not now, when?"*

Theresa Delfalto, former SNCC organizing secretary: *Our media have trained us only to look at the surface. They told us about Martin Luther King, but they never told about the people who stood and got beaten, the people who sat in meetings in Mississippi, risking their lives for the Freedom Democratic party, the people who made the movement strong. For years the media have told us the movement is dead, that there is apathy in campuses, because King is dead and SNCC is gone. But they don't see what is really happening in this country. Every time there is a threat to clean air or to peace or to your schools or your freedom, people will pick up a placard and march. The media don't tell you that thanks to the civil rights movement and to the movements that went on before that in the twenties and the thirties, protest is a way of life in this country. Now a new movement is growing. One of these days the media will notice it, and they'll say, "Where did that come from?" It was there all the time.*

Scott Williamson, student at Yale Divinity School: *Keep on moving. . . . We've got a lot of energy. Now we have to channel our energy and we can change the world.*

The late Septima Clark, founder of the first citizenship schools: *I don't expect to ever see a utopia. I think there will always be something that you're going to have to work on. That's why when we have chaos and people say, "I'm scared. I'm scared," I say, "Don't worry. Out of this will come something good." It will, too. . . . Things will happen and things will change. The only thing that's really worth-while is change. It's coming.*

Alma John, New York City community leader and radio personality: *If you know, teach.*

If you don't know, learn.

Each one—teach one.

Diane Nash: *There is a terrible danger in this belief we have in the great charismatic leader. Sometimes it is a benevolent figure—like Martin Luther King. But that same mentality will allow a Hitler to emerge. The only answer is for us to take on responsibility for our own lives, to realize that the answer is in us; the leaders are us.*

This Little Light of Mine

One of the greatest of the old-time songs, this was also the favorite of one of the greatest individuals of the civil rights movement, Mrs. Fannie Lou Hamer of Mississippi. A short, blunt woman, she was also short and blunt in her speeches: "I'm sick and tired of being sick and tired." A country person, she insisted on her right to vote in spite of many threats and several bad beatings. She was an inspiration to all who met her.

The arrangement we give here tries to imply how one person usually starts a song, and others gradually join in, adding harmony. The melody is never twice the same, as inspiration hits different people, who lead off with different verses. It became common to start with the name of the city or state one was singing in at the time, and then broaden the geographical area, or shrink it to become ever more specific. Thus a series of verses might be:

> All over the state of Georgia . . .
> All over the southland . . .
> All over America . . .
> All over the world now . . .

Or it could be:

> All over the state of Georgia . . .
> All over the city of Atlanta . . .
> On this street called Peachtree . . .
> Here in this building . . .
> Deep in my heart . . .

And at various points, repeat the opening verse as a chorus.

Profile: BOB MOSES

Bob sits eating eggs in a coffee shop in Cambridge, Massachusetts, near the house where he lives with his wife, Janet, and four children. He speaks quietly and thoughtfully. He has a full beard now, peppered with gray; behind his spectacles, his eyes still shine with the same focused intensity that movement people remember from twenty-five years ago.

Bob grew up in New York, in the shadow of Yankee Stadium. He studied math, earning his master's degree at Hamilton College, where he was the only black student.

During this time I went to some Pete Seeger concerts and hootenannies, and I began to see that I wasn't on this world just for myself—I had an obligation to make things better.

In 1960, while teaching math at the Horace Mann School, Bob visited the South and decided to give all of his free time to the movement.

That summer, I went to Atlanta to help SCLC. I was doing office work, sending out fund-raising letters and stuffing envelopes. Jammed into the office was one desk for SNCC. I talked a lot to Jane Stembridge, who was at the SNCC desk—she was the only paid staff for the organization—and she asked me if I wouldn't take a trip for SNCC through Alabama and Mississippi and Louisiana, looking for people to come to their fall conference. See, SNCC had no contact with the Deep South yet. I said OK, so Ella [Baker] drew up a list of names of contacts that she had gotten during all her years. Then Jane called up the people and told them that I was coming.

I went through Birmingham and spoke to Shuttlesworth and went to Talladega College in Alabama and went to Clarksdale. I was going to head up to the north end of Mississippi, to Holly Springs, but instead, I went south to Cleveland to see Amzie Moore.

For me, meeting Amzie Moore was a turning point. If I hadn't met him, there is no way I'd have gone down and stayed in Mississippi. I had to come back and work with him. If SNCC had rejected the project, I'd have come back on my own.

After his teaching contract at Horace Mann ran out, Bob returned to work full-time in Mississippi.

I went down to work in Amite County, in southern Mississippi. It was a trial heat of what Mississippi really meant in terms of fighting us—a real opposition. It was around mid-August; there were a series of events—they ran the gamut. First they arrested me. They could keep me in jail, but I refused to pay anything, so they let me go after a few days. Then, that didn't work, so they roughed us up, and that didn't work; and all the time, they were meeting in the courthouse, hundreds of Klansmen and Citizens Council members from all over the state, trying to figure out how to stop us. Finally, there was a murder. They killed Herbert Lee, a neighbor of the Steptoes, a man who had helped us. This little program of ours really threatened them.

Something like that forces you to come to grips within yourself—whether you have it in you to continue. You're out there in a really rural area, no electricity, no radio, no running water. Everything moves very slowly, and you really have time to go into yourself. You begin to realize how long this is going to take and how hard it is going to be. You're in a deep-sea-diver situation, and you wonder how long can you stay under water under this heavy pressure.

I think I remember when I realized I was going to last it out. I remember it was the day I was driving down to the courthouse—the first day we took some people down to register. The tension had been building up and up. Steptoe lived a few miles from the courthouse. As we were driving I remembered that song—Jacob's Ladder. I sang it in my mind again and again like a mantra. "Every rung goes higher higher. Every rung goes higher higher. . . ." On the one hand it was spiritual and on the other hand it had a wider political meaning, and it was all connected in this act of driving down to courthouse.

Bob stayed in Mississippi for three years, through Freedom Summer and part of the following year. After that, though he remained nominally in SNCC, he felt that it was time for him to move on. He worked with Staughton Lynd and Dave Dellinger in organizing the first mass resistance against the war in Vietnam.

In 1965, Bob visited Africa. In 1966, he organized a conference in the South to familiarize American movement people with the liberation movements in Africa. When he was drafted that year, at the age of thirty-two, he realized that the government meant to make an example of him, so he moved to Canada and then to Tanzania. That's where most of his children were born. In 1976 he returned to Cambridge, Massachusetts, where he has lived ever since.

Many people were bitter about the results of the Freedom Summer and the Freedom Democratic party. But we changed the Democratic party. What we started brought in millions of new voters and changed the rules of the convention. By 1968 all of the delegations were integrated. A lot of the energy that had been in the movement began to get focused into politics—people like John Lewis and Andy Young and Marion Barry got involved. But the grass-roots energy that we had in the Freedom Democratic party wasn't translated up north. Up north, politics has remained pretty traditional. Jesse Jackson's campaign is an attempt to bring some of the grass-roots energy onto the national arena, but it is not building an ongoing grass-roots organization—

Bob Moses, 1965.
© Joe Alper, courtesy Jackie Gibson Alper

it's more the SCLC model of mobilizing people around specific events or short-term campaigns. But the other model, that was coming more out of the tradition of Ella Baker of developing community organizations, has not translated yet into mass movement.

Grass-roots organizations now are what Howard Zinn called "pockets of resistance"; at least we can keep a leash on government abuses. I had said it would take fifty years to change the Democratic party; and it's twenty-five years and there have been changes. Maybe Jesse's role is helping to accelerate the process. Maybe it won't take all fifty.

I think the big challenge is economic. The whole shift into what some people call the information age or the computer age means that large numbers of people who don't have training, who don't have education, will be economically on the outside. In the sixties, people who couldn't read and write didn't count politically—they were nonexistent. We're heading for a situation where the same thing will happen to people without technological or computer literacy. That's why I've been developing ways to teach algebra to inner-city school children beginning in the fourth and fifth grades. If we can raise them to a point of literacy, at least they can start to make demands. As it is now, an inner-city kid without this literacy is doomed to always being on the outside of the economic system—never being able to make a demand. Unless there is a way found to teach this literacy to our children, you'll have 50 percent of our black population just shuffling from one McDonald's-type job to another or, if they want money, shifting into dope dealing and crack dealing. When you face a whole life of entry-level jobs, with not enough cash to have an apartment or raise a family, selling dope looks pretty good to some people.

I've recently gotten involved with a group of local people who are dedicated to community work in the Boston area, the kind of grass-roots that Ella Baker spoke of. It's a group of Harvard graduates, most of them black, trying to work in the community in much the same way we did in SNCC. See, in SNCC we never got past being students. We were just beginning to broach the problem of how to do our work while being parents and raising a family, when the organization started to collapse in on itself in '65 and '66. These people are facing that problem. We're trying to take the best of SNCC and see if they can make it work here.

The main thing is not to set out with grand projects. Everything starts at your doorstep. Just get deeply involved in something. There is so much to do that people may not look at this little bit here as important. I got started with this algebra project because I was concerned with my children and their education. Soon we involved the school, and now part of the Boston school system. Some major institutions are getting involved. It grows. It all began with one parent and his nine-year-old daughter trying to learn algebra. You throw a stone in one place and the ripples spread.

Jacob's Ladder

Africans in America had many freedom songs long before there was such a thing as a civil rights movement—*Go Down Moses, Didn't My Lord Deliver Daniel*. Furthermore, they had for a long time been adopting their traditional songs, with slightly different words, as union songs. Many early unions were all-white and frankly racist. But more farsighted union leaders had long said that white workers could not win their rights without uniting with black workers. In the 1930s the hymn beginning "Jesus is my leader, I shall not be moved" became, with new words, better known as a union song.

West Virginia miners sang, "We have worked in dark and danger, workers in the mine," using the tune of *Jacob's Ladder*. A few years later, North Carolina textile workers were singing, "We are building a strong union, workers in the mill." Now, in 1989, we make so bold as to end this book with two verses from the original song, a last line composed in 1973, and some new verses put together by women in Milwaukee. And let singers of the future—black, white, red, and brown, men and women, young and old, east and west, north and south, ashore or afloat—decide how they want to change it or add to it or translate it.

My best songwriting of 1973 was to discover three words that made a new last line. The well-known spiritual was perhaps originally put together by people with chains around their legs. And we who sometimes have too-tight white collars can learn from them. Many people in this world still think heaven will come in one big bang, one opening of the gates, one great revolution. Historically, scientifically, we know there'll be many steps. A *New Yorker* cartoon showed a big ladder ascending into the clouds, and a tiny little ladder connecting two of the big rungs.

I've written the song here as I usually do it, with a strong guitar bass starting it off. Throughout, a song leader's few words interjected between the phrases of the song may make the difference between a group of people's singing well, or not. If a crowd of people is halfway warmed up, this song can give them hope for struggles to come, as the harmony develops like a great organ.

—*Pete Seeger*

(Optional words for the song leader are in italics.)

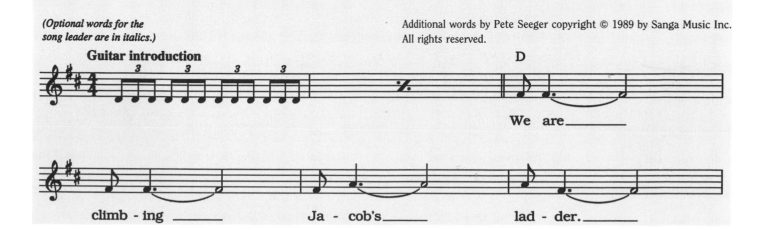

sis - ters, (all) all._____ (We are danc - ing Sa - rah's cir - cle)

We are dancing Sarah's circle . . .
   Sisters, brothers, all.

Every round a generation . . .
   Sisters, brothers, all.

Struggle's long but hope is longer . . .
   Sisters, brothers, all.

People all need jobs and justice . . .
   Sisters, brothers, all.

We are climbing Jacob's ladder . . .
   Brothers, sisters, all.

Alabama, 1965.
© 1978 Dan Budnik / Woodfin
Camp & Associates

More Reading, Listening, Looking, and Doing

READING

Belfrage, Sally. *Freedom Summer*. New York: Viking, 1965.

Branch, Taylor. *Parting the Waters: America in the King Years, 1954–63*. New York: Simon and Schuster, 1988.

Cagin, Seth, and Philip Dray. *We Are Not Afraid*. New York: Macmillan, 1988.

Carawan, Guy and Candie. *We Shall Overcome*. New York: Oak Publications, 1963.

———. *Ain't You Got a Right to the Tree of Life*. New York: Simon and Schuster, 1967.

———. *Freedom Is a Constant Struggle*. New York: Oak Publications, 1968.

Carson, Clayborne. *In Struggle: SNCC and the Black Awakening of the 1960s*. Cambridge, Mass.: Harvard University Press, 1981.

Clark, Septima. *Ready from Within*. Ed. Cynthia Stokes Brown. Navarro, Calif.: Wild Trees Press, 1986.

Farmer, James. *Lay Bare the Heart*. New York: Arbor House, 1985.

Forman, James. *The Making of Black Revolutionaries*. New York: Macmillan, 1972.

Friedman, Leon. *The Civil Rights Reader*. New York: Walker, 1968.

Garrow, David J. *The FBI and Martin Luther King, Jr.* New York: Norton, 1981.

———. *Bearing the Cross: Martin Luther King and the Southern Leadership Conference*. New York: William Morrow, 1986.

Good, Paul. *The Trouble I've Seen*. Washington, D.C.: Howard University Press, 1975.

Griffin, John H. *Black Like Me*. New York: Signet, 1962.

Gwaltney, John L., ed. *Drylongso: A Self-Portrait of Black America*. New York: Random House, 1980.

Hamer, Fannie Lou. *To Praise Our Bridges: An Autobiography*. Jackson, Miss.: KIPCO, 1967.

Hansberry, Lorraine. *The Movement*. Ed. Elizabeth Sutherland. New York: Simon and Schuster, 1964.

Harding, Vincent. *The Other American Revolution*. Ed. Robert A. Hill. Los Angeles, Calif.: Center for Afro-American Studies (UCLA), 1980.

Hersey, John. *The Algiers Motel Incident*. New York: Knopf, 1968.

Holt, Len. *The Summer That Didn't End*. New York: William Morrow, 1965.

Huie, William Bradford. *Three Lives for Mississippi*. New York: WCC Books (New York Herald Tribune Inc.), 1965.

King, Coretta Scott. *My Life with Martin Luther King, Jr.* New York: Avon Books, 1969.

King, Martin Luther, Jr. *Why We Can't Wait*. New York: Harper and Row, 1964.

———. *Where Do We Go from Here: Chaos or Community*. New York: Harper and Row, 1967.

King, Mary. *Freedom Song*. New York: William Morrow, 1986.

Mars, Florence. *Witness at Philadelphia*. Baton Rouge: Louisiana State University Press, 1976.

McCord, William. *Mississippi: The Long, Hot Summer*. New York: Norton, 1965.

Mendelson, Jack. *The Martyrs: Sixteen Who Gave Their Lives for Racial Justice.* New York: Harper and Row, 1966.

Moody, Anne. *Coming of Age in Mississippi.* New York: Dial Press, 1968.

Oates, Stephen B. *Let the Trumpet Sound.* New York: Harper and Row, 1982.

Peck, James. *Freedom Ride.* New York: Simon and Schuster, 1962.

Raines, Howell. *My Soul Is Rested.* New York: Putnam, 1977.

Reagon, Bernice Johnson. *We'll Never Turn Back.* Washington, D.C.: Smithsonian Institution Press, 1980.

Schulke, Flip, ed. *Martin Luther King, Jr.* New York: Norton, 1976.

Sellers, Cleveland. *The River of No Return: The Autobiography of a Black Militant and the Life and Death of SNCC.* New York: William Morrow, 1973.

Silver, James W. *Mississippi: The Closed Society.* New York: Harcourt, Brace and World, 1966.

Sutherland, Elizabeth. *Letters from Mississippi.* New York: McGraw-Hill, 1965.

Von Hoffman, Nicholas. *Mississippi Notebook.* New York: David White Co., 1964.

Watters, Pat. *Down to Now.* New York: Pantheon, 1971.

Webb, Sheyann, and Rachel West Nelson, as told to Frank Sikora. *Selma, Lord, Selma.* Tuscaloosa: University of Alabama Press, 1980.

Wilkins, Roy, with Tom Mathews. *Standing Fast: The Autobiography of Roy Wilkins.* New York: Viking, 1982.

Williams, Juan. *Eyes on the Prize.* New York: Viking, 1987.

Zinn, Howard. *SNCC: The New Abolitionists.* Boston: Beacon Press, 1964.

LISTENING

Folkways Records

Birmingham, Alabama—Mass Meeting. Produced by Guy and Candie Carawan, 1963.

Nashville Sit-in Story. Produced by Guy and Candie Carawan, 1960.

Sea Island Folk Festival. Produced by Alan Lomax and Guy and Candie Carawan, 1966.

Sing for Freedom. Produced by Guy and Candie Carawan, 1964.

Story of Greenwood, Mississippi. Produced by Guy and Candie Carawan, 1965.

We Shall Overcome: Songs of the Freedom Movement. Produced by Guy and Candie Carawan, 1963.

Smithsonian

Voices of the Civil Rights Movement, 1980.

Mercury

Freedom Singers Sing of Freedom Now. Produced by Chad Mitchell, 1964. Includes voices of SNCC members.

Keep an eye out for records of Matt Jones, Bernice Johnson Reagon, Sweet Honey in the Rock, Jane Sapp, Serious Bizness, and others who sing songs of the movement from the 1950s on up to the present.

LOOKING

A Class Divided. Yale University Films.

Eye of the Beholder. Post-Newsweek Films of Florida, 1987.

Fundi. Fifty-minute documentary on Ella Baker. New York: Fundi Productions, 1978.

Keep Your Eyes on the Prize. Six-hour documentary on the movement. Boston: Blackside Inc., 1985.

My Past Is My Own. After School Special produced by WCBS-TV, January 1989.

We Shall Overcome. Seventy-five-minute documentary on the movement, past and present. Jim and Ginger Brown, PBS, 1988.

A World of Difference. Series of films produced by WCBS-TV, 1988–89.

The fight for equal opportunity and dignity goes on today. Most large cities have legal-defense groups, voter-registration groups, and educational groups. If there are no such groups in your community, get together with friends and see if you can start one.

If you are a student, whatever your heritage or skin color, take part in the black- and African-studies programs at your school. If you are a parent, get involved with your school board to make sure that the stories of all of our nation's people are taught—African, Asian, Latino, and native American as well as European.

Most of all, if you see prejudice around you, or if you yourself are a victim, challenge it: Write letters to your local newspaper; ask a national organization like the NAACP, SCLC, or Urban League for advice; get help from a lawyer; join with others to take action. The poet Ariel Dorfman said that when you speak out, "you are freeing one little space. Many little spaces make a large space. Courage is contagious. . . . Hope is contagious."

Notes

In addition to interviews and private papers, the following sources have been used in the narrative.

CHAPTER 1
Septima Clark, *Ready from Within,* ed. Cynthia Stokes Brown (Navarro, Calif.: Wild Trees Press, 1986); Martin Luther King, Jr., *Stride toward Freedom* (New York: Harper, 1958); Stephen B. Oates, *Let the Trumpet Sound* (New York: Harper and Row, 1982); Howell Raines, *My Soul Is Rested* (New York: Putnam, 1977); Juan Williams, *Eyes on the Prize* (New York: Viking, 1987).

CHAPTER 2
Seth Cagin and Philip Dray, *We Are Not Afraid* (New York: Macmillan, 1988); Clayborne Carson, *In Struggle: SNCC and the Black Awakening of the 1960s* (Cambridge, Mass.: Harvard University Press, 1981); Mary King, *Freedom Song* (New York: William Morrow, 1986); Raines, *My Soul Is Rested;* Williams, *Eyes on the Prize;* Howard Zinn, *SNCC: The New Abolitionists* (Boston: Beacon Press, 1964).

CHAPTER 3
James Farmer, *Lay Bare the Heart* (New York: Arbor House, 1985); Oates, *Let the Trumpet Sound;* Raines, *My Soul Is Rested; Southern Exposure* (magazine), Vol. IX, No. 1 (Spring 1981); Williams, *Eyes on the Prize;* Zinn, *SNCC: The New Abolitionists.*

CHAPTER 4
Oates, *Let the Trumpet Sound;* Raines, *My Soul Is Rested;* Pat Watters, *Down to Now* (New York: Pantheon, 1971); Williams, *Eyes on the Prize;* Zinn, *SNCC: The New Abolitionists.*

CHAPTER 5
Martin Luther King, Jr., *Why We Can't Wait* (New York: Harper and Row, 1964); Oates, *Let the Trumpet Sound;* Raines, *My Soul Is Rested; Southern Exposure* (Spring 1981); Watters, *Down to Now;* Williams, *Eyes on the Prize.*

CHAPTER 6
Cagin and Dray, *We Are Not Afraid;* James Forman, *The Making of Black Revolutionaries* (New York: Macmillan, 1972); Watters, *Down to Now;* Zinn, *SNCC: The New Abolitionists.*

CHAPTER 7
Edwin King, *The Children's Crusade* (unpublished); Anne Moody, *Coming of Age in Mississippi* (New York: Dial Press, 1968); Raines, *My Soul Is Rested;* James W. Silver, *Mississippi: The Closed Society* (New York: Harcourt, Brace and World, 1966). *Southern Exposure* (Spring 1981); Williams, *Eyes on the Prize;* Zinn, *SNCC: The New Abolitionists.*
Papers in the Fannie Lou Hamer Collection, Tougaloo College, Tougaloo, Mississippi; papers in the Edwin King Collection, Tougaloo College; collections in the library of the University of Mississippi (Oxford campus), University, Mississippi.

CHAPTER 8
Sally Belfrage, *Freedom Summer* (New York: Viking, 1965); Forman, *The Making of Black Revolutionaries;* Lorraine Hansberry, *The Movement,* ed. Elizabeth Sutherland (New York: Simon and Schuster, 1964); William Brad-

ford Huie, *Three Lives for Mississippi* (New York: WCC Books [New York Herald Tribune Inc.], 1965); Mary King, *Freedom Song;* William McCord, *Mississippi: The Long, Hot Summer* (New York: Norton, 1965); *Southern Exposure,* Vol. XV, No. 2 (Summer 1987); Elizabeth Sutherland, *Letters from Mississippi* (New York: McGraw-Hill, 1965); Nicholas Von Hoffman, *Mississippi Notebook* (New York: David White Co., 1964); Watters, *Down to Now;* Williams, *Eyes on the Prize;* Zinn, *SNCC: The New Abolitionists.*

CHAPTER 9
Guy and Candie Carawan, *Freedom Is a Constant Struggle* (New York: Oak Publications, 1968); Raines, *My Soul Is Rested;* Watters, *Down to Now;* Shey-ann Webb and Rachel West Nelson, as told to Frank Sikora, *Selma, Lord, Selma* (Tuscaloosa: University of Alabama Press, 1980).

INTERLUDE: JULY 4, 1964
King, *Freedom Song.*

CHAPTER 10
Paul Good, *The Trouble I've Seen* (Washington, D.C.: Howard University Press, 1975); Cleveland Sellers, *The River of No Return: The Autobiography of a Black Militant and the Life and Death of SNCC* (New York: William Morrow, 1973).

INTERLUDE: MARTIN LUTHER KING, JR.
Ben Joravsky, "A Moment of Truth," *Chicago,* August 1986.

CHAPTER 11
John Hersey, *The Algiers Motel Incident* (New York: Knopf, 1968); Oates, *Let the Trumpet Sound;* Raines, *My Soul Is Rested;* Flip Schulke, ed., *Martin Luther King, Jr.* (New York: Norton, 1976).

Index

Page numbers in *italics* refer to illustrations.